TRADITION AND TENSION

MCGILL-QUEEN'S STUDIES IN THE HISTORY OF RELIGION
Volumes in this series have been supported by the Jackman Foundation of Toronto.

SERIES ONE G.A. RAWLYK, EDITOR

1 Small Differences
Irish Catholics and Irish Protestants, 1815–1922
An International Perspective
Donald Harman Akenson

2 Two Worlds
The Protestant Culture of Nineteenth-Century Ontario
William Westfall

3 An Evangelical Mind
Nathanael Burwash and the Methodist Tradition in Canada, 1839–1918
Marguerite Van Die

4 The Dévotes
Women and Church in Seventeenth-Century France
Elizabeth Rapley

5 The Evangelical Century
College and Creed in English Canada from the Great Revival to the Great Depression
Michael Gauvreau

6 The German Peasants' War and Anabaptist Community of Goods
James M. Stayer

7 A World Mission
Canadian Protestantism and the Quest for a New International Order, 1918–1939
Robert Wright

8 Serving the Present Age
Revivalism, Progressivism, and the Methodist Tradition in Canada
Phyllis D. Airhart

9 A Sensitive Independence
Canadian Methodist Women Missionaries in Canada and the Orient, 1881–1925
Rosemary R. Gagan

10 God's Peoples
Covenant and Land in South Africa, Israel, and Ulster
Donald Harman Akenson

11 Creed and Culture
The Place of English-Speaking Catholics in Canadian Society, 1750–1930
Edited by Terrence Murphy and Gerald Stortz

12 Piety and Nationalism
Lay Voluntary Associations and the Creation of an Irish-Catholic Community in Toronto, 1850–1895
Brian P. Clarke

13 Amazing Grace
Studies in Evangelicalism in Australia, Britain, Canada, and the United States
Edited by George Rawlyk and Mark A. Noll

14 Children of Peace
W. John McIntyre

15 A Solitary Pillar
Montreal's Anglican Church and the Quiet Revolution
Joan Marshall

16 Padres in No Man's Land
Canadian Chaplains and the Great War
Duff Crerar

17 Christian Ethics and Political Economy in North America
A Critical Analysis
P. Travis Kroeker

18 Pilgrims in Lotus Land
Conservative Protestantism in British Columbia, 1917–1981
Robert K. Burkinshaw

19 Through Sunshine and Shadow
The Woman's Christian Temperance Union, Evangelicalism, and Reform in Ontario, 1874–1930
Sharon Cook

20 Church, College, and Clergy
A History of Theological Education at Knox College, Toronto, 1844–1994
Brian J. Fraser

21 The Lord's Dominion
The History of Canadian Methodism
Neil Semple

22 A Full-Orbed Christianity
The Protestant Churches and Social Welfare in Canada, 1900–1940
Nancy Christie and Michael Gauvreau

23 Evangelism and Apostasy
The Evolution and Impact of Evangelicals in Modern Mexico
Kurt Bowen

24 The Chignecto Covenanters
A Regional History of Reformed Presbyterianism in New Brunswick and Nova Scotia, 1827–1905
Eldon Hay

25 Methodists and Women's Education in Ontario, 1836–1925
Johanne Selles

26 Puritanism and Historical Controversy
William Lamont

SERIES TWO IN MEMORY OF GEORGE RAWLYK
DONALD HARMAN AKENSON, EDITOR

1 Marguerite Bourgeoys and Montreal, 1640–1665
Patricia Simpson

2 Aspects of the Canadian Evangelical Experience
Edited by G.A. Rawlyk

3 Infinity, Faith, and Time
Christian Humanism and Renaissance Literature
John Spencer Hill

4 The Contribution of Presbyterianism to the Maritime Provinces of Canada
Edited by Charles H.H. Scobie and G.A. Rawlyk

5 Labour, Love, and Prayer
Female Piety in Ulster Religious Literature, 1850–1914
Andrea Ebel Brozyna

6 The Waning of the Green
Catholics, the Irish, and Identity in Toronto, 1887–1922
Mark G. McGowan

7 Religion and Nationality in Western Ukraine
The Greek Catholic Church and the Ruthenian National Movement in Galicia, 1867–1900
John-Paul Himka

8 Good Citizens
British Missionaries and Imperial States, 1870–1918
James G. Greenlee and Charles M. Johnston

9 The Theology of the Oral Torah
Revealing the Justice of God
Jacob Neusner

10 Gentle Eminence
A Life of Cardinal Flahiff
P. Wallace Platt

11 Culture, Religion, and Demographic Behaviour
Catholics and Lutherans in Alsace, 1750–1870
Kevin McQuillan

12 Between Damnation and Starvation
Priests and Merchants in Newfoundland Politics, 1745–1855
John P. Greene

13 Martin Luther, German Saviour
German Evangelical Theological Factions and the Interpretation of Luther, 1917–1933
James M. Stayer

14 Modernity and the Dilemma of North American Anglican Identities, 1880–1950
William H. Katerberg

15 The Methodist Church on the Prairies, 1896–1914
George Emery

16 Christian Attitudes towards the State of Israel
Paul Charles Merkley

17 A Social History of the Cloister
Daily Life in the Teaching Monasteries of the Old Regime
Elizabeth Rapley

18 Households of Faith
Family, Gender, and Community in Canada, 1760–1969
Edited by Nancy Christie

19 Blood Ground
Colonialism, Missions, and the Contest for Christianity in the Cape Colony and Britain, 1799–1853
Elizabeth Elbourne

20 A History of Canadian Catholics
Gallicanism, Romanism, and Canadianism
Terence J. Fay

21 The View from Rome
Archbishop Stagni's 1915 Reports on the Ontario Bilingual Schools Question
Edited and translated by John Zucchi

22 The Founding Moment
Church, Society, and the Construction of Trinity College
William Westfall

23 The Holocaust, Israel, and Canadian Protestant Churches
Haim Genizi

24 Governing Charities
Church and State in Toronto's Catholic Archdiocese, 1850–1950
Paula Maurutto

25 Anglicans and the Atlantic World
High Churchmen, Evangelicals, and the Quebec Connection
Richard W. Vaudry

26 Evangelicals and the Continental Divide
The Conservative Protestant Subculture in Canada and the United States
Sam Reimer

27 Christians in a Secular World
The Canadian Experience
Kurt Bowen

28 Anatomy of a Seance
A History of Spirit Communication in Central Canada
Stan McMullin

29 With Skilful Hand
The Story of King David
David T. Barnard

30 Faithful Intellect
Samuel S. Nelles and Victoria University
Neil Semple

31 W. Stanford Reid
An Evangelical Calvinist in the Academy
Donald MacLeod

32 A Long Eclipse
The Liberal Protestant Establishment and the Canadian University, 1920–1970
Catherine Gidney

33 Forkhill Protestants and Forkhill Catholics, 1787–1858
Kyla Madden

34 For Canada's Sake
Public Religion, Centennial Celebrations, and the Re-making of Canada in the 1960s
Gary R. Miedema

35 Revival in the City
The Impact of American Evangelists in Canada, 1884–1914
Eric R. Crouse

36 The Lord for the Body
Religion, Medicine, and Protestant Faith Healing in Canada, 1880–1930
James Opp

37 Six Hundred Years of Reform
Bishops and the French Church, 1190–1789
J. Michael Hayden and Malcolm R. Greenshields

38 The Missionary Oblate Sisters
Vision and Mission
Rosa Bruno-Jofré

39 Religion, Family, and Community in Victorian Canada
The Colbys of Carrollcroft
Marguerite Van Die

40 Michael Power
The Struggle to Build the Catholic Church on the Canadian Frontier
Mark G. McGowan

41 The Catholic Origins of Quebec's Quiet Revolution, 1931–1970
Michael Gauvreau

42 Marguerite Bourgeoys and the Congregation of Notre Dame, 1665–1700
Patricia Simpson

43 To Heal a Fractured World
The Ethics of Responsibility
Jonathan Sacks

44 Revivalists
Marketing the Gospel in English Canada, 1884–1957
Kevin Kee

45 The Churches and Social Order in Nineteenth- and Twentieth-Century Canada
Edited by Michael Gauvreau and Ollivier Hubert

46 Political Ecumenism
Catholics, Jews, and Protestants in De Gaulle's Free France, 1940–1945
Geoffrey Adams

47 From Quaker to Upper Canadian
Faith and Community among Yonge Street Friends, 1801–1850
Robynne Rogers Healey

48 The Congrégation de Notre-Dame, Superiors, and the Paradox of Power, 1693–1796
Colleen Gray

49 Canadian Pentecostalism
Transition and Transformation
Edited by Michael Wilkinson

50 A War with a Silver Lining
Canadian Protestant Churches and the South African War, 1899–1902
Gordon L. Heath

51 In the Aftermath of Catastrophe
Founding Judaism, 70 to 640
Jacob Neusner

52 Imagining Holiness
Classic Hasidic Tales in Modern Times
Justin Jaron Lewis

53 Shouting, Embracing, and Dancing with Ecstasy
The Growth of Methodism in Newfoundland, 1774–1874
Calvin Hollett

54 Into Deep Waters
Evangelical Spirituality and Maritime Calvinist Baptist Ministers, 1790–1855
Daniel C. Goodwin

55 Vanguard of the New Age
The Toronto Theosophical Society, 1891–1945
Gillian McCann

56 A Commerce of Taste
Church Architecture in Canada, 1867–1914
Barry Magrill

57 The Big Picture
The Antigonish Movement of Eastern Nova Scotia
Santo Dodaro and Leonard Pluta

58 My Heart's Best Wishes for You
A Biography of Archbishop John Walsh
John P. Comiskey

59 The Covenanters in Canada
Reformed Presbyterianism from 1820 to 2012
Eldon Hay

60 The Guardianship of Best Interests
Institutional Care for the Children of the Poor in Halifax, 1850–1960
Renée N. Lafferty

61 In Defence of the Faith
Joaquim Marques de Araújo, a Brazilian Comissário in the Age of Inquisitional Decline
James E. Wadsworth

62 Contesting the Moral High Ground
Popular Moralists in Mid-Twentieth-Century Britain
Paul T. Phillips

63 The Catholicisms of Coutances
Varieties of Religion in Early Modern France, 1350–1789
J. Michael Hayden

64 After Evangelicalism
The Sixties and the United Church of Canada
Kevin N. Flatt

65 The Return of Ancestral Gods
Modern Ukrainian Paganism as an Alternative Vision for a Nation
Mariya Lesiv

66 Transatlantic Methodists
British Wesleyanism and the Formation of an Evangelical Culture in Nineteenth-Century Ontario and Quebec
Todd Webb

67 A Church with the Soul of a Nation
Making and Remaking the United Church of Canada
Phyllis D. Airhart

68 Fighting over God
A Legal and Political History of Religious Freedom in Canada
Janet Epp Buckingham

69 From India to Israel
Identity, Immigration, and the Struggle for Religious Equality
Joseph Hodes

70 Becoming Holy in Early Canada
Timothy G. Pearson

71 The Cistercian Arts
From the 12th to the 21st Century
Edited by Terryl N. Kinder and Roberto Cassanelli

72 The Canny Scot Archbishop James Morrison of Antigonish
Peter Ludlow

73 Religion and Greater Ireland
Christianity and Irish Global Networks, 1750–1950
Edited by Colin Barr and Hilary M. Carey

74 The Invisible Irish
Finding Protestants in the Nineteenth-Century Migrations to America
Rankin Sherling

75 Beating against the Wind
Popular Opposition to Bishop Feild and Tractarianism in Newfoundland and Labrador, 1844–1876
Calvin Hollett

76 The Body or the Soul?
Religion and Culture in a Quebec Parish, 1736–1901
Frank A. Abbott

77 Saving Germany
North American Protestants and Christian Mission to West Germany, 1945–1974
James C. Enns

78 The Imperial Irish
Canada's Irish Catholics Fight the Great War, 1914–1918
Mark G. McGowan

79 Into Silence and Servitude
How American Girls Became Nuns, 1945–1965
Brian Titley

80 Boundless Dominion
Providence, Politics, and the Early Canadian Presbyterian Worldview
Denis McKim

81 Faithful Encounters
Authorities and American Missionaries in the Ottoman Empire
Emrah Şahin

82 Beyond the Noise of Solemn Assemblies
The Protestant Ethic and the Quest for Social Justice in Canada
Richard Allen

83 Not Quite Us
Anti-Catholic Thought in English Canada since 1900
Kevin P. Anderson

84 Scandal in the Parish
Priests and Parishioners Behaving Badly in Eighteenth-Century France
Karen E. Carter

85 Ordinary Saints
Women, Work, and Faith in Newfoundland
Bonnie Morgan

86 Patriot and Priest
Jean-Baptiste Volfius and the Constitutional Church in the Côte-d'Or
Annette Chapman-Adisho

87 A.B. Simpson and the Making of Modern Evangelicalism
Daryn Henry

88 The Uncomfortable Pew
Christianity and the New Left in Toronto
Bruce Douville

89 Berruyer's Bible
Public Opinion and the Politics of Enlightenment Catholicism in France
Daniel J. Watkins

90 Communities of the Soul
A Short History of Religion in Puerto Rico
José E. Igartua

91 Callings and Consequences
The Making of Catholic Vocational Culture in Early Modern France
Christopher J. Lane

92 Religion, Ethnonationalism, and Antisemitism in the Era of the Two World Wars
Edited by Kevin P. Spicer and Rebecca Carter-Chand

93 Water from Dragon's Well
The History of a Korean-Canadian Church Relationship
David Kim-Cragg

94 Protestant Liberty
Religion and the Making of Canadian Liberalism, 1828–78
James M. Forbes

95 To Make a Village Soviet
Jehovah's Witnesses and the Transformation of a Postwar Ukrainian Borderland
Emily B. Baran

96 Disciples of Antigonish
Catholics in Nova Scotia, 1880–1960
Peter Ludlow

97 A Black American Missionary in Canada
The Life and Letters of Lewis Champion Chambers
Edited by Hilary Bates Neary

98 A People's Reformation
Building the English Church in the Elizabethan Parish
Lucy Moffat Kaufman

99 Towards a Godless Dominion
Unbelief in Interwar Canada
Elliot Hanowski

100 Finding Molly Johnson
Irish Famine Orphans in Canada
Mark G. McGowan

101 Apparition Fever
Observing the Virgin Mary in Belgium
Tine Van Osselaer

102 Tradition and Tension
The Presbyterian Church in Canada, 1945–1985
Stuart Macdonald

Tradition and Tension

The Presbyterian Church in Canada, 1945–1985

STUART MACDONALD

McGill-Queen's University Press
Montreal & Kingston • London • Chicago

ISBN 978-0-2280-2469-9 (paper)
ISBN 978-0-2280-2534-4 (ePDF)
ISBN 978-0-2280-2535-1 (ePUB)

Legal deposit second quarter 2025
Bibliothèque et Archives nationales du Québec

Printed in Canada on acid-free paper that is 100% ancient-forest-free, containing 100% sustainable, recycled fibre, and processed chlorine-free.

This book has been published with the help of a grant from the Federation for the Humanities and Social Sciences, through the Awards to Scholarly Publications Program, using funds provided by the Social Sciences and Humanities Research Council of Canada.

Funded by the Government of Canada | Financé par le gouvernement du Canada

Canada Council for the Arts | Conseil des arts du Canada

We acknowledge the support of the Canada Council for the Arts.

Nous remercions le Conseil des arts du Canada de son soutien.

McGill-Queen's University Press in Montreal is on land which long served as a site of meeting and exchange amongst Indigenous Peoples, including the Haudenosaunee and Anishinabeg nations. In Kingston it is situated on the territory of the Haudenosaunee and Anishinaabek. We acknowledge and thank the diverse Indigenous Peoples whose footsteps have marked these territories on which peoples of the world now gather.

Library and Archives Canada Cataloguing in Publication

Title: Tradition and tension: the Presbyterian Church in Canada, 1945–1985 / Stuart Macdonald.

Names: Macdonald, Stuart, 1957- author

Series: McGill-Queen's studies in the history of religion. Series two; 102.

Description: Series statement: McGill-Queen's studies in the history of religion. Series two; 102 | Includes bibliographical references and index.

Identifiers: Canadiana (print) 20250114593 | Canadiana (ebook) 20250114607 | ISBN 9780228024699 (paper) | ISBN 9780228025351 (ePUB) | ISBN 9780228025344 (PDF)

Subjects: LCSH: Presbyterian Church in Canada—History—20th century. | LCSH: Canada—Church history—20th century.

Classification: LCC BX9001 .M314 2025 | DDC 285/.271—dc23

This book was designed and typeset by Marquis Interscript in 10.5/13 Sabon. Copyediting by Rachel Taylor.

McGill-Queen's University Press
Suite 1720, 1010 Sherbrooke St West, Montreal, QC, H3A 2R7

Authorized safety representative in the EU: Mare Nostrum Group BV, Mauritskade 21D, 1091 GC Amsterdam, the Netherlands, gpsr@mare-nostrum.co.uk

To Gale

Contents

Figures and Tables

FIGURES

TABLES

Acknowledgments

This book began in the classroom. Since 1997 I have taught the Presbyterian history course at Knox College, a true privilege. Year after year the course changed as new themes and new questions emerged. I am deeply grateful to my students for all of the questions, comments, essays and interest. One example: Jo-Ann Dickson's master of theological studies thesis on women's ordination convinced me there was more to that story than was currently known. To all my students, thank you. The course was also taught interdenominationally, the first year with three of us (Alan Hayes speaking to the Anglican tradition) and for many years with Phyllis Airhart (the United Church of Canada). I learned so much from my teaching colleagues.

I want to express thanks to my research assistants. Mark Godin did the initial photocopying related to church extension (around 2002). Robert Revington collated and indexed the overtures to the General Assembly from 1945 to 1985. Incredible research support was given by Anne Miller (never officially a research assistant). Anne entered the denominational statistics of the Presbyterian Church in Canada on to Excel spreadsheets, which facilitated the computer mapping and other research that provides some of the deep background for chapters 2 and 7, as well as the demographic analysis throughout the book. Anne also indexed three decades of the *Presbyterian Record* and provided me with pages of photocopies of articles or items in the denominational magazine that she knew I would find of interest.

Librarians and archivists are invaluable to all historians. I want to thank the staff of the Presbyterian Church in Canda Archives for their invaluable support and encouragement. Kim Arnold (archivist), Bob Anger, Nicole D'Angela, and Alex Kay: Thank you. I am also grateful to the staff of the Anglican Church of Canada's General Synod Archives for their warm welcome. Being part of the University of Toronto has provided access to the amazing library collection and to the research resources, including support for using GIS software provided by Marcel Fortin. The staff of the Caven Library deserve special thanks: Joan Pries, Susan Sheridan, Laura Alary, and Anne McGillivray. The Caven staff have always gone above and beyond to support this project. I am grateful to the Knox staff as a whole, for their interest and their patience as I explained my latest discovery. I also want to express my special gratitude to Laura Alary for providing invaluable feedback on chapters 4 and 8, and to John Vissers for doing the same on chapters 5 and 9.

My thanks to those in the clerk's office in the Presbyterian Church in Canada, Victor Kim, Stephen Kendall (now retired), Don Muir, and Terrie-Lee Hamilton. I am also grateful to Peter Coutts, whose analysis of the Presbyterian Church's demographics has always been insightful and with whom I have been engaged in spirited conversations about these numbers and trends for over twenty years. My thanks to William J. Adamson, Stephen Hayes, A. Donald MacLeod, and Susan Shaeffer; to the members of the denomination's national history committee; and to all in the denomination who have shared their wisdom and insights.

The historians who go before us are the ones who shape the story. I am truly grateful for the work of John Moir, and share with him the frustration that so little has been written about the Presbyterian Church in Canada in the period after church union. I am grateful to Brian Fraser, Peter Bush, and all who have tried to fill in the gaps in our knowledge. I also want to thank Gil Stelter of the University of Guelph, who taught me about urban history and suburbanization. My academic colleagues at Knox College have listened, supported, and encouraged, as have my colleagues who were part of the then history department at the Toronto School of Theology. Brian Clarke deserves a special note of thanks, not only for working with me on *Leaving Christianity* but for supporting me over the years and encouraging me in writing this book. I am also grateful to my colleagues in the Canadian Society of Church History and the Canadian Society of Presbyterian History. Their friendship and support are greatly appreciated.

Knox College has allowed me not only to teach about Canadian Presbyterians but to research and write as well. I am grateful to the Board of Governors of Knox College for their ongoing support of research and of academic freedom through sabbaticals and conference and book allowances,. I offer my thanks to the principals of Knox – Arthur Van Seters, Dorcas Gordon, John Vissers, and Ernest van Eck – who have supported this project and provided special financial support to bring it to completion.

I want to thank all who helped in the process of transforming the manuscript into a book. I am grateful to Jon Cleland for his work editing the manuscript for submission to the publisher. At McGill-Queen's University Press, I have been privileged again to work with Kyla Madden, who has supported this project with her wisdom at every step. Thank you. My thanks as well to Rachel Taylor, my copy-editor, and to Kathleen Fraser, the managing editor, for their guidance, patience, and support. Thanks to Stephen Ullström for his expertise in producing the index. I am also deeply grateful to the anonymous readers who provided great insight and made this a much better manuscript because of their comments.

Finally, to my family. To my children, Meaghan and Brendan, who saw the early stages of this research but are now long settled in their own lives and careers: if nothing else, this book helps explain their father. And to my wife Gale, who has lived through the writing process and offered invaluable support. My deep thanks and love.

TRADITION AND TENSION

Introduction

"Here it is – 1975!"

This announcement from the executive director of the Presbyterian Church in Canada's Centennial Committee marked the beginning of an important year for Canadian Presbyterians. Their denomination was 100 years old. Dr Finlay G. Stewart called the church not only to celebration but to reflection, gratitude, and service, and suggested the year would be "a test of our worthiness in this generation." Stewart asked his readers to approach the centennial celebrations as they did the Lord's Supper, "in gratitude and penitence" and with a "spiritual understanding" that would lead to a deeper purpose. Remembering the denomination's history was important, primarily to spur the church on to action in the present:

> With this study will come vision and dedication, developed and enriched by warm hearted fellowship and evangelism. You will make the discovery that you matter and your church matters today in your community and your world. You will discover that you are both the object of God's love and instrument of his love. In other words that you are the body of Christ and the kingdom of God is within you. This will mean a new day of evangelism in our Presbyterian family. It will not be a self righteous dividing faith. It will be happy, contagious and satisfying in every way. We have services of renewal taking place in many congregations and in presbyteries and in groups of congregations and it is most encouraging.[1]

The denomination's centennial, it was believed, would lead to positive action and renewal. But the hoped for renewal did not happen.

Three years after celebrating their centennial, Canadian Presbyterians created a committee to look into the state of the church. Confidence had been shaken. The Presbyterian Church in Canada was worried about its current situation as well as its future.

This book explores this history of the Presbyterian Church in Canada in the period immediately following World War II up to the middle of the 1980s. This denomination was one of Canada's largest Protestant denominations. It also had been and remained one of Canada's most culturally dominant churches. The period under study, 1945–85, marked a dramatic change in the fortunes of this denomination. Canadian Presbyterians expanded significantly, only to find themselves in the early 1960s unexpectedly seeing fewer in their pews on a Sunday morning and losing members, children, and youth. Canadian Presbyterians were not unique in experiencing this dramatic shift at this particular moment. What is noteworthy is how they responded to this challenge. What did they do to grow so successfully in the immediate post-war period? What adjustments did they make or attempt to make when it became evident that they were no longer growing? How did the denomination itself change in this crucial period? These questions are important. At the same time, they often feed into the narrative of "what went wrong" that have become the lore within the denomination itself as well as within broader conversations concerning the changing place of Christian churches within Canadian society. Some within the denomination suggest, "We became too liberal. That's why they left." Others add, "We stopped doing evangelism. We became too political." Others argue a contrary position, "No. We wouldn't change anything. We were too stuck in the past." The arguments continue and have for years, even decades.

What was the Presbyterian Church in Canada like in this forty-year period? Did it, as some accuse, abandon evangelism? Was it theologically liberal or politically progressive? Was it too stuck in the past? How did Canadian Presbyterians see themselves, and how did they adjust their mission during this forty-year period? These are some of the questions this book hopes to answer by exploring important themes in the life of the denomination during these years. One of these themes is how the church built new congregations. This was a time when Canadian Presbyterians were aggressively involved in beginning new congregations. How did they do this? Who was in charge? Did they succeed? Did this approach change over time? In exploring this theme, many of the questions raised in the conversation about "what went wrong" are indirectly referenced. This, I would argue, is the best way to address these questions. We need to know what happened and what was done before we judge too quickly what went wrong. We need to know the facts first. The facts are fascinating, at times supporting our preconceived notions, at other times challenging them.

This book takes a thematic approach. The first chapter gives crucial background that is necessary if we are to understand the Presbyterian Church in Canada in 1945. The denomination established in 1875 had divided in 1925, with roughly two-thirds participating in the church union that created the United Church of Canada. This book follows the fortunes of the roughly one-third who continued as the Presbyterian Church in Canada. Given its significance, it is important to consider the background to the events of 1925, as well as how continuing Presbyterians rebuilt their denomination. Only with an awareness of this can we truly engage the history of the denomination after World War II.

The four themes explored in this book are: church extension; the church's sense of identity (how it related to other Christians, how it understood its mission, how the denomination did its work); the place of women in the church; and theology and worship within the denomination. These themes were not chosen randomly. This book has emerged out of teaching students the history of the denomination at Knox College for over twenty-five years. These are the themes that have in various ways emerged as the most significant ones that need to be considered for this particular period. Research into the overtures sent to the denomination in this period, as well as reading the yearly reports of the General Assembly in the *Presbyterian Record*, confirmed that these were key themes. This does not mean that there are no other themes that might be considered or other ways to tell this story. One additional theme that might be considered is the foreign missions work of the denomination. Overseas mission is touched on in this book. A more extensive coverage, one that would require looking at it over a much broader number of years than just those four decades, would be a project on its own. Other themes might also be proposed. The belief is that by considering in depth these four themes, an overall sense of the history of the denomination in this period will emerge. It is also true to say that some topics that have emerged as central in our own times – most notably the involvement of the Presbyterian Church in Canada in the residential school system – were not as prominent in those decades. Presbyterian missions to Indigenous Peoples in

Canada began in the mid-to-late nineteenth century. Whereas Methodists and Anglicans had established missions to Indigenous Peoples in the maritime provinces, Lower Canada, and Upper Canada, Canadian Presbyterians had seemingly done no such mission work.[2] It was with the opening of the prairies and the overall enthusiasm about mission work of the nineteenth century that the denomination began to work with Indigenous Peoples, alongside their work with other communities. One key part of that work involved residential schools. Canadian Presbyterians would begin eleven residential schools in total. Some of these had a brief history. Others became the responsibility of the United Church of Canada after Church Union.[3] In the period after World War II, the Birtle Residential School in Manitoba and the Cecilia Jeffrey Residential School near Kenora, Ontario, were the two residential schools operated by the Presbyterian Church in Canada under the direction of the Women's Missionary Society Western Division. This work, when it was noted, was discussed under the general mission work of the denomination, as one feature alongside work with Hungarian, Ukrainian, or Chinese Canadians. Residential schools were noted in passing in the period between 1945 and 1985, and largely spoken of positively, but were not the major concern they are today.

Why those four decades? Why not take the story up to the present day? These are questions I have faced, both in planning this book and in conversations about it. There are some personal as well as pragmatic reasons. I was ordained in 1985. Being involved in a different way after 1985, it seemed more challenging to tell the story of those years. There was also the very pragmatic reason that there was more than enough material to discuss in the period from 1945 to 1985. A longer period would have required a much longer, and different, book. Most significantly, these forty years were not just any forty years. They were a crucial forty years. Indeed, with a few notable exceptions, one could argue that most of what has occurred in the years since 1985 in the Presbyterian Church in Canada is a natural outgrowth of what happened during these crucial decades. Membership decline, the creation of many small suburban churches, the ordination of women as ministers and elders; increased divisions within the denomination on specific issues – these all were crucial features that developed in these forty years. If this is the case, it becomes imperative that we look in greater depth and detail at what happened during those crucial decades. For all these reasons this current study has focused on what is a vital period that we need to understand.

Denominational histories have proven their worth. The value of a broader perspective, as seen in Patrick Allitt's *Religion in America since 1945: A History* and Brian Clarke's "English-Speaking Canada from 1854," is clear.[4] The debt owed to *Leaving Christianity*, an exploration by Brian Clarke and myself of religious change in Canada since World War II, will be evident.[5] *Leaving Christianity* provides the context needed in order to interpret the actions and responses of the Presbyterian Church in Canada. Broader studies are important. There is also value in a close study of a denomination, something ably demonstrated by Michael Wilkinson and Linda Ambrose in *After the Revival*, Michael Wilkinson in *Canadian Pentecostalism*, Kevin Flatt in *After Evangelicalism*, Adam Stewart in *The New Canadian Pentecostals*, and Terrence Fay in *A History of Canadian Catholics*.[6] The last major history of the Presbyterian Church in Canada, John Moir's *Enduring Witness*, was published in 1974 to mark the centennial of the denomination the next year. Two subsequent editions of this book have been produced, each adding additional chapters to cover more recent developments.[7] Other large Canadian Protestant denominations have produced more recent studies. Alan Hayes's *Anglicans in Canada* has provided a very useful history of the Anglican tradition, one that, similar to this study, uses a thematic approach.[8] Two recent books have also been published on Canada's largest Protestant denomination, the United Church of Canada. A decade-by-decade exploration of the denomination by various authors in *The United Church of Canada: A History* was edited by Don Schweitzer. Phyllis Airhart, in *Church with the Soul of a Nation*, focused on the early period of the United Church of Canada's history and the developing challenges posed by the late 1950s and 1960s.[9] This book owes a debt of gratitude to these studies and all of these authors for demonstrating in different ways the continued usefulness of in-depth studies of a particular denomination.

This study challenges some conventional understandings and provides detailed discussions of crucial topics from this historical era. The idea that the Presbyterian Church in Canada never recovered after church union has become not only part of denominational lore but an example for those who wish to argue for long-term secularization. As will be argued, there is no evidence for this conclusion. Similarly, we see evidence that Canadian Presbyterians saw themselves in partnership with the government on key issues. They expected to be listened to when tensions arose. They also saw themselves as having a privileged place within Canadian Christendom. Church, state, and culture were still interwoven in the early post-war period. What we see over time is the beginnings of an emerging distance between culture, state, and church. The changing place of women is an important theme that deserves serious discussion. Too many discussions of the role of women in this period seem to start and end with the issue of the ordination of women as clergy. The case of the Presbyterian Church in Canada offers an opportunity to look beyond this to the role that all women played (or did not play) in the decision-making processes of the denomination. The discussion of the active discrimination against women, even after the decision had been made and the attempt to reverse or renegotiate what had been agreed to, is, as far as I am aware, unique. The book also provides an extensive and unique discussion of how a North American denomination expanded into the emerging suburbs in the post–World War II period, deliberately setting out to build new churches in areas where new housing was being concentrated and communities were growing.

The Presbyterian Church in Canada expanded and grew in the years immediately following World War II. That growth was real and significant. The denomination was intentional in its desire to be a major Reformed denomination open to all Canadians. This is one of the major arguments of this book. At the same time, the Presbyterian Church in Canada was hampered in this desire by their own culture, which looked back in particular to the Westminster Confession of Faith and their system of governance. This could make any change difficult. This was particularly evident in some of the debates about how the denomination should be administrated and financed and in the torturous path taken to produce a statement of faith in contemporary language. Presbyterians did change in this period. They accepted women as ordained elders and ministers in the church. They stood by this decision when it was challenged in the late 1970s and early 1980s. The tension was between the desire to move forward and the compulsion to look back.

The structure of this book is straightforward. The first chapter provides essential background on the events of 1925 and the challenging task of rebuilding the denomination in the years immediately following. The book is then divided into two sections, the first looking at developments to the mid-1960s, and the second taking the story up to 1985. Each section explores the four themes: church extension (new church development), identity, the place of women, and theology and worship. There is no clear-cut date that divides the two sections, though the chapters generally divide in the period between 1965 and 1967. It should also be noted that in the second section, the theme of identity is explored before turning to look at church extension. The arguments of the book are developed along the way, and then briefly summarized in the conclusion.

1

Rebuilding (1925–1945)

The moment has become iconic. On the night of 9 June 1925, as midnight grew closer, Canadian Presbyterians gathered within Knox Presbyterian Church on Spadina Avenue. They were holding a vigil. At midnight, as 10 June began, the laws of Canada stated that a new denomination, the United Church of Canada, would come into being and the Presbyterian Church in Canada, established in 1875, would become part of that denomination and thus cease to exist. Those gathered at Knox Presbyterian Church begged to differ. In their eyes, *they were* the Presbyterian Church in Canada. Certainly, some Presbyterians had left their denomination to join another, but as 10 June began, those present knew that they were the true Presbyterian Church in Canada. And they were continuing. The General Assembly had not, despite what those leaving the denomination asserted, ended on 9 June when it met at College Street Presbyterian Church. Those in charge of that meeting may have adjourned it. They may have refused to let the "Protest and Claim of Right" be read during the official meeting. But that meeting had not been adjourned – "finis." Commissioners intent on continuing the Presbyterian Church in Canada had continued to meet in that church. They had elected a new Moderator, D.G. McQueen. These continuing Presbyterians then ended their meeting, but not before they had stated their next time of meeting and location – which was now, the evening of 9 June 1925, and at this location, Knox Presbyterian Church in Toronto. This was the General Assembly of the Presbyterian Church in Canada and it was continuing. And so, they and their supporters gathered. Songs were sung. And as a new denomination came into being, those gathered refused to let their denomination die. For those who continued as the Presbyterian Church in Canada, it was an iconic moment indeed.[1]

But how had it come to this? What was "church union," or as those who continued as the Presbyterian Church in Canada after 10 June 1925 preferred to call it, "the disruption," all about? The union of denominations that created the United Church of Canada in 1925 was one of the most significant moments in twentieth-century Canadian church history. At its birth, the United Church of Canada became by far the largest Protestant church in Canada. Since the Reformation period, when various groups broke away from the Roman Catholic Church to form their own churches, Protestants had continued to divide. Lutherans. Reformed Christians, who then divided further between Congregationalists and Presbyterians. Baptists. Mennonites. English Protestants, who came to be known as Episcopalians or Anglicans. Methodists broke from the Anglican church. Methodists then divided, and divided again, and again. Presbyterians had done the same. English-speaking Presbyterians were divided not only by national boundaries (Ireland, England, Scotland, and various American colonies) but by their understanding of how they should relate to the state – in particular, how much the state should support the church and thus, through that support, control the church. Who was in control of the church, Jesus or the King? Presbyterians divided. They brought their divisions to what became Canada. They continued to divide once they arrived in Canada, the largest such division happening in 1844 when the Free Presbyterians broke away from those in connection to the Church of Scotland, echoing a division that had occurred the year previously in Scotland. But divisions that made sense in Britain did not make sense in the British colonies. If nothing else, the sheer vastness of the colonies and the scattered populations dimmed the zeal of those holding onto old points of principle. There was also the challenge of Roman Catholicism (which Presbyterians opposed), not only in Lower Canada (Quebec) but also throughout the colonies. As a result, different kinds of Presbyterians discovered they had more in common with each other than they first realized. They also came to an awareness that they could do more together than they could separately. Gradually, Presbyterians started uniting rather than dividing, until in 1875 they came together to form the Presbyterian Church in Canada.[2]

This remarkable success in overcoming what had previously been principled points of division was one of the great successes achieved by Canadian Presbyterians. And they were not alone in this. Methodists had followed a similar path to unity. As the twentieth century began, the two largest denominations in Canada were the Presbyterian Church in Canada and the Methodist Church, followed at some distance by the Church of England in Canada (Anglicans).[3] This was one of the major factors which led to the belief that, if some unity had been a good thing, more unity would be even better. A second major factor encouraging denominations to believe that a unified Protestant church was something they should consider and even create was the reality that theological differences between these Protestant traditions were muted by their common evangelical Protestant culture. Methodists, Congregationalists, Anglicans, Baptists, and Presbyterians all believed that Christians should make a commitment to Jesus Christ and then live that commitment out each day. They all believed in revivals. They cooperated in the same social causes. They worked in the temperance movement for the prohibition of alcohol because they believed this was God's will and would result in a better society. They fought – with considerable success – to restrict business on Sundays to allow people to attend church and to honour what they believed to be the Lord's Day.[4] They shared common causes and common fears. The goal was building a Christian Canada. The fear was that this would be ruined not only by the nefarious liquor interests but by the Roman Catholic Church. Canadian Protestants were particularly worried about immigrants arriving who were Roman Catholic. They feared these immigrants just as they feared the Roman Catholic Church. Given that they already shared the same evangelical ethos, the same goals and causes, and the same opponents, unity made sense. One unified Protestant church would be more effective in opposing the one Roman Catholic tradition. It would have greater success in converting those immigrants to the Protestant faith. One unified Protestant church would also be more efficient. This was the third factor encouraging the dream of unity: efficiency. It was something that made sense inside the church, but it was also something strongly encouraged by the external cultural forces at the time. What had the creation of Canada been, after all, but a merger of disparate and different British colonies? And it had been a success. Businesses were merging. Larger organizations were seen to be more effective. It made sense, particularly as the church moved into new areas such as the prairies, to imagine that building one common Protestant church where fifty people could gather to worship God, rather than building three competing Anglican, Methodist, and Presbyterian congregations, each struggling to exist with a dozen or so in worship. Efficiency. Common culture and a common opponent. Previous success in overcoming divisions. All of these led to the belief among Protestants in Canada that a unified denomination would be not only a good idea but what God was calling the church to do.

The vision of a unified Protestant church for Canada made a great deal of sense. What this vision underestimated or overlooked entirely was how challenging this would be. It was one thing to bring together congregations and denominations who shared a common heritage – for example, who saw themselves as following in the footsteps of John Wesley, the founder of Methodism; it was another thing entirely to bring those who looked to John Wesley together with those who looked to John Calvin, the key leader for Presbyterians. This was to be a union across traditions, not a union within traditions. There was a common evangelical ethos; however, there were also major differences in theology on a variety of issues. Baptists, who at one point were invited to join the discussions, had a completely different understanding of baptism than Methodists or Congregationalists. Anglicans, who were also invited to consider being part of this united Protestant church, had a completely different understanding of ordination. Great dreams frequently collapse due to details. The dream of one Protestant church encompassing everyone was too bold a dream. The idea of uniting the Methodists, Presbyterians, and Congregationalists was bold enough.[5]

For some Presbyterians, it was a step they would not take. Was it because they looked down on the Methodists because they were of a lower social class and had been less educated? Was it because of subtle cultural differences between the traditions? Presbyterian congregations chose ("called") their ministers, while Methodist congregations had their ministers appointed. Was it because these Presbyterians refused to give up their theological heritage, specifically the Westminster Confession of Faith and related documents? The answers were not clear at the time, nor have they become clearer with time. People opposed church union for different, sometimes contradictory, reasons. The reality is that those Presbyterians who went into church union look remarkably like those Presbyterians who stayed out, and suggestions that it was because those supporting church union were more "liberal" or were supporters of the "social gospel" do not stand up under close scrutiny.[6] For multiple reasons, Presbyterians divided on whether or not to support church union. They divided, as we shall see, regionally. They divided based on other factors. What makes it even more challenging is that two different stories emerged. Those arguing this was a disruption told a very different story from those who suggested this was a church union. These narratives emerged at the time and they have continued to shape how we understand what happened on 10 June 1925. It is thus important that we discuss the debates within the Presbyterian Church in Canada over church union as this directly affected decisions by individuals and congregations to either move into the United Church of Canada or attempt to continue as a distinct Presbyterian denomination. Despite careful planning, those who wished to continue as a distinct Presbyterian denomination faced significant challenges. This chapter will discuss the debates about union and the events of 1925 itself, then turn to consider what remained and the difficult process of rebuilding the denomination. The basic structures were in place by 1928, though the denomination was very different from what the Presbyterian Church in Canada had looked like in 1924. Continuing Presbyterians were concentrated in central Canada, weaker in the Maritimes, and decimated in the prairies. This reality was one that not all in the denomination wished to accept. Efforts were made to rebuild in the prairies. All of these efforts ran straight into the economic depression of the 1930s and then the new challenge of World War II. It was during the war that finances finally stabilized. It was also during this period that the denomination successfully affirmed their identity, notably in winning the right to call itself the Presbyterian Church in Canada. This chapter will look at each of these periods in turn. Despite all of the challenges it faced, the continuing Presbyterian Church in Canada was able to successfully rebuild the denomination and, as peace returned, was prepared to move forward.

CHURCH UNION DEBATES IN THE PRESBYTERIAN CHURCH IN CANADA

The story of church union should be a simple one. A proposal for discussion on a possible union was made. Committees were struck, met to discuss issues, and successfully created an agreement on how the churches might merge. The individual denominations met and voted on this proposal. The union either went forward or did not. The story should be simple and clear. And in some ways, this is exactly what we do see: a proposal to consider union, an agreement on terms, and then the voting on this union. All of these elements can be seen in the period from 1902 to 1925. But wait. Should we begin with 1902? Did this not really all begin in 1899 with discussions on cooperating on the home mission fields? Two narratives have developed, with different understandings of the origins of this movement, concerning who began this move to church union (or disruption), and whether or not it was ever properly authorized in the first place. There are different stories about the votes within the Presbyterian General Assembly and what they mean. There are different stories about the organized opposition. There are sections within this story that are relatively straightforward, such as the negotiations on the terms of agreement and what became known as the basis of union. The votes approving the deal within the Presbyterian Church in Canada were a different matter entirely.

This is not a book about church union; rather, this is a book about those who continued as the Presbyterian Church in Canada.[7] At the same time, in order to understand how the church continued, it is important to understand what happened in these fateful years, beginning with the two origin stories. For unionists, organic church union was part of a natural outgrowth of increasing cooperation between the denominations, going back to the 1899 request from the Presbyterians for greater cooperation in home missions in Canada. Those supporting union would also point to the three speakers – official delegates from the Presbyterian Church in Canada, including the moderator who had spoken at the 1902 Methodist gathering. By contrast, those opposed to the union saw the origins as illegitimate and outside all due processes. While it might be noted that there were three speakers at the 1902 Methodist conference bringing fraternal greetings, the focus was largely on William Patrick and what he supposedly stated. Patrick was new to Canada and had no official authority to propose a possible union. Yet, as suggested by those opposed to church union, his unauthorized comments are what began the entire church union movement.

Conversations on an interdenominational union began in 1904. The negotiations on the agreement, known as the basis of union, took place over four years. The basis of union laid out the terms of union and how the new church would operate. It also included a statement that defined the theology of the new denomination. Once the basis of union had been approved, it was necessary for all of the denominations to pass this agreement according to the laws of each denomination. In the case of the Presbyterian Church in Canada, this involved something called the Barrier Act. The Barrier Act was a process, adapted from the Scottish Presbyterian tradition, that guaranteed that changes in doctrine or polity needed to be carefully considered. One General Assembly could not change the confessional heritage of the denomination. Instead, if a change was desired, the General Assembly would agree to send this issue down for consideration and vote by the various presbyteries. A first vote then sent the remit (proposal) down to the presbyteries. Presbyteries could only vote yes or no to the remits. The vote on these remits was reported to the next General Assembly. If the majority of presbyteries approved, and if these presbyteries also included a majority of the members of the denomination, the remits were put to a vote at this second General Assembly. If this General Assembly approved the motion, it became the polity or doctrine of the church. Change was not swift. But the Barrier Act did ensure that the majority of Canadian Presbyterians approved of what was being proposed.

As the basis of union involved changes to both the polity and the doctrine of the church, the Barrier Act was used. In 1910, the General Assembly supported a motion to approve church union – 180 delegates supported the motion and seventy three opposed. This was then sent down under the Barrier Act to the presbyteries. The results were reported to the next Assembly: of seventy presbyteries, fifty were in favour and sixteen were against, with four not replying. This vote would have given a double majority: a majority of the presbyteries were in favour, and they would have represented the majority of the membership of the denomination. What should have happened next needs to be noted – a vote should have been taken again, and if this passed, the Presbyterian Church in Canada should have moved into the proposed union. Instead, and contrary to the normal practices of the denomination, a plebiscite of the membership was held to see what percentage were in favour of church union. The results were reported in 1912 with 70 per cent of those who voted supporting union. The next few years saw a series of motions and actions, all, it seems, intended to increase the percentage of those in favour of church union. Minor changes were made to the basis of union in 1914. A second plebiscite was held in 1915, again with the majority supporting the move to church union. Finally, the vote that should have taken place in 1911 happened in 1916. The General Assembly in 1916 voted (406/90) to move forward with church union. As this was now in the midst of World War I, it was agreed that union would take place at the conclusion of the war.[8] The obvious question is why was the second vote not taken on this matter in 1911? Why did Canadian Presbyterians hold a plebiscite, indeed two of them, rather than simply hold a second vote at General Assembly, as was the requirement of the Barrier Act? Why the delay?

It is here that the discussion has become confused, both at the time and since. There was clearly opposition to the proposed union. There often is opposition to an issue at a General Assembly, and this does not usually prevent the denomination from making changes. While not discounting the suggestions of the various historians who have emphasized different concerns and different personalities, the real issue was not church law. The problem was civil law – in particular, a decision made in the British House of Lords that is known commonly as the Overtoun decision. In 1900, the United Presbyterian Church and the Free Church of Scotland united as the United Free Church of Scotland. Within the Free Church of Scotland there had been a minority strongly opposed to the union, and although they lost the vote on this union (643/27), they claimed that they continued as the Free Church of Scotland – it was those who had voted in the majority who had left the denomination. As such, they contended that all of the property – congregational buildings, funds, theological colleges, endowments – belonged to them. In 1904 the House of Lords found in favour of the minority. It was a remarkable and surprising decision, one that required an Act of Parliament in the United Kingdom to sort out the mess that was left. This decision, though taken in Great Britain, applied to the Canadian situation, as the House of Lords in Britain was the final arbitrator in these situations.

What the decision did was three things. First, it established key principles about what the state and courts believed needed to happen when denominations merged. It was not enough that a denomination follow its own policies and procedures. The state added additional tests to determine which of the bodies was the true denomination and was thus entitled to the assets and properties. Canadian Presbyterians who were opposed to church union were very aware of the decision and its implications. Ephraim Scott, the editor of one of the denominational magazines *The Presbyterian Record* and a strong opponent of church union, made direct reference to this British legal case in *"Church Union" and the Presbyterian Church in Canada*, declaring that it "was one of the most important [legal cases] ever decided by a

British court" and noting that its judgment was directly relevant to the situation in Canada.[9] He cited with approval Lord Chancellor Halsbury's judgement that "the identity of a religious community described as a Church must consist in the unity of its doctrine. Its creeds, confessions, formularies, tests, and so forth are apparently intended to ensure the unity of the faith which its adherents profess, and certainly among all Christian Churches the essential idea of a creed or confession of faith appears to be a public acknowledgment of such and such religious views as the bond of union which binds them together as one Christian community."[10] Those opposed to church union were very aware that this case applied to Canada and aware of what they needed to do to meet these new standards. The second impact of the Overtoun decision was that it removed any necessity for those opposed to union to compromise. They had a remarkably strong hand. They simply needed to say "no." Third, to avoid or at least mitigate the inevitable disputes over property, it was now clear that legislation would be needed to divide the property. This, again, strengthened the hand of those opposed to union as it allowed them to make the argument that church union was not about God but was simply a legal arrangement, one that needed to be passed by parliament.

Why was there a plebiscite? Why were there delays on the side of the Canadian Presbyterians that meant that union was not realized until 1925? The legal consequences that arose from the Overtoun decision was the crucial factor. Had it followed its own polity and rules of governance, the Presbyterian Church in Canada could have approved union in 1911. After this, the necessary steps could have been taken and the United Church of Canada could have been established in the next few years. The Overtoun decision ensured that those who opposed church union might either derail the enterprise entirely, or, if union succeeded, be able to continue and continue with buildings and assets. It is no wonder that organized opposition to church union, in the form of the Presbyterian Church Association, gathered strength after the vote on union in 1916. While the battle might not have been won, there was much to be gained from fighting.

The Presbyterian Church in Canada had voted in 1916 to move forward with church union but not until after the war had concluded.[11] It was not until 1921 that a vote to proceed with church union was approved (414/107).[12] This vote should be understood as procedural; the process of church union had already been passed under the Barrier Act, with the second vote taken in 1916. In 1921 the Presbyterian Church Association was reactivated. For the next four years it fought against church union or, should this first fight fail, for the best possible results in terms of property and finances for those who wished to continue as Presbyterians. In 1923 the draft legislation passed the General Assembly.[13] As noted, the Overtoun decision meant that laws had to be passed federally as well as in every province. As these legal disputes evolved, a key determination was made: in most provinces congregational votes were taken if requested, and congregations had to vote whether to go into church union. This was a blow for those who believed that, because the denomination had according to its polity joined the new denomination, all congregations automatically went into that denomination. They might later vote to leave; however, they were all part of the new entity. As noted, this was not what was decided. In many parts of the country, notably Alberta, Saskatchewan, and Manitoba, many congregations did not hold votes as everyone agreed that they would be moving into church union. In other regions congregational votes were held and sometimes bitterly contested.[14]

The Presbyterian Church Association engaged in legal battles to oppose church union and to allow those who wished to stay outside of the United Church to continue as Presbyterians. This organization also kept track of the votes across Canada. This encouraged those who wished to dissent. It also was crucial in organizing those who planned to continue as the Presbyterian Church in Canada. The Presbyterian Church Association laid plans for a Presbyterian church to continue after the Act of Union came into place on 10 June 1925.[15]

In June 1925, as the General Assembly of the Presbyterian Church in Canada moved into its final days at College Street Presbyterian Church, another group of Presbyterians gathered at St Andrew's Presbyterian Church. The "Pre-Assembly Congress of the 'Continuing' Presbyterian Church in Canada" opened on the evening of 8 June at St Andrew's (King Street). The Pre-Assembly Congress was very much the creation of the Presbyterian Church Association. Its president, Principal D.J. Fraser, noted this in his welcoming address. The gathering reconvened the next day, 9 June, at St Andrews. In the morning the business was a report on "Congregations and Minority Groups, by Presbyteries, from the

Figure 1.1 Those committed to preserving the Presbyterian Church in Canada gathered in Toronto in a Pre-Assembly Congress of the "Continuing" Presbyterian Church in Canada, 8 June to 10 June 1925. This is a selection of the photograph of those who gathered.

Synod of the Maritime Provinces." In the afternoon the focus shifted to the same groups in the synods in western Canada. In the evening two public meetings were held. The public meetings adjourned at 10:00 p.m., but the evening was not over. The iconic meeting at Knox Presbyterian Church, with which we began this chapter, followed. Many went from these early evening meetings to participate in the vigil over the midnight hour. The midnight vigil sitting of Assembly adjourned in the early hours of 10 June and planned to meet again at St Andrews Church the following day, Wednesday, 11 June. The Pre-Assembly Congress had already planned another full day of meetings for 10 June. As the new United Church of Canada held its opening sessions on 10 June, delegates to the Pre-Assembly Congress met to consider reports from the three synods in Quebec and Ontario. These reports on which congregations and groups were continuing across Canada were followed in the evening by inspirational addresses in two different churches, St Andrew's and Cooke's.[16] The General Assembly reconvened on 11 June at St Andrew's Presbyterian Church to continue its new work of rebuilding the denomination and met until 16 June.[17] Also on 11 June, the Women's Missionary Society of the continuing Presbyterian church met at Knox Church.[18]

Table 1.1
Presbyteries, congregations, and membership, Presbyterian Church in Canada, 1924, 1925

	1924				*1925*		
Synod	Presbyteries	Congregations	Membership	Synod	Presbyteries	Congregations	Membership
Maritimes	10	639	51,457	Maritimes	5	224	16,802
Montreal and Ottawa	6	400	52,660	Montreal and Ottawa	6	170	23,561
Toronto and Kingston	14	671	104,784	Toronto and Kingston	10	308	54,777
Hamilton and London	9	363	72,706	Hamilton and London	9	228	43,157
Manitoba	8	489	33,985	Manitoba	3	36	3,657
Saskatchewan	15	876	27,731	Saskatchewan	3	58	2,779
Alberta	10	572	16,025	Alberta	3	60	4,751
BC	5	387	18,608	BC	2	56	4,759
Total	77	4,397	377,956	Total	41	1,140	154,243

Sources: For 1924 data, *A&P* (1925), 471; for 1925 data, *A&P* (1926), 192.

Note: Congregations and membership in the Synod of the Maritimes excludes those in the presbytery of Trinidad, on which see *A&P* (1925), 298–9.

A CONTINUING PRESBYTERIAN CHURCH: WHAT REMAINED

Despite all of their planning and considerable efforts, those continuing as the Presbyterian Church in Canada faced significant challenges. They had lost the legal right to use this name. They had good but incomplete data about how many churches would be joining the continuing denomination. What they clearly knew was the size of their church before church union. On 31 December 1924, the Presbyterian Church in Canada had a membership of 377,956 and a church school enrolment of 285,926.[19] But what did it look like after June 1925? In two provinces, New Brunswick and Manitoba, congregations only voted on whether to go into or stay out of union after 10 June 1925.[20] A year later in June 1926 there was a better sense of the membership of the denomination (slightly over 154,000, or less than half of what it had been previously) and the size of their church schools. There was a clearer sense of the structures of the denomination across the nation. The regional synods remained as they had prior to union (see table 1.1). The number of pastoral charges was less than a third of those that had existed previous to church union. What was more devastating was the loss of entire presbyteries, particularly in the Maritimes and in western Canada. In the Maritimes there had been ten presbyteries before union; now there were only five. Central Canada was largely stable, though one of the central synods was down four presbyteries. Western Canada saw the most dramatic losses: Manitoba fell from eight presbyteries to three, Saskatchewan from fifteen to three, Alberta from ten to three, and finally, British Columbia went from five presbyteries to only two. Two provinces deserve particular attention. In Nova Scotia, only the Presbytery of Pictou survived on the mainland. The presbyteries of Truro, Lunenburg and Yarmouth, Wallace, and Halifax had all joined the United Church of Canada. Scattered congregations and minority groups remained in these regions. Another province that had a strong Presbyterian presence before union was the province of Saskatchewan. This was no longer the case. Of 859 congregations, only 25 voted to stay out of church union. In Saskatchewan 750 congregations, representing nearly 14,000 members, had not even taken a vote.[21] Where the membership had been over 27,000 throughout the province, the membership of the congregations that had rejected union stood at 2,356 (less than a tenth).[22] This is not the number given in table 1.1, but the number the

Presbyterian Church Association tabulated in its recording of votes in various areas and regions of Canada.[23] Despite the challenge of differing statistics in this period, it was clear that the Presbyterian Church in Canada no longer had strong support across all the regions of Canada. It was now a church heavily concentrated in the provinces of Ontario and Quebec, with some strength in regions of the Maritimes, and a scattered population across western Canada. Presbyterians did not want to accept this. Ephraim Scott proclaimed in 1926 in the *Presbyterian Record* that the denomination's membership was "fairly evenly divided from ocean to ocean." This was simply not true. The numbers made this clear, even those that Scott cited: "West of the Great Lakes, where we were so often told our Church would be no more, there were in December last 210 Presbyterian preaching stations, with 9,039 families, 15,916 communicant members, and 14,917 in Sabbath Schools and Bible classes."[24] A comparison with what had been in 1924 was not given, nor was the data on churches in central Canada provided. With this information (see table 1.1), readers of the *Presbyterian Record* would have been aware of how great the losses in western Canada had been, and that their denomination was actually not "fairly evenly divided" across the country as was claimed.[25]

By 1928 the Budget Committee of the Board of Administration reported that the denomination had seemingly stabilized. Communicant membership stood at 172,000 in December 1927, up from 154,000 in 1925. Money was being raised, though more money was needed: "It is not extension or new work that is concerning us at present; it is the meeting of the expenses for which we are committed."[26] The numbers reported in 1928 give us a clearer picture of what the continuing Presbyterian denomination looked like (table 1.2). As the Budget Committee reported, membership was up from what it had been. Two other notable changes can also be seen. One presbytery had been added to each of the Maritimes and British Columbia synods. In Nova Scotia there was now a second presbytery on the mainland, encompassing all of the congregations from Halifax to Lunenburg. In British Columbia, the Presbytery of Kootenay had been created. New congregations had been established in most of the synods. In many cases these were congregations made up of minority groups from surrounding congregations. This kind of scenario happened across Canada. Another scenario was one where there had only been one presbyterian congregation in a community. In some cases,

Table 1.2
Presbyteries, congregations, and membership, Presbyterian Church in Canada, 1925, 1927

	1925				*1927*		
Synod	Presbyteries	Congregations	Membership	Synod	Presbyteries	Congregations	Membership
Maritimes	5	224	16,802	Maritimes	6	250	17,358
Montreal and Ottawa	6	170	23,561	Montreal and Ottawa	6	179	27,012
Toronto and Kingston	10	308	54,777	Toronto and Kingston	10	315	60,247
Hamilton and London	9	228	43,157	Hamilton and London	9	245	47,356
Manitoba	3	36	3,657	Manitoba	3	54	5,261
Saskatchewan	3	58	2,779	Saskatchewan	3	85	4,191
Alberta	3	60	4,751	Alberta	3	92	5,308
BC	2	56	4,759	BC	3	61	5,785
Total	41	1,140	154,243	Total	43	1,281	172,518

Sources: For 1925 data, *A&P* (1926); for 1927 data, *A&P* (1928).

the minority who wished to stay out of union established another congregation. In other cases, the majority found itself with a congregation and property as part of the continuing denomination, but a much smaller congregation to pay the expenses. Frequently, there was also no minister, as ministers had tended to favour the church union project. What the numbers from this period also confirm was the regional imbalance within the continuing Presbyterian Church in Canada. This was a denomination with strength in central Canada, particularly Ontario, but many fewer congregations and members west of the Ontario border.

Rebuilding occurred community by community, congregation by congregation, and presbytery by presbytery. The national institutions that the denomination shared and supported also needed to be rebuilt. Prior to church union, the Presbyterian Church in Canada had supported several denominational magazines. After 10 June 1925 only one remained, the *Presbyterian Record*, edited by eighty-year-old Ephraim Scott. Scott had been a staunch and vocal opponent of union. It was not surprising that he continued to publish the *Presbyterian Record*. It was perhaps also not surprising that a different version of the magazine briefly appeared in July 1925, which offered a completely different picture of what had happened at the 1925 General Assembly.[27] Even after he beat back this challenge, Scott had an enormous problem. The *Presbyterian Record* no longer had a clear sense of its subscribers or mailing list.[28] It took time to sort this out. Theological colleges had to open in the fall, in many cases with new faculty and new leadership, and they had to recruit students who wished to serve in the denomination. Missions, both domestic and international, had become central to the life of the denomination. But which mission fields remained? Untangling the foreign mission fields took longer. As Zander Dunn has demonstrated, missionaries on the foreign mission field did get to express their opinions, but those served by the missionaries in India, Korea, Trinidad, China, and other places were not asked their opinions on whether they wanted to continue as partners with the Presbyterian Church in Canada or work instead with the United Church of Canada.[29] The mission fields were divided. Continuing Presbyterians ended up with mission fields in two regions of India, British Guiana (Guyana), and Formosa (Taiwan).[30] They also ended up with a mission field working among Koreans in Japan. This latter field emerged because the missionary, Luther Young, went to Japan instead of returning to Canada and began a new mission there.[31] There were church school curriculums to create and youth programs to establish.[32] Did the denomination own the copyright to their hymnbook, the *Book of Praise*? The answer was no. There were national positions to fill supervising the work in Christian education, worship, finance, theological education, and various aspects of mission. At the same time as these tasks had to be done, the denomination also continued to work to protect the property of the denomination – both in terms of buildings such as congregations, theological colleges, and other institutions, and in terms of financial endowments.[33] Rebuilding was a massive task. Even with the determined preparation that had preceded the division of the denomination in 1925, it took several years to return to something resembling stability.

One other major task that Canadian Presbyterians engaged in during these years was fighting for their identity, particularly in terms of their ecumenical partnerships. Canadian Presbyterians were determined that they would be recognized by other Reformed denominations as a legitimate denomination and part of the Alliance of the Reformed Churches throughout the World Holding the Presbyterian System (known as the Alliance of Reformed Churches), the international community representing their theological heritage. They were adamant that they receive this recognition. One of the important committees during this period was the Committee on Correspondence with Other Churches. The denomination carefully recorded the greetings it received from other denominations. For example, in 1927, greetings to the "Presbyterian General Assembly" were received from the moderator of the Presbyterian Church in the USA. A reply offering thanks was sent from the Presbyterian Church in Canada.[34] The denomination continued to insist that it was entitled to this name and politely reminded others of this claim. Stuart Parker reported in 1928 on a difficult meeting of the Western Section of the Alliance of Reformed Churches held in the United States. The greatest challenge was that the Alliance had failed "to accord us our proper designation in its minutes." Continuing Presbyterians wanted to be known as the Presbyterian Church in Canada. This slight was met by a motion from Assembly that a committee be created "to investigate the matter of the name of our Church, to take legal counsel, if required," and to report the results at the next General Assembly.[35] The name meant identity. It conveyed what had happened before, during, and after 1925. Presbyterians were adamant that their understanding be accepted. When the report was heard at the next General

Assembly it was unanimously agreed: "We are the same church as before the disruption of 1925, not having changed in either doctrine or policy. Those who went out from us could not divest us of either. Being therefore the same Church and being the only Presbyterian Church in Canada, in Assembly we consistently re-affirmed the name, *The Presbyterian Church in Canada*."[36] At the conclusion of the report, it was noted that both the Church of Scotland and the United Free Church of Scotland had requested delegates using the correct name, Presbyterian Church in Canada.[37]

ADVANCE: 1928–30

In a bold and important symbolic move, the General Assembly held their 1928 General Assembly in Regina, Saskatchewan. The success of mission expansion in Saskatchewan had been one of the prides of the church prior to union. The denomination gathered that year in Saskatchewan to offer moral support to those in that province who had remained within the denomination. As was the custom, Assembly began on the Wednesday evening. What was unique was what happened on the weekend: The "ministerial commissioners available were scattered abroad so that the greater number of the congregations and missions stations in the province heard a representative of the Assembly."[38] This had taken money and careful planning. All of this effort was considered worth it as this "assured to the province and our congregations in particular the largest possible benefit from this first General Assembly to be held within the bounds of Saskatchewan."[39] As well as those scattered across the province, Presbyterian ministers preached at First Church Regina (the Assembly church), Northside Presbyterian Church, First Baptist Church, and Cameron Memorial Baptist Church. There was also a "Sunday School Rally" in the afternoon at First Church. No United Church pulpits were included even though some United churches in Regina had invited Presbyterians to preach. The reason, the denominational magazine explained, was that the United Church had sponsored a speaker from the *Christian Century* in Chicago, who had made "unchristian pronouncements upon our Church's motives and conduct in the recent crisis" while in the province, and the United Church had failed to "repudiate" his comments. "Amazement" was expressed that such a request had even been made.[40]

Holding the General Assembly in Saskatchewan was intended to send a message: the Presbyterian Church in Canada was not going to die, but was continuing to consolidate. More than that, it intended to expand, grow, and renew the mission it believed it continued to have. Two years later, the denomination received the welcome news that one of its most contentious legal cases, involving the Salt Spring's pastoral charge in Nova Scotia, had been resolved in favour of the Presbyterian Church in Canada.[41] More good news followed. The Committee on Correspondence with Other Churches had continued to work to guarantee the denomination's "proper recognition throughout the world" and had achieved a major success. The previous year's gathering in Boston of the Alliance of Reformed Churches had agreed to refer to the denomination as the Presbyterian Church in Canada, although the resolution (which was printed) had a noteworthy caveat: "until an authoritative decision has been reached and made effective, the Council shall designate this Church as The Presbyterian Church in Canada, and shall protect its own records by a footnote to the effect that this designation is in dispute and is here used without prejudice, implying neither approval nor disapproval on the part of the Council." Despite the news that there was "a footnote" or asterisk, this news was met with a "hearty cheer from the Assembly."[42] Progress was also being made in the number of charges in the denomination. For example, in the Maritimes there had been 118 charges in 1925; now, in 1929, it was reported, there were approximately 130.[43] Membership and finances overall had improved: the net gain in membership across Canada was over 25,000.[44] The General Board of Missions reported that "requests to extend were coming for all our fields" where mission work was being done in Canada as well as overseas. Personnel and financial resources were all that was lacking. Positions were being filled where possible. The committee was clear that it was time to move forward in all these areas: "We dare not think of retrenchment; forward must be our watchword."[45]

The moderator, the Rev. Frank Baird, summarized the situation in a message to the denomination that was printed in the August 1930 *Presbyterian Record*. He outlined the many things that were going well with the denomination. Success in legal decisions and in gaining wider recognition of the correct name of the denomination and its right "*to advance under its own banner*" were noted. More ministers were needed, and it was reported that the Colleges and committees of the church were working on this in order to "provide the men necessary for our vacant pulpits." Missions were moving forward. The challenges of the budget were faced directly. Growth in membership was noted and compared to the growth of 8 per cent reported by the United Church of Canada, and it was suggested there was "no cause for discouragement" here: "At the same time there is urgent call to every minister and Session to put forth the utmost effort for the enlargement of communion rolls. Next to growth spiritually, there must be increase numerically."[46] The denomination was set to expand, yet the choice of moderators created some difficulties. The denomination throughout this period was intent on honouring those who had fought in key places and over many decades against church union. While commendable, this meant that those elected moderator were older, with Ephraim Scott, who was eighty when elected moderator, as only one example. Moderators kept dying while in office. The honouring of those who had fought so hard against union was understandable, but in this period and the early 1930s, the result was it often being reported to General Assembly that the previous moderator was either ill or dead.

Canadian Presbyterians were advancing. They were also reconstructing their theology. Those who had opposed church union had represented diverse theological positions, ranging from the staunch creedalism of Ephraim Scott to the theological liberalism of D.J. Fraser, principal of Presbyterian College. The "Fathers of 1925," as Alan Farris has noted, were a diverse group.[47] The role of Walter Bryden, professor and later principal of Knox College, in the renewal of the denomination's theological engagement was notable. As John Vissers has written of Bryden: "He taught a generation of ministers to think theologically and thereby contributed to a theological awakening in the church."[48] It was through his students, including Joseph McLelland, Gordon Peddie, and James Smart, that Bryden's influence was felt. While contributing original ideas himself, he also opened his students and the denomination itself to a sympathetic reading of theologians such as Karl Barth who were working with similar goals, rejecting both the liberalism and fundamentalism of the early twentieth century. This contributed to a positive vision for the denomination as it moved forward: not only was it against something (church union), it also had a renewed and revived theology. In terms of their identity, a renewed theological vision, and their numbers, Canadian Presbyterians were not only growing but moving forward as the decade of the 1920s ended and the 1930s began.

Table 1.3
Congregations in the Presbyterian Church in Canada, selected years (1928, 1932, 1937, 1942, 1945)

	Self-sustaining	*Augmented*	*Mission fields*	*Total number of congregations*
1928	633	316	339	1,288
1932	626	320	374	1,320
1937	567	320	426	1,313
1942	578	271	387	1,236
1945	606	256	332	1,194

Sources: For 1928 data, *A&P* (1929), 280; for 1932 data, *A&P* (1933); for 1937 data, *A&P* (1938), 290; for 1942 data, *A&P* (1944), 288; for 1945 data, *A&P* (1946), 306.

GREAT DEPRESSION AND WORLD WAR II

The timing could not have been worse. By 1928 the Presbyterian Church in Canada had largely recovered; two years later the denomination was beginning to envision expanding. All of these plans faltered as the economic crisis that was affecting Canada and the entire world began to be felt. Over the course of the next twelve years almost 100 congregations would be lost. The impact of the Great Depression on the Presbyterian Church in Canada can be seen in table 1.3. As well as the total number of congregations, the various types of congregations categorized by the denomination are noted. Self-sustaining congregations were congregations that could pay all of their expenses independently. These were the largest congregations in the denomination. Augmented congregations were congregations that could pay some of their own way, but needed assistance to pay the rest of these costs. Mission fields were congregations that, for a variety of reasons (frontier congregations, a ministry to an ethnic or linguistic minority, or financial assistance), needed significant support from the denomination. What this table demonstrates is a very modest increase from 1928 to 1932 in the total number of congregations, followed by a gradual and then intensifying decrease. Self-sustaining congregations remained relatively stable as a percentage of the total number of congregations in the denomination. They reached their lowest proportion at the height of the depression, then improved their number during World War II. Augmented congregations declined throughout this period, both in real numbers and as a percentage of the total. The mission charges tell a different story: they increased in total numbers and as a proportion of the total in the early years, only to decrease significantly during World War II. What is clear is that the growth the denomination had been making in the 1920s and early 1930s was lost over the course of the next twelve or so years. An economic depression and war took their toll on the number of congregations within the Presbyterian Church in Canada. These also took their toll on the number of members in the denomination. As figure 1.2 illustrates, after the clear recovery that followed union, membership peaked in the early 1930s, then declined during the rest of that decade and throughout the war years. A similar pattern, only more dramatic, can be seen in the membership in church schools (figure 1.3). The depression not only stalled the growth of the denomination but pushed back some of the significant recoveries made after 1925.

The effect of the depression on the denomination was noted over the course of the 1930s. The 1931 Assembly was considered a crucial one. There had as yet been no "retrenchment" in any of the areas of the denomination's work but it was noted that under the "stress and strain of these trying days" many institutions throughout society were struggling.[49] A report on the relief work the denomination had done in prairie areas affected by drought during the past three years was given to the Assembly in 1932.[50] The Assembly in 1932 also received overtures asking that salaries and minimum stipend be reduced.[51] This was not done, but by the next year the financial situation of the denomination led to a major dispute between the Mission Board, responsible for paying the stipends of all those serving overseas as missionaries as well as all those in Canada on minimum stipend, and the Commission of Assembly that was responsible for the budget. It was agreed that minimum stipend would stay at $1,800 plus a manse; however, presbyteries were allowed to appoint new ministers at the reduced rate of $1,600 plus manse.[52] Two years later, it was clear that many different groups in the church were struggling to raise money and pay their bills.[53] The impact of the depression was clearly being felt by 1935. The denomination had cooperated with other churches in providing relief to the areas of the prairies devastated by drought.[54] It was also noted that there had been a decrease in church schools and enrolment due, in large part, to the "movement of population in the West, from the south to the north."[55] The General Board of Missions in 1936 reported that it "was constrained in view of the limited resources available for its work" in what it could do, and appealed to members to give more generously.[56] On the eve of World War II, the denomination

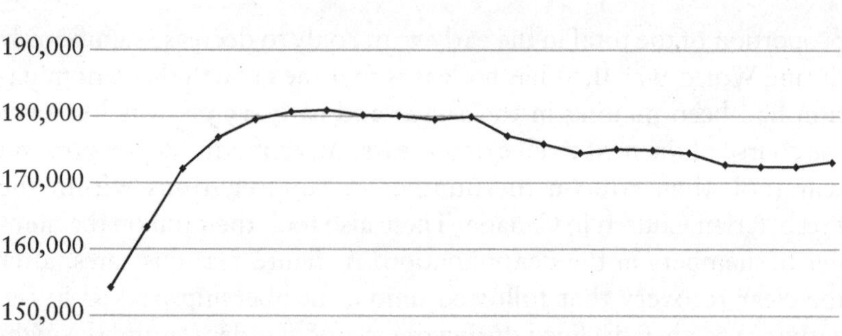

Figure 1.2 Membership in the Presbyterian Church in Canada, 1925–45

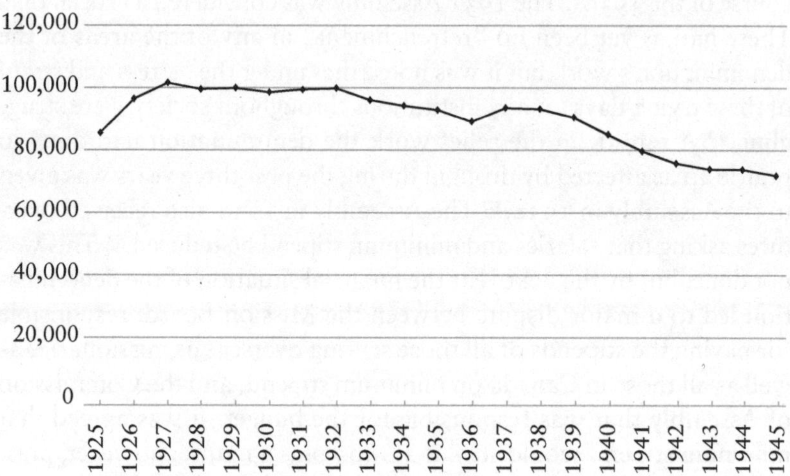

Figure 1.3 Church school membership, 1925–45

received an update on the impact the depression had on the prairies: "The Western Synod, on account of the economic conditions and crop failures with a consequent shifting of the population presented a serious problem and to save the situation Presbyteries were requested to do their utmost by way of amalgamation of congregations and mission stations. Satisfactory results have followed this effort."[57]

As was the case in Canadian society as a whole, war brought new challenges for Canadian Presbyterians. They also benefited from an improved economy. By 1943 the denomination was cautious but clear that finances were in a much better situation. One clear indication of this was the restoration of salaries to the denominational officials who had seen their salaries reduced by 10 per cent since 1933.[58] The next year it was reported that the stipends had increased for those serving in augmented and ordained mission field appointments.[59] Church finances had improved, although the denomination was extremely cautious in how it spoke of these improvements. There was no call for celebration; nevertheless, there are numerous signs that as World War II drew to a close the Presbyterian Church in Canada was in much better shape than it had been for over a decade and was ready, as it had been in the late 1920s, to advance and expand.

It was in the midst of the Great Depression that the Presbyterian Church in Canada celebrated its sixtieth anniversary. Marking their Diamond Jubilee in 1935 allowed Canadian Presbyterians to do many things. It allowed them to stress their continuity with the church that had existed before 1925; they were making the argument that they were the continuation of the Presbyterians who had united in 1875, and not any other body. It also allowed the denomination to mark ten years since "the disruption." Finally, it allowed the denomination to seek external validation both to their existence as a church and to their right to be called the Presbyterian Church in Canada. A "Thanksgiving and Rededication" service was held (tellingly) on 10 June 1935 as part of the General Assembly. The July issue of the *Presbyterian Record*, usually focused on the current Assembly, went into elaborate detail regarding the events of 1875. The denominational magazine also published greetings that were received from other Reformed churches throughout the world. The United Presbyterian Church of North America and the Presbyterian Church in the USA extended good wishes on the occasion to the Presbyterian Church in Canada. The Presbyterian Church in Wales dodged the issue of the name (intentionally or otherwise) but did congratulate the denomination on its "sixtieth year of service." The Presbyterian Church of England and the Presbyterian Church of Ireland both noted the Diamond Jubilee and used the correct name for the denomination. The same was done by others: the United Original Secession Synod in Scotland, the General Synod of the Evangelical and Reformed Church, the United Free Church of Scotland, the Free Church of Scotland, and the General Presbyterian Alliance. Missionary partners in India and North Formosa also sent greetings: in the latter case, there may have been a challenge in translation as the telegram message read: "Congratulations Jubilee and Tenth Anniversary." Despite this error, this was printed alongside the other greetings.[60] This had all been carefully orchestrated. As the Committee on the Correspondence with Other Churches noted in its report: "Other churches were informed of the fact that this is the Diamond Jubilee of our Church, with the result that many messages were presented on the evening of the special celebration. These have been reported in the July *Record*."[61] One notable absence had been a greeting from the Church of Scotland. This, it was reported in the July issue, had been due to an illness of the Clerk of that denomination; it was assured a message was on its way.[62] Canadian Presbyterians effectively used this anniversary to reaffirm their identity, not only in their own eyes but in the eyes of their peers.

The issue of the name remained. The United Church had challenged the right of continuing Presbyterians to use it, but Canadian Presbyterians continued to insist they were the Presbyterian Church in Canada and should be known by this specific name.[63] A key breakthrough was reported in 1938. The Committee on Correspondence with Other Churches reported that the "asterisk" – that is, the notation that there was a dispute as to whether the Presbyterian Church in Canada could be known by this name – had been removed by the Alliance of Reformed Churches. It was also noted that this had been done "with the co-operation of the United Church representatives."[64] Representatives of the Alliance were greeted at the next year's Assembly, as were two delegates from the United Church of Canada.[65] Even more significantly, it was reported that legislation approving the incorporation of "The Trustee Board of the Presbyterian Church in Canada" had been passed in April at the federal level, followed by provincial legislation in Ontario. The significance of this was noted: "The way is now open for the first time since 1925 to have the business of the Church, and all matters connected with the holding or disposing of property, funds and securities placed on a sound and permanent basis for the future, and to get free from many of the legal and technical difficulties of recent years."[66] This had all been made possible as a result of negotiations with the United Church of Canada which had resulted in the amendment of the United Church of Canada Act.[67] Through this work, the denomination was able to move forward as the Presbyterian Church in Canada – the name it demanded – and normalize relations with the United Church. It represented an enormous achievement, and is rightly noted by Keith Clifford in his study of the Presbyterian resistance to church union as the end of the story of that resistance.[68]

CONCLUSION

The vision of uniting with Methodists and Congregationalists to form a larger Protestant denomination to make mission more effective and to provide a more united front against the Roman Catholic Church was too radical a vision for many Canadian Presbyterians. For a variety of reasons (unfortunately there is no one reason that explains why some Presbyterians went into church union and others did not), they chose to stay outside of the United Church of Canada and continue as the Presbyterian Church in Canada. It was this decision, however, that shaped the denomination in the years preceding and following 1925. They developed their own story of how this union process began, how it had been against the laws of their denomination (something that was not quite accurate), and how the voice of the people had been ignored. Even as they railed against the proposed church as being created by the state, those opposed to union benefited enormously from a civic legal decision in Scotland that allowed religious minorities in these situations considerable advantages as long as they could argue they were maintaining the theology and polity of their religious denomination. It was the attempt to deal with these issues, as well as the outbreak of war, that delayed church union. Those opposed to union organized, not only to oppose union but also to continue their denomination after 1925. Despite their work, rebuilding was an enormous task at the local, regional, and national level. It was only in 1928 that things began to stabilize; however, this new normal was markedly different from the denomination that had existed previously. Canadian Presbyterians were now concentrated in central Canada, weaker than they had been in the Maritimes, and diminished in western Canada. This reality was not accepted or acceptable to many in the denomination. Their vision required a national denomination and they took steps, such as holding their General Assembly in Regina, Saskatchewan, to make claims of strength and then begin to change the reality on the ground. They were not content staying as they were. This desire to be a national church would continue to shape the denomination. They made plans to advance. These plans were interrupted, and then reversed, as the impact of the economic depression continued. A new crisis, the outbreak of another war, improved the financial situation but not the membership. The Presbyterian Church in Canada in this period had won major victories – including the right to its name – in preserving its identity and rebuilding its institutions. As World War II ended, it was ready, able, and prepared to advance the mission that it believed it had.

These arguments, made throughout this chapter, differ from some of those made by John Moir in *Enduring Witness*. The major difference relates to the success of the recovery. Reading Moir's chapter "Survival and Reconstruction" one is given a picture of failure, of a weakened, crippled, divided denomination, that survived union, but not in a way that would allow it to flourish afterwards. This portrait is best summed up in the conclusion to Moir's chapter:

> In 1926 it had had forty-five presbyteries – in 1946 it reported only one more. Its membership in 1926 had been 160,000 – twenty years later that figure had grown only by one per cent, a figure that could not be, like finances, blamed on the Depression. Obviously the church had failed to retain a proportionate measure of that dynamism and popular appeal which had less than two generations earlier made it the largest Protestant denomination in the Dominion. These were the hard, cold and cruel facts of life from which no comfort could be drawn as the Presbyterian Church in Canada faced the challenges and opportunities of the post-war era.[69]

As has been demonstrated, the impact of the depression, and later the war, on membership was much greater than Moir allowed. There is also an error in Moir's math. As we have seen, numbers in this period are a challenge; however, an increase of 1 per cent of the 1926 membership would mean the membership in 1946 would be approximately 165,000. In fact, it was approximately 174,000. More significantly, as a closer look at the denominational membership has shown, the depression significantly reversed the membership gains made in the period after church union. The denomination had grown only to decline during the depression. Despite the enormous challenges which have too often been underestimated, the Presbyterian Church in Canada had successfully rebuilt itself. It was a different denomination, in particular in terms of its regional strengths. It had, as most denominations do, divisions within its leadership and membership. Nonetheless, it had succeeded in establishing a core identity and shared story of its fight against union, in winning the right to its own name, and had created structures that could be built upon.

The denomination was ready for the post-war world and ready to expand.

2

Expansion and Growth

Local Initiative and Building New Congregations

As World War II drew to a close, the presbytery responsible for Canada's second largest city was taking initiative. The Presbytery of Toronto believed it needed someone working full-time to start new churches. In January 1945 they appointed the Rev. J.B. Thomson to serve as the full-time presbytery church extension worker. "Church extension" was what Presbyterians called establishing new congregations or new church development. This appointment was not the beginning of church extension work in the presbytery; indeed, the presbytery was already working with an emerging congregation in Leaside, and was taking steps to purchase land in the Kingsway. This appointment demonstrated that the presbytery was anticipating a need for a significant number of new Presbyterian congregations, enough to require a full-time staff person. They were taking a determined step to ensure that these congregations were developed.[1]

The Presbytery of Toronto took this important step for the simple reason that the development of new congregations was their responsibility. It was up to the presbytery to do the challenging task of surveying the need for a church in an area, renting space, appointing a minister, finding land, purchasing the land, constituting a congregation and a session, helping with providing a building, and all of the other steps that were required to create a new congregation. Local initiative was key. Local decisions drove the process. Church extension did not become denominationally coordinated until the first national director of church extension was appointed in 1963. Prior to this the work was done at the local level under the direction of the individual presbytery. In 1945 the denomination's responsibilities were limited. It provided assistance through the synod ministry convenor and the national home missions committee. This could include assistance in funding staff positions but it was still up to the presbytery to take these key steps in whatever order fit the particular situation. What synods and presbyteries looked to the national denomination for was qualified staff and resources: "men" (ministers for these new congregations) and "money" (essentially seed money to begin the process). Both of these were essential if new congregations were to be established. Ministers were needed. So too were financial resources. There were operational costs. The stipend (salary) of a minister had to be paid. There were also considerable capital expenditures. Land had to be purchased. Buildings needed to be constructed. New church development required considerable investment. The denomination struggled in the 1950s and early 1960s to both provide the necessary ministers and to raise the capital it believed was necessary. But these challenges did not take away from the reality that it was up to individual presbyteries across Canada to start new congregations if they believed there was a need and potential for growth. In January 1945, the Presbytery of Toronto vigorously took up this challenge.

The Presbyterian Church in Canada established new congregations between 1945–63. This is unquestionable. But how many did they build? Where did they build them? How many succeeded and how quickly? Did any fail? Were more built in Toronto than in Montreal? What about in British Columbia, or Alberta, or even the Maritimes? These are all important questions but they have remained stubbornly difficult to answer. A system that left the initiative at the local level (presbytery or synod) created few central records. It has not been possible to determine every congregation built across Canada in this period. We will begin with a look at some projects started in different localities in the early period after World War II. It is possible to get a glimpse of the denominational picture during the mid-1950s, thanks to a series of articles published in the denominational magazine by John McNab, the *Presbyterian Record*'s editor. By the late 1950s, finances had become a serious concern. The creation of Synod Corporations provided a temporary solution but did not resolve the problem. The challenge of finances, alongside the desire for better coordination, led the denomination to freeze new church extension projects briefly and centralize the planning function within the national offices. This shift from local control to central control marks a clear break in how the Presbyterian Church in Canada established new congregations. What needs to be recognized is how successful this early phase of church extension was. The Presbyterian Church in Canada successfully established new congregations in the suburbs of major and smaller cities. These congregations became significant for the life of the denomination in the decades that followed. Critiques, at the time and subsequently, should not blind us from seeing how the denomination transformed itself by successfully meeting the challenge of church extension in this period.

A GROWING CHURCH ACROSS CANADA

Synod reports in the aftermath of World War II speak to the need to develop new congregations. Among the mission reports made to the General Assembly in 1946, the Synod of Toronto and Kingston reported on its mission work. It noted that under the direction of the "Extension department" a building and property had been purchased for the Kingsway congregation. The committee also reported "splendid progress has been made in the new Leaside Church under the ministry of Charles Hay, and St Matthews under J.K. MacDonald has also marched forward."[2] In Manitoba, a survey had been done in the summer of 1945 by a deaconess, Helen Scott, and this encouraged the synod mission committee to begin "aggressive work" in an area of the Presbytery of Brandon.[3] Church extension work was being planned and undertaken, but the reporting to the General Assembly was scattered and incomplete. The Synod of Toronto and Kingston neglected to note that there was a full-time extension worker in the Presbytery of Toronto nor did they bother reporting on their activities in the three years from 1948 to 1950. One might conclude nothing was being done, but this was not the case at all. In Toronto the two presbyteries, East and West Toronto, established eight new congregations in these three years.[4] At the same time reports which expressed concern for growth did not necessarily mean a synod was actively engaged. In 1948 the Synod of Montreal and Ottawa spoke of the challenges they faced: "In the City and District of Montreal there are four or five localities where we ought to initiate mission work if our Church is to keep pace with the development of the City. There are certain industrial centres throughout the Province where we would be justified in opening new work. The question is how can we expand unless we have more men and money."[5] Four years later, in 1952, the synodical missionary, Allan Reid, again described the needs within the Synod of Montreal and Ottawa. He noted six sites within the Presbytery of

Montreal that were promising; only one of them, it would seem, was able to be developed. In the Presbytery of Quebec, Reid suggested mission work could be undertaken in Three Rivers (Trois Rivieres), Shawinigan Falls, Grand Mere, and other areas of expanding industrial and resource development. He mentioned three obstacles, two of which were familiar: men and money. The new obstacle that he discussed was the emerging problem of obtaining suitable land.[6] Reid was hopeful that the current denominational financial appeal – Christian Outreach – would help resolve the issue of money. He was less sure what to do about the issue of the shortage of ministers, as he argued student ministers could not do the task: "experience seems to show us that there is no purpose in trying to develop these places by student supply, and the only way in which the work can be done is by an ordained minister who is fitted for such mission work."[7]

Synod reports noted the challenges. They are not a reliable guide to what was actually being done. It is not clear in Reid's report what experience he was referring to, given that by his own admission the Presbytery of Montreal, responsible for Canada's largest city, was only involved in one church extension project in the suburbs of that city.[8] As we will discuss later, the presbytery responsible for Canada's largest city took much longer to become involved in actively building congregations than the presbytery in Toronto, Canada's second largest city. While there may have been problems, what is notable is how they are portrayed as virtually insurmountable, with therefore nothing proposed or any work in church extension (other than the one project) actually undertaken.

Challenges faced all presbyteries in this period. What is remarkable is how they set about establishing new congregations. The many steps involved can be seen by considering how one congregation was established in the Maritimes. In June 1951 the student minister at Musquodoboit Harbour was directed by the Presbytery of Halifax–Lunenburg to do a survey of a particular area of Tuft's Cove to "assess the possibilities of our starting some work there." The first response of the presbytery to the results of the survey was mixed: the convenor of the committee was negative, but other members of the committee saw more potential. When the issue of starting a church in this area was reconsidered in December it was agreed that an application would be made for the services of a deaconess to begin a work in the area. Estelle McCausland was appointed to the task. She was assisted by a student deaconess, Beryl Miller, and together they developed the project: "These two girls made a grand team; new families were found as they entered the district and the work progressed by leaps and bounds." A grant of $500 was obtained by the presbytery to assist with the costs of the survey. After a successful summer, an advisory committee was established and two further grants were sought: one for a building lot, another for the Sunday school. Two Sunday schools were established, one in the Odd-Fellows Hall and the second in a local home. Attempts were made to find a building in which to hold services and eventually they received permission to use the "newly completed Odd-Fellows Hall." The first worship service was held just prior to Christmas 1952. After this, things "progressed at a more rapid rate." The first women's group met in early January. The presbytery recognized this new congregation at the March 1953 meeting. An assessor session was formed. The first "Pantry sale" to raise money took place. A preparatory service was held with thirty-one members placing their names on the communion roll and on the next Sunday fifty-one people took communion. The first congregational meeting was held on 8 May 1952, and managers were elected by the congregation to take charge of the financial and building needs. A student minister was appointed, one assumes for the summer. In October the presbytery formed a planning committee "to oversee the Extension work in the Halifax and Dartmouth area." The question was not if the congregation would build a church, but where the church would be located. The building lot chosen by the congregation was accepted by the presbytery in November and permission was given to purchase it and seek a grant to build a new church. By May 1954 plans for the church building were in hand, and permission was given to borrow $25,000 (later increased to $62,000). That September Estelle McCausland, the deaconess who did so much work and seems to have been the constant presence on the ground, was given permission to be transferred. The congregation was named in June 1955 – St Andrew's, Dartmouth – and the cornerstone for the new building was laid in September of that year. The new building was dedicated on 22 January 1956.[9] The entire process, from considering the need to create a congregation to constructing a church building, took under five years.

This is but one example of what Canadian Presbyterians were doing in this period. Was it typical? It is difficult to say if anything was "typical" as different presbyteries approached the challenges in different ways. What this does illustrate is how involved the process was and how active a presbytery needed to be for a new congregation to be established. This was a costly venture in terms of time and money. In Toronto, given the number of congregations involved, a full-time worker was kept busy. These new congregations followed the suburbs as they expanded outwards.[10] In the western portion of Toronto, Alderwood (Browns Line north of Lake Shore Boulevard) was established in 1952, Rexdale (at Islington and Rexdale) in 1953, and Hillview (Martin Grove and Rathburn area) in 1955. Park Lawn, closer to the core of Toronto, was established in 1952. The Presbytery of West Toronto also established a congregation in a neighbourhood northwest of the intersection of Keele and Lawrence in 1953 called North Park. Presbyterians were establishing these congregations in neighbourhoods. Very few of the new congregations were established on major roads. The major intersections have been provided as a convenience to the reader, but in many cases the congregation was imbedded in a neighbourhood. Hillview, for example, was on Ravenscrest Drive, across from Glen Agar Park. This was not a major thoroughfare but a winding neighbourhood street.[11] Presbyterians also built a lot of congregations. They did not anticipate that regional congregations with larger parking lots might be a different option. In the eastern part of the city, three congregations were established in 1952: Trinity in York Mills, Wexford in Agincourt, and St David's in Scarborough. Congregations followed at Claire Lee Park in Scarborough in 1953 and St Mark's in Don Mills in 1954, and a Hungarian congregation was established in Oshawa in 1956. The two Toronto presbyteries followed an aggressive plan for expansion in this period.

EXPANDING ACROSS CANADA

Initiative was local. The denomination was not provided with a national picture of church extension until John McNab, the editor of the *Presbyterian Record*, began a series of articles in December 1954 summarizing the activity throughout Canada. This series of articles gives us a sense of how church extension was viewed in this period and of the progress being made across the nation. McNab began with Toronto and discussed "Evangelizing the Growing Suburbs" in both East and West Toronto. The various projects in Toronto were described, as well as the work of the two ministers who were coordinating the church extension work in Toronto across the presbytery boundaries.[12] The next month McNab turned his focus to the

Presbytery of Hamilton, discussing developments in the areas surrounding that growing city. Indeed, McNab suggested the only parallel in terms of "the extension effort that prevails" was in Windsor, Ontario. Hamilton had not waited "for the leadership of larger presbyteries" but forged ahead, under the leadership of a lay person and retired teacher, W.J. Moffat, who served as the chair of the Church Extension Committee. Under Moffat's leadership, a careful plan had been devised: at each site there was "sufficient space on the site for off-street parking" and each proposed site was approximately two miles apart. The article detailed the energy and commitment of the Mission's Committee of the Presbytery of Hamilton, which supervised the Church Extension Committee. The presbytery also established a fund to purchase church property with a goal of $200,000 to be raised for church extension. Detail was then provided on each of the new or proposed congregations, beginning to the east of Hamilton at Aldershot. A congregation had been organized eighteen months previously and was currently meeting in a school. There were seventy-six members and thirty children, and the congregation was active in raising funds and had organized a Vacation Bible School the previous summer with 180 children attending. A building lot had been purchased with plans for the new congregation. Roxborough Park was the next project described. A student minister had knocked on over 800 doors and discovered 186 families who would welcome a Presbyterian service. At that first service, again meeting in a school, seventy adults and eighty children were present. A building lot had been purchased and plans were moving forward. There was a challenge in this section of the city as it contained an existing church. St Columba was a new church development begun immediately after the war. While the congregation had raised money and had a church school of 250 that was overflowing its crowded facilities, it was also judged to be in the wrong location and too close to some of the other proposed works. Would it not be better, the article speculated, for St Columba to "go into this new district and with its present membership, perhaps double the congregation in a short time?" The details of the work in Hamilton continued, moving up the Niagara Escarpment (known in Hamilton as the "mountain") to the new developments being built there. Congregations were being planned at Eastmount, Southgate, and Westmount, and land had been purchased in each of these areas. These lots now had signs on them indicating that a future Presbyterian church would soon be constructed. It was noted that none of these sites was "on the principal thoroughfares, but they are very close." The pictures that accompanied the article showed overcrowded church school classes, young parents and their children, and the minister and his mother at the sod-turning at the Southgate site. The article also showed a picture of W.J. Moffat, the elder responsible for this, as an example of what "a consecrated layman, who has made extension work his chief interest for the past two years" could do, perhaps in the hope that other presbyteries might use this as an example.[13]

The story was quite different in the Maritime region, as the March issue of the *Record* detailed. The rural population was moving to urban areas in the Maritimes. The success of the new congregation started at St Andrews, Dartmouth, was highlighted. Several surveys of the need for new churches were being taken in other areas in the Maritimes, but no concrete plans were described. Instead, the article turned to the needs of frontier areas along the Labrador coast and the need for the church to be established in this remote area.[14] While these were "new frontiers" they also fit comfortably into the denomination's own experience of home missions. Expansion into frontier areas also began the discussion in September on church extension in British Columbia. The incredible growth of Kitimat, where the world's largest aluminum plant was being built, was detailed. The article described how a site for a manse and a church had been granted, and how a minister was already serving a congregation in this booming town. All three photographs that accompanied the article focused on aspects of the new church. After this powerful opening, John McNab turned to try to explain to his readers the differences he had discovered between the experiences of the church in eastern Canada (by which he meant central Canada) and western Canada. The kind of "phenomenal growth" where a "church school may be opened and in a few weeks' time 60 to 80 pupils may be enrolled" was unknown in "many parts of the prairies." He also noted that the "Sects have invaded the western provinces and British Columbia" in a manner clearly different from what he had seen in Toronto and Hamilton. He noted that in his travels in western Canada "I found the feeling that in some places consolidation was even more necessary than church extension. While I disagree with that philosophy, I feel that we have to help consolidate some of the weaker churches already in existence. But we have got to push further into the new developments *immediately* if the Church is going to expand as it should in western Canada." After this attempt

Figure 2.1 The "portable" sanctuary at Rexdale Presbyterian church, Toronto, Ontario. Moving to the suburbs meant using whatever space was available for Sunday worship. The congregation worshipped at Elmlea School prior to the completion of this building.

to explain some of the differences he had witnessed in the west, which informed not only this article but the ones that would immediately follow, McNab turned to describe the extension work being undertaken. He began in the more remote areas of British Columbia (Kimberley and Prince George) before turning to the suburbs around Vancouver: "Practically every self-supporting congregation is renovating or expanding or rebuilding." A new church had been built in New Westminster, with First Church replacing the former St Stephen's and St Andrew's Church. West Point Grey had been rebuilt and extended, and St Paul's (New Westminster) extended. Kerrisdale was not only an ambitious extension project but now had "the largest membership of any congregation." New work was being planned in Park Crest–Brentwood, on the north shore, in West Vancouver, in the Fraserview district, and in Whalley, a suburb of New Westminster. The article also noted with pride the construction of a Presbyterian residence, St Andrew's Hall, on the campus of the University of British Columbia.[15]

Figure 2.2 St David's Presbyterian Church, Kelowna, BC, 1950s. A modern church building in the suburbs, complete with office space and Church school classrooms. The large brick building would be the sanctuary, though there is no cross, no steeple, and no stained glass. The smaller building would be for church activities.

The tour of extension in Canada next turned to explore work in Alberta and the Synod of Manitoba (which included northwestern Ontario). Money began the conversation, specifically the amount of money owed by congregations in the west to "the central funds of the Church." What seems unique was that this region lacked "strong congregations to help the needy." McNab worried about what might happen, given that there were fewer strong congregations in this region of Canada than in the eastern regions: "Does this mean that we are going to have a strong Church at the centre and leave the western provinces or even new areas isolated and without the ordinances of the Gospel? Certainly the men who are pioneering, and it is pioneer work, in Manitoba, Saskatchewan, Alberta and British Columbia, need a central reservoir from which they can draw loans or grants in an hour of opportunity."[16] After laying out this challenge, he turned to consider what was happening in Alberta. He noted that, unlike Saskatchewan and Manitoba, strong central churches came through church union in both Calgary and Edmonton. First Church, Edmonton, was one example of a church still doing well. Other congregations in Edmonton were also doing well. Rupert Street had replaced the "dilapidated church building that I saw eight years ago" with a modern structure. Strathcona Park, Westmount Church, and St Andrews were all portrayed as being strengthened, while proposed new work in other parts of the city were noted. "Non-Anglo Saxon" ministries to Hungarian and Ukrainian congregations were described, with a particularly positive discussion of the large Hungarian congregation in Lethbridge. The issue of relocation of the congregations in Calgary was raised. These congregations were not currently well situated within the city. Relocating any of these congregations would be a challenge but one that was being discussed.[17]

In the Synod of Manitoba, frontier work in Atikokan was noted, as were various projects in Port Arthur, Fort William, Winnipeg, and Brandon. The moving of "our Indian school" by the government from Lake of the Woods to Kenora was noted: "The missionary in charge started a small Presbyterian cause here, and the congregation has gone ahead rapidly," with $20,000 having been raised for a building fund and the hope that they would "become self-supporting in a few years."[18] (When a new fellowship centre was dedicated in Kenora in 1971, a stained-glass window was dedicated within this church to the staff and students of the Cecilia Jeffrey Residential School. There was nothing expressed in the news item that would convey any sense that the residential schools had been in any way problematic.)[19] Overall, it was not a particularly exciting picture, with few success stories or future projects to hold up as exemplary. Instead, McNab felt it necessary to note the challenges ("undoubtedly, the small and struggling congregations in some western cities need to be strengthened and consolidated") before concluding: "Throughout my travels in the west it was emphasized that our Church has not had enough daring in extension work; nor enough faith in the possibilities; nor enough courage to go forward, and not enough money to assist those who are pioneer-minded and anxious to establish new causes."[20]

The editor of the *Record* concluded his tour and the series, addressing the issue of church extension in Saskatchewan. He assured his readers that the Synod of Saskatchewan was "aware of their church extension problem" and had plans to raise $200,000 and "build six much-needed churches and six manses."[21] Building lots, thanks to a generous donation, had been purchased in Regina's Lakeview district. In Saskatoon, St Andrew's Church enjoyed an excellent central location. The newly established Calvin Church in the southwest part of the city had a membership of 87 and a church that could seat over 200, and was beside an area with an anticipated housing development. The city's two other churches, St Paul's and Parkview, were noted as dating back to the union crisis and having buildings that were "inadequate and depressing." More hope was held out for a development in the Albert Park area, where six lots had been purchased, and plans were being made under the supervision of the minister of Calvin Church. The particular challenges of doing extension work in the prairies was noted. One challenge was the need (as noted in other articles dealing with the west) to consolidate before expanding. Another challenge was the reality that in some provinces and cities, "public school authorities will not permit the schools to be used for Sunday school or church purposes."[22] While there were unique problems, McNab used this final article in the series to highlight challenges he saw in church extension in general. He quoted one minister in Saskatoon as proclaiming, "We need men and we need money, but we need Jesus Christ far more. If our people were enthusiastic followers of their Saviour, we could get all the money we need for church extension in this one city."[23] Later in the article McNab summed up his findings, suggesting that there were "three faults" in the way Canadian Presbyterians were doing church extension: first, they were not "getting into an area at the right time"; second, presbyteries needed to step up, and if necessary relocate churches, even at the risk of annoying some members of those congregations; and third, they had to deal with a seeming personnel issue ("certain catechists who, if they are not a menace, will never let anything but an anaemic type of Christianity seep through the bloodstream of the Church"). He noted that synods needed to be made stronger, with "more devolution" in terms of administration.[24]

Through these six articles, the editor of the *Presbyterian Record* gave Canadian Presbyterians a survey of church extension work across Canada. These articles give us the best national picture of church extension in this period. Several things need to be noted. One is that, through it all, there was never a doubt raised that this is what the church should be doing. John McNab was clear that Canadian Presbyterians needed to be building new congregations and needed to be doing it as rapidly as they could. McNab shared with his readers the rationale for expansion that emerged during his discussion with ministers he met in Vancouver: "The ministers believe that the Church catholic needs the kind of witness that the Presbyterian Church can give. This was said in no arrogant nor boastful fashion ... The ministers also felt that if our Church maintains its theological emphasis and depth for the next 25 years, other denominations may become more reformed in their theology than they are today."[25] Canada needed, according to Canadian Presbyterians, the Reformed voice and theology they offered.

Second, and despite this clear vision, the denomination seemed confused as to whether it should be expanding on the frontier, as it has done in its glorious past, or dealing with the reality of expanding cities. The omission in this series of any discussion of Canada's largest city – Montreal – and what was happening there is worth noting. The Labrador coast and the company town of Kitimat, British Columbia, were expected to fire Presbyterian imagination more than the expanding suburbs on the west part of the island of Montreal. Or so it seemed. McNab's articles reflected a desire to show expansion and opportunity across Canada. In reality, the opportunity was limited (as his own articles demonstrated) in the Maritimes and in other parts of Canada as well. Frontier resource towns were places new congregations might be started. But the greatest challenge was the expansion around urban areas. These growing suburbs might be found, to some degree, around smaller towns and cities but they were concentrated around Canada's largest cities – Montreal, Toronto, Vancouver, and to a lesser extent Edmonton, Calgary, and Ottawa. As much as one might want all regions of Canada to be equally involved, this was not a realistic goal.

Third and finally, the importance of local initiative was clear throughout the series. In places where the synod, or in more cases the presbytery, had taken aggressive steps, new congregations were being organized and church extension was moving forward. Expansion was locally driven. At the same time, the articles do highlight various challenges faced by the denomination nationally; the need for more ministers to staff these congregations; and the need for money. The challenge of money was a particular challenge – and one to which we will turn, after we fill in one obvious gap in our understanding of what the church was doing nationally in terms of church extension: what was happening around Montreal?

Two years later, in an article similar to the series published in 1954–55 detailing church extension across Canada, McNab gave a picture of what was happening in Canada's largest city. The article was included in the March 1957 issue, which was a special issue highlighting home missions. The cover of the issue included a picture of a new congregation, St Giles in St Catharines, and included updated articles on church extension in British Columbia and in Toronto. The article on Montreal began by stating that "only one Presbyterian church has been erected in the burgeoning suburbs of Montreal in the past ten years," before going into the story of that congregation. St Laurent was started under the leadership of the Rev. Eric Beggs, who had come to Canada from Northern Ireland. The church had met in a school before building a Christian education building in 1955. Plans to pay off the debt and complete a sanctuary were underway. The congregation numbered 400 families and was filled with activities and organizations. While St Laurent was the furthest along, other congregations were also being planned or were in various stages of development: St Columba-by-the-Lake (close to Point Clair and Dorval) which had begun in 1952 and now had a full-time minister and a membership of 157; St Giles, Baie d'Urfe, a congregation with a membership of 100 which had a building site; and a possible congregation on Île-Perrot, near St Anne de Bellevue. McNab had met with the Home Missions Committee of the presbytery. This committee expressed its critique of the denomination's work in church extension: "Our whole pattern of Church extension thus far has been '19th century.' We have not considered the effect of the automobile on the Church." The chair of the committee, Dr William Stanford Reid, expressed his belief that church buildings needed to have a seating capacity of about 300 (otherwise heating could be too expensive) and be more "contemporary" in architectural style rather than gothic.[26] A more extensive review of the situation in Montreal was provided two years later.[27] The article covered much of the same material as before but added more detail. It was noted that a congregation had been established in Mount Royal just at the end of World War II. It noted that neither this work in Mount Royal nor the congregation at Ville St Laurent had been "the result of extension work by the presbytery," but had arisen because of local support. The development of the congregation at Valois (which became St Columba-by-the-Lake) had been supported by donations from two established Montreal congregations. It was also noted that the head of the extension subcommittee, the Rev. F.R.M. Anderson, had surveyed the "suburban areas near Montreal" in 1955 and suggested "ten strategic locations" for Presbyterian congregations, four of which were now being developed. The presbytery created a separate extension committee in October of that year with Stanford Reid as the chair. Funds were raised so that by 31 March 1959, slightly over $150,000 was available.

Several projects, in addition to those outlined in the *Presbyterian Record* article two years previously, were mentioned. In addition, it was noted that the Rev. A. Ross MacKay was now being supported by the General Board of Missions to serve as the extension secretary of the presbytery.[28] The pictures of new buildings or their congregations that ran alongside the article made the point that the church was growing in the areas around Montreal.

McNab's surveys gave the most comprehensive picture Canadian Presbyterians would have had of their denomination's expansion – that they were growing would not have been a surprise. Month after month the denominational magazine carried news items and pictures of new building lots being purchased, new congregations being established, new sanctuaries being constructed, and services of dedication being held. These new buildings were not all new congregations. Some were older congregations who found themselves surrounded by growing towns or suburbs and responded by improving their facilities. What was clear to anyone reading the denominational magazine was that the Presbyterian Church in Canada was a growing, vibrant denomination.

FUNDING CHALLENGES

The denomination was expanding. At the same time, Canadian Presbyterians in the 1950s had run up against a serious problem in terms of how their denomination was structured and how finances were raised and spent. Growth and mission were not what the Presbyterian system, which they prized and for which they had fought so hard, naturally did. The Presbyterian system, as Presbyterians in Canada would have proudly noted, was a hierarchy of church courts – but what exactly did that mean? Well, they would have pointed out, the head is Jesus Christ, as "the only King and Head of the Church." This was one way of saying they did not place either a monarch or an individual (the pope) as head of the church, as Anglicans and Roman Catholics respectively did. Presbyterians would then have explained that there was a General Assembly, a gathering of the entire denomination with equal representation from both the clergy and the laity. Beneath this were the regional synods. More significant were the presbyteries. A presbytery was a regional gathering of the minister and elders from each congregation in a designated area and it served the functions a bishop would exercise in an episcopal system. As meetings needed to take place regularly, a presbytery was usually limited in size so that ministers would be able to gather together for monthly meetings to do important business. Every congregation in that region belonged to the presbytery, which gave oversight to the session which was responsible for the local affairs of the congregation. This was the system that had developed during the Reformation in the sixteenth century and that Canadian Presbyterians had inherited from their European ancestors. This was the system which had been affirmed in theological documents, including at the Westminster Assembly in the mid-seventeenth century, as the one Christ intended for the church: this was not just *any* system for organizing the church, this was the *divinely mandated* one.

But what did it mean to call this a hierarchy of "church courts"? And how did a national office fit within this structure? And how did this system help or hinder the ministry of the church as Canada grew and expanded in the period after World War II? These questions were much harder to answer. Most Canadian Presbyterians would not have known that their entire system in the sixteenth, seventeenth, and early eighteenth century had been focused on church discipline and its main function had been as courts. This was what it had been designed for – preserving the correct moral behaviour and doctrine of the communities in which the church was placed. It was not a system designed to raise money. In Scotland, one of the nations from which the Presbyterian system came to Canada, the minister's stipend (salary) and the cost of the church building were paid for by the local noble or in urban settings by the burgh or city government. This system had adapted as it was imported into Canada. There was no local nobility to pay for the church or minister, so local congregations had to work out how to raise money. Vital institutions – for example, theological colleges – were paid for by special appeal and subscription. In the nineteenth century there were few organizations that needed to be paid for above the congregational level. There was no national office or national staff.

Missions changed this. The desire to fund missionaries, either across the ocean or on the frontier, required a different structure. This developed somewhat organically. Indeed, many of the ministers who came to colonial Canada came because of the Glasgow Colonial Society, a voluntary society organized in Scotland, that paid the stipends of ministers so they could serve on the frontiers of Nova Scotia, Prince Edward Island, New Brunswick, and the Canadas, as well as other British colonial possessions.[29] This model of a voluntary society running in parallel to the church became one way for the church to become involved in missions. As the number of missionaries grew and the resources needed to keep them in the field expanded over the course of the nineteenth century, denominations began to require full-time staff to manage this work. National offices began, with committees required to make sure the money was being well spent. Money needed to be raised to pay the stipend of, for example, someone like the mission superintendent for the prairies, James Robertson. The tension between these missionaries and the national church were frequently noted.[30] What was not always considered was how uneasily this system worked, and how it was one model (a centralized business structure, complete with boards with specific functions with officers overseeing those functions) grafted on to a hierarchy of church courts. It might be more accurate to say a national office had been duct-taped on to the General Assembly. In many ways, the vision of church union had included an attempt to adjust this, to create a system that worked more effectively in twentieth-century Canada, as opposed to seventeenth-century Scotland. Yet this was one of the aspects – the supposed "centralization" of the United Church of Canada and its bureaucracy – against which continuing Presbyterians had rallied opposition to church union. Instead, they had spoken of the wonders of their own Presbyterian system. And so, that was what they were stuck with. As the 1950s drew to a close, the duct-tape seemed to be stretched to a breaking point.

Money is always an issue for churches. How do you raise the money to pay for what you believe God is calling you to do? How do you ensure that this money is wisely spent? And how do you find the money for new projects – or, to be very specific to the issue facing the Presbyterian Church in Canada in the 1950s, for establishing new congregations? Governments have taxes (however popular they may be) to do this. To cite the most common example, when a government decides to go to war, it pays for the war by taxing its citizens. A general "tax" on the denomination was not possible for Canadian Presbyterians for one simple reason: the General Assembly did not (and does not) have the power to tax. This power rests with the presbytery and with the synod. Each of these levels of church government can tax: the synod and presbytery "dues" are a requirement that each congregation must pay to the courts directly above them. The national offices – to which the church looks to provide "men" and "money" – did not, through the General Assembly, have the ability to tax the denomination in order to provide the necessary funds. The tools at their disposal were much more limited. Appeals for the national budget were made. Suggested amounts (cleverly entitled "assessments") that a congregation should give based on its membership were provided. Special appeals were made. Yet the reality was that this money was always voluntary. The General Assembly could not require it as a "tax."

As the Presbyterian Church in Canada entered the post-war period, it clearly wanted to continue to grow and expand. Its vision of itself was of a national denomination, one spread from sea to sea. It spoke of wanting to build new congregations and expand its missions work in foreign countries. It wanted to build the internal infrastructure that any self-respecting Protestant denomination at the time required (lay-training centres, church school curriculums, youth resources, publications, evangelism projects). In 1945 the Presbyterian Church in Canada wanted to expand but it seems clear that no one had truly imagined the scale of church extension that would be required across Canada in this period. Nor did anyone anticipate how much money this would require. Even if there had been adequate clergy to staff the high number of developments, the cost of land and buildings alone was beyond what could easily be afforded by voluntary giving.

The drive of church extension throughout this period was to build new congregations, while always in the background there was the challenge of funding these projects. In the early years, thanks to seed money given by the very generous donations of established congregations close to the new project, these challenges were met. But as there was less available money from these congregations, as the anticipated demands continued, as the denomination was stretched, and as the cost of land and buildings grew, there was a point at which there would be a crunch. It could also be said that the manner in which the denomination went about new church development might also have been a problem. In hindsight we may see this with greater clarity than those who at the time were muddling through the fog of expansion. The decision continued to be – in the Presbytery of Hamilton, the Presbytery of Montreal, and in the two presbyteries in Toronto – to build smaller congregations, seating 200 to 300. At no point did anyone suggest it might be wiser to build larger congregations at more strategic locations on major thoroughfares, rather than simply close to them. This might have been too much to ask. The vision in the local communities was for neighbourhood churches. And so, resources were spent on multiple sites. In the later 1950s the challenge of finances came to a head. One result was the establishment of Synod Corporations to help fund church extension. The other result was a crisis at the denomination level, related to how the church was administered and funded (discussed in chapter 3).

ONE SOLUTION: SYNOD CORPORATIONS

Awareness of the financial challenge and its impact on church extension developed gradually.

The resources at the national level needed to purchase land and construct new buildings were proving inadequate for the amount of expansion underway within the denomination. In 1955 the Presbytery of West Toronto overtured Assembly to consider the possibility of issuing bonds as one way of raising the money necessary to build new congregations.[31] It was the Synod of Alberta that first developed a solution to the need for enough capital to fund new construction. In the face of a situation where it became impossible to borrow money to build new churches, the Presbytery of Calgary had investigated a solution followed by some American Presbyterians in the Synod of Washington. At its annual meeting in the fall of 1957, the synod established a Synod Corporation, incorporated under Alberta law. The corporation immediately undertook to finance projects that had been stalled because of a lack of finances, allowing for loans to be made in 1957 to Chalmers (Calgary), Westmount (Edmonton), and St Andrew's (Lethbridge). Loans over the next few years followed to St Giles (Calgary) and Knox (Calgary).[32] It also served as an example for other synods who quickly copied the model.

The idea was relatively simple. A corporation was formed and registered under provincial law. Capital was then raised. This capital was then used as collateral for loans. The collateral was leveraged so that up to ten dollars could be borrowed against each dollar in capital held by the Synod Corporation. In October 1957 the Synod of Toronto and Kingston responded to similar needs and adopted the same model. A few months later the province granted a charter and gave royal assent to the Synod Corporation on 27 March 1958. The synod's goal was to raise $250,000 to use as collateral so that it could loan up to $2,500,000. The plan was to raise this capital over five years. The money was to be raised by soliciting donations (which could be designated to support specific extension congregations) from established congregations or presbyteries, as well as soliciting funds from each congregation in the presbytery. By the end of the first fiscal year of the corporation, on 31 August 1959, a little over $68,000 had been raised. The challenge, as the first annual report noted, was that by far the largest proportion had been given by donations from established congregations and presbyteries, with the assessments raising only a little over $10,000.[33] The Synod Corporation sought to promote their work in order to raise more resources. In its third annual report it noted that capital of nearly $150,000 had been raised; however, of that amount only 45 per cent had been given from ordinary contributions (that is, assessments on congregations) with the remaining 55 per cent coming from special contributions (individual donations or special donations from congregations).[34] While the disappointment of those involved in the Synod Corporation should be noted, the expectations they had for the congregations in the presbytery also need to be considered. The assessment (that is, the amount the Synod Corporation expected individuals to contribute) was 15 per cent of what they were being asked to contribute to the General Assembly budget; not only that, this was all on top of the amount they were being called to give to their local congregation.[35]

As with the Synod of Alberta, the Synod of Toronto and Kingston did not wait to receive all of the capital before they began using that capital for loans to congregations. Congregations could use this money as collateral for further loans. The expectation was always that this money would be repaid, and repaid as soon as possible, so the capital could be loaned out to other congregations so they could purchase land and build or renovate churches. The motivation was clear. The Presbyterian Church in Canada was a "missionary Church." The challenge was not only that Ontario was growing (a fact which the Synod Corporation highlighted in its report) but that the population was shifting, with rural areas losing population and the population becoming increasingly urbanized: "This results in the disturbing fact that we have Church buildings where the people are not living and not enough Church buildings where the people are living." The corporation existed because there was "not enough money for this purpose [building new churches] in the Capital Funds" of the denomination; nevertheless, it was essential that money be raised in order to meet the challenge – that is, in order to meet the need for churches of "Presbyterian Families." The synod wrote, "We should be planning now and sacrificing now so that we may be in a position to take our share of Christian work with the other Denominations."[36]

The Synod Corporation's promotional material highlighted new congregations, providing sketches of new buildings and details on the history and financial needs (including the amount of loan provided) of the congregations developing around Toronto and throughout the synod. The new building and new congregation at Elliot Lake was one example that fit the traditional understanding of expanding into a frontier area. The profiles of other congregations provided quite a different picture. For example, in Guelph a new congregation had been founded in 1958 called Westminster–St Paul's. Westminster had begun as a Sunday school organized by one of the established churches, Knox, Guelph. It had been organized in May of 1958 as a congregation, with 133 charter members. A church site had been donated by one individual in an area where there was ongoing housing development. The congregation of St Paul's was amalgamated with this congregation in 1959 to create the current congregation, Westminster–St Paul's, which in 1960 opened a new building with a seating capacity of 350.[37] A similar story was developing in the nearby city of Kitchener. St Andrew's, Kitchener, had sponsored a Sunday school beginning in 1957 which had by 1960 developed into Calvin Presbyterian Church, a congregation with fifty-four charter members, a church school of sixty-two, their own minister, and plans to move out of the public school where they were currently meeting and construct a new building. Another Calvin Presbyterian Church had been established in Sudbury, beginning as a church school in "New Sudbury" in 1951. The congregation began meeting in a public school in 1952, purchased and erected a portable church (better understood as a prefabricated church) in 1956, and now had a new building under construction.[38] These different examples show the variety of places and different ways in which Presbyterian congregations were established and growing in this period. What was also clear was that money was needed to allow for this growth to continue This was the rationale for the Synod of Toronto and Kingston to create a Synod Corporation.

The neighbouring Synod of Hamilton and London followed suit. Its promotional material notes with gratitude the support of David McCullough, the church extension coordinator employed by the Presbyteries of East and West Toronto. The Synod of Hamilton and London's goals was more modest – they hoped to raise $100,000 – but the intention of using that money to allow for more money to be accessed was the same. The synod noted that the needs were not equal across the synod. The rural presbyteries (Stratford, Huron-Maitland, and Bruce) were losing population, as the overall national trend of "the drift to the cities" continued. There was thus "little need for church extension work in these Presbyteries but there is a good deal that could be done, and should be done, in the matter of improving our existing church buildings in this area." It was in the presbyteries of "Niagara, Hamilton, Paris, London, Chatham and Sarnia" where new congregations were being established and "these congregations need money urgently." The corporation was being created to meet this need, following very much the template already established by the corporations in Alberta, and Toronto and Kingston. The corporation laid out clearly how the fund worked, as well as its expectations that the individual presbyteries would play a central role in vetting all projects to ensure that any building constructed would "be suitable for a Presbyterian Church" and "a credit to our denomination," and that the funds would be able to be repaid. While noting that loans could be made for "the construction of any Church building" within the synod, the priority of buildings for new congregations was clearly expressed.[39] It was through these Synod Corporations that Canadian Presbyterians worked to build new churches in this period. It is also through the documents they produced that we get a glimpse of what was happening on the ground – and an understanding of the motivations behind this expansion.

Synod Corporations provided an effective response to the capital needs of church extension, focusing that need at the local level. But the broader financial challenges continued, particularly in covering the operating costs supported by the denomination. The first clear indication of this crisis was an emergency action taken after the 1957 Assembly to reduce the minimum stipend (the amount paid to ministers, in particular those in mission charges which included extension congregations). This resulted in a flurry of overtures to the 1958 Assembly and the creation of a special committee to deal with the administrative issues of the church (see chapter 3). For the purposes of our discussion of church extension, this financial uncertainty slowed, then froze church extension in the denomination between 1963 and 1965. When the denomination began actively building churches again after 1965 it did so with a national staff person responsible for planning and assisting the establishment of new churches. This ushered in a distinct and different period of church extension in the denomination's history (see chapter 7).

Figure 2.3 Victoria Presbyterian Church, c. 1950. This was an example of one of the older churches seen in many of the towns and cities across Canada. In larger cities these older churches saw their membership disappear as their neighbourhoods changed and younger families moved to the suburbs.

A DENOMINATION TRANSFORMED

Canadian Presbyterians successfully established new congregations from 1945 through to the early 1960s. They did this based on the local presbyteries being responsible for determining where congregations should be established and overseeing the buildings of those congregations. Some presbyteries, for example Toronto and Hamilton, were more organized than others, yet across Canada presbyteries established new congregations where they determined there was a need. In the background of this work taking place, there always loomed the challenges of finding enough clergy and money. There was also the assumption that the need for these new congregations would always be there. The period immediately after World War II was a period of religious revival for Canadian Protestants, one where church membership and participation grew. "If you build it, they will come" was true of many situations. The example of Hopedale Presbyterian Church in Oakville, Ontario, illustrates this well.[40] On 11 December 1956 a decision was made to rent Orr Public School in the southwest of Oakville. T.H. McKennell, a graduating Knox College student, was appointed to serve as the minister, beginning 1 May. Services at Hopedale began in March 1957 with ten attending the first Sunday, twenty-five the next, thirty-five the subsequent Sunday, and eighty the final Sunday of the month. Given this progress, the presbytery appointed an interim moderator and elders from Knox Presbyterian Church, Oakville, to serve as an assessor (temporary) session until the congregation was established. In May the presbytery gave permission for four building lots to be purchased. On 16 June the new congregation of Hopedale Presbyterian Church was formed with forty-three charter members. The next year, in 1958, the presbytery approved the change of a site, giving them permission to sell the land they had purchased and to purchase a different parcel of land of the same size.[41] In this period it received financial support from the neighbouring Knox Presbyterian Church in Oakville, as well as an established Toronto congregation, Parkdale Presbyterian Church. Hopedale continued to expand and grow. By 1961 – four years after it was established – it had a membership of 430 and a Sunday school of 280.[42] Five years later, and less than a decade after its founding, it had become the fourth largest congregation in the newly established Presbytery of Brampton, with a membership of 585 and a church school of almost 300.[43]

Such dramatic expansion reflected the enthusiasm for Protestant churches in this period, in particular in the suburbs surrounding Canada's growing cities. The Presbyterian Church was able to establish new congregations. Existing congregations also thrived when they found themselves in the fortunate situation of development happening on their doorstep. Islington Presbyterian Church had been established in the fall of 1922 with seventy-nine members. Two years later a "concrete block basement structure" was built and dedicated. For the next decade the congregation was linked to Dixie Presbyterian Church. During the depression it became linked to a different Presbyterian church, Mimico. By its own admission, the congregation struggled along in this period. Things changed after the conclusion of the war. In 1948 a building fund was established and plans for a new building commenced. The name was changed in 1952 to St Andrew's Presbyterian Church, Islington, and a new building was opened and dedicated that year. The congregation had almost 400 members by 1956. Additional property was acquired after it became available due to some reconfiguration of traffic, and a Christian education building was then built and dedicated in September 1966.[44] At the other end of the metropolitan area, St Andrew's, Scarborough, one of the oldest congregations in the Toronto area, witnessed similar changes.[45] This was also a period when existing congregations added a Sunday school hall, remodeled their sanctuary, or in some other way transformed themselves, particularly if the expanding suburbs provided them with the opportunity. The establishment of new congregations was only one aspect of the overall denominational growth and expansion.

But not all churches were growing. Rural churches shrank as their population moved to more urban areas of the province or country. Urban churches, once full, found themselves with fewer members and greater financial challenges. In 1946 Parkdale Presbyterian had a church school of 347 and was one of six Presbyterian congregations in central Toronto with a membership of more than 1,000, in their case 1,070. Twenty years later, in 1966, there were no congregations in central Toronto with a membership over 1,000. Parkdale had a membership of only 439.[46] Local decisions to build new congregations were vital for the future direction of the Presbyterian Church in Canada. It is striking how many of the congregations established in this period, or renewed as the suburbs expanded to their doorstep, played a vital role in denominational developments in the 1960s, 1970s, and 1980s. These became the congregations that provided children for church camps, leadership for church programs, innovative ideas, and even served as recruiting ground for clergy. The Presbyterian Church in Canada took advantage of the religiosity of this period to successfully establish new congregations. In the process, the denomination was strengthened and transformed.

3

Proud to Be a Presbyterian

The May 1957 *Presbyterian Record* has arrived in the mail. This is the special issue on the Christian home; the theme is clearly expressed on the cover. A father sits in a comfortable chair in the living room surrounded by his family. His youngest son is wearing a bow tie and sitting on his knees. His elder son is sitting behind the youngest in a tie while the daughter is sitting on the other arm of the chair, wearing the uniform (blouse and neckerchief) of one of the denomination's girl's organizations, the Explorers. The mother is pictured behind the chair, looking on supportively as her husband reads the Bible to everyone. This, the denomination's magazine suggests, is the ideal Christian family. And it is one that those who read the magazine that month would have affirmed. They would have been pleased to be seen as part of the denomination, a growing church that was reaching out in mission around the world as well as in Canada. And the contents of the *Presbyterian Record* would have told that story of a vital denomination.

The Presbyterian Church in Canada was a growing denomination in the early post-war period. Year after year, the denomination was able to report successful growth in terms of the number of members, the number of children in church or Sunday school, the number of baptisms, the number of families associated with the denomination, the number of professions of faith, and virtually every other statistic that the denomination recorded. While the leadership might (and did) bemoan that the denomination was not holding its own against the overall population growth of Canada at that time, for most young Presbyterian lay women and men this would not have been their concern. They would have witnessed – in their congregations and on the pages of the denominational magazine – a vital, growing denomination. These were exciting times.

But what kind of church was the Presbyterian Church in Canada in the period from 1945 to the mid-1960s? How did Canadian Presbyterians see themselves in relationship to other churches and in relationship to Canadian society? What did they believe the church should be doing? How did they see their denomination functioning? This chapter will explore these and related questions, beginning with the questions connected to how Canadian Presbyterians saw themselves in relation to other Christian denominations. Presbyterians had a clear vision of themselves as a church. However, they disagreed amongst themselves concerning what other Protestant denominations they should be associated with. Should they limit those associations to others who looked to the Westminster Standards, or could they associate more broadly? This was an area of considerable disagreement. Where they agreed was on the work of the church. The denomination continued to welcome as members new immigrants from many countries, to focus on home and foreign mission ventures, to participate in evangelistic efforts, and to voice social concerns. The denomination continued to grow, but the financial and administrative structures seemed unable to balance income with expenditures. The late 1950s witnessed a major financial crisis. New systems were put in place. Deeper issues were not addressed. All of these developments took place as the denomination was growing. In the early 1960s, uncertainty grew, and questions began to be asked. Canadian Presbyterians were not alone in raising issues at this particular moment. This chapter will explore all of these topics, beginning with how Canadian Presbyterians related to other Christians.

CANADIAN PRESBYTERIANS AND OTHER CHRISTIANS

Presbyterians were proud to be part of a church. They were not a sect; they were a church. They expressed this conviction without always clearly defining what they meant by either the pejorative "sect" or the word "church." From context it was clear what was meant: churches were the respectable Christians with an educated clergy, proper buildings, and social status within the Christian community. They would include Anglicans, Lutherans, most Baptists, and, though Canadian Presbyterians might disagree with them on certain issues, the United

Figure 3.1 Dr and Mrs J.A. MacInnis at the Queen's Coronation, 2 June 1953. Christendom was alive and well, and Canadian Presbyterians were proud of their place as one of the major denominations in the dominions.

Church of Canada. These churches cooperated together, including in the Canadian Council of Churches, and expected to be treated with great respect and to be listened to by the Canadian government. As part of an important church, it was only right that the denomination's moderator, the Rev. J.A. MacInnis, attended the coronation of the new Queen, Elizabeth II, in 1953 (see figure 3.1). As one of the significant churches in Canada, one of the important dominions in the Commonwealth, this was only appropriate. The Presbyterian Church in Canada was one of the major denominations in the country, something which its members were both proud of and determined to defend.

The threat of Roman Catholicism was one of the things Canadian Presbyterians guarded against. While they might disagree with their fellow Protestants, they shared with them a commonly held anti-Roman Catholic sentiment, seeing the Roman Catholic Church as something completely alien. They believed Roman Catholicism posed a distinct threat, both to themselves as individuals and to the Canadian nation as a whole. Some of these beliefs had deep historical roots, going back to the sixteenth-century Reformation. Other concerns were more contemporary. Presbyterians worried about mixed marriages – marriages between their members and Roman Catholics. Alongside the perceived threat of communism in the early 1950s, they worried about the power of the Roman Catholic Church. In 1954 the movie *Martin Luther* was banned in Quebec by the Quebec Board of Censors. Canadian Presbyterians responded by showing the movie in various congregations in Westmount, Montreal. Pictures of Canadian Presbyterians defying the censor board in their suits and hats were published in the denominational magazine. The Presbyterian perspective was made very clear. The *Record* challenged the Quebec Board of Censors' explanation that they had in the past done similar things with other films deemed "offensive to various religious groups": "Nevertheless, films like *The Song of Bernadette*, *Going My Way* and *The Bells of St. Mary's*, and other definitely Roman Catholic films have been shown without question in the Province of Quebec."[1] At issue was not free speech – Presbyterians would gladly have banned any number of films they considered objectionable – but religious freedom, fairness, "national unity," and the power relationships between Roman Catholics and Protestants.[2] The *Record* commented that one result of defying the censor board had been to "reveal that the Protestants in this majority Roman Catholic city cannot be pushed around."[3] The rhetoric of freedom versus oppression was clear.

Presbyterians were clear they were a church. They opposed the Roman Catholic Church. There was a high-handed superiority to those like the Nazarenes, the Brethren, and the Pentecostals who they would have considered as "sects." But how should they – as Reformed Christians – be related to other Protestant denominations, not only in Canada but overseas? This was one issue where the Presbyterian church lacked consensus. There were two related yet somewhat distinct concerns. The first was a fear, bordering on paranoia, of being dragged into some form of church union. The second was the question of which other denominations Presbyterians should relate to. There seems to have been a clear consensus that Canadian Presbyterians should be part of any international alliance of Reformed churches. Beyond this, there was division. The position of those opposed to the denomination's participation in the Canadian Council of Churches was made clear in an overture from the Presbytery of Miramichi in 1945: by cooperating with the Canadian Council of Churches the denomination "sacrifices our distinct Presbyterian testimony." The presbytery was skeptical that this venture would be able to "solve the problems of our Churches, or increase the effectiveness of our witness and influence to the nation as a whole" and worried that "such connections have led and may lead us into further efforts that are not of our own choosing, or hinder our initiative in any given line of missionary effort." The latter concern reflected the fear that cooperation might lead to far more than originally intended. Clearly opposed, the presbytery suggested the denomination "refuse ratification of the Constitution of the Canadian Council of Churches and withdraw all connection with said organization" and instead to proceed with the denomination's own work "keeping ourselves entirely free for such initiatives and actions as we wish to take."[4] A more expansive overture focused on a variety of cooperative bodies was presented the next year at the Synod of the Maritime Provinces. The overture listed eight cooperative ventures, including the Canadian Overseas Mission Council, the Foreign Missions Council of North America, the Home Mission Council of Canada, and the Church of Christ in China, and argued that cooperating in these and other listed movements "must ultimately result in the emasculation and obliteration of our Doctrinal Standards." As in the overture from Miramichi, issues of the "constitutionality" of the process were raised, as was the suggestion that "such co-operation must in the last analysis lead to Union with other bodies whose Doctrinal Standards are not our Standards" and destroy "the spirituality and power" of the denomination, as well as denying its heritage. This overture met with considerable opposition and even dissents at the synod before it was transmitted to the General Assembly.[5] The overture from the Synod of the Maritime Provinces was rejected by the General Assembly.

Behind the overture from the Maritimes, the mover A.A. Murray later explained, was opposition to the denomination's acceptance of a relationship with the Church of Christ in China, a new denomination that had not accepted the Westminster Standards.[6] Not everyone in the denomination shared this concern. In a strongly worded overture the next year, the Presbytery of Montreal asked the denomination to "repudiate the action" of those who had raised these issues as they were "responsible for creating and fostering within the Church the very uneasiness, dissatisfaction and fear, which they so emphatically deplore." The overture expressed a strong commitment to ecumenical cooperation, suggesting that the General Assembly,

> while maintaining steadfastly, in harmony with the re-affirmation made by the General Assembly in 1925 its adherence to the ancient and historic standards of the Presbyterian faith, nevertheless places itself on record as interpreting these standards in harmony with the best traditions of the Church, that is to say, as not only encouraging but enjoining as a duty the fullest possible co-operation with all other Christian bodies for the glory, not primarily of Presbyterianism, but for the glory of God and the triumph of His purpose among men.[7]

Two other overtures received at the 1947 General Assembly, from the presbyteries of Saskatchewan and Quebec, reflected an opposing position, one more aligned with those that had emerged from the Maritimes.[8] John Moir has suggested that this debate, focused on the Church of Christ in China, "assumed the proportions of a civil war" within the denomination. Moir also notes that one of the dissenters at the Presbytery of Montreal where the overture passed was Dr William Stanford Reid, who would, in Moir's words, "soon assume the role of spokesman for the anti-ecumenists."[9]

This debate continued at various times over the next decade. Tight control was kept over any committee meeting with other denominations, in particular the Inter-Church Relations Committee. In 1961 the committee reported its work in clarifying "the position of Presbyterians with regard to relations with other communions" and stated that the committee's purpose was "to encourage study of the distinctive Presbyterian witness to Christian unity and the catholicity of the church and to clarify the thinking of our members about the true character of the Presbyterian position so that we may be faithful in making the witness to which God is calling us today."[10] The committee did this by relating to specific groups. These included the Alliance of Reformed Churches, the World Council of Churches, the Canadian Council of Churches, and various denominations.

Ecumenism was to be undertaken with great caution and was a point of dispute within the denomination in this period.[11]

Fear of stumbling into another union was expressed frequently. As a result of a minor dispute with the United Church over the establishment of a new congregation, a committee of representatives of both denominations was established to resolve the issue. The Inter-Church Relations Committee reported to the Assembly in 1964 on this meeting:

> At this meeting, the chairman of our Inter-Church Relations Committee entered a caveat drawing to the attention of the assembled representatives the action of the 89th General Assembly which specifically forbade any conversations between representatives of our church and representatives of any other communion which might lead to the consideration of organic union. Our position was simply that the United Church had asked us to meet with them to discuss areas of tension, particularly, the matter of Rocky Mountain House, Alberta, and that we were quite prepared to do this, but not to discuss the matter of union at all. The United Church representatives agreed to meet with us on these terms, in fact insisted upon them, and negotiations are proceeding.[12]

The United Church of Canada again appeared on the committee's agenda as the United and Anglican communions discussed union. In 1967 the General Assembly allowed representatives to observe these discussions under very strict conditions – "but take no action which would commit our church to organic union without the consent of the Assembly." When the invitation was extended to the Presbyterians to take a more active role, they withdrew.[13] Fears of what some believed had happened in the past led to an extreme caution in terms of ecumenism.

THE WORK OF THE CHURCH: MISSION, EVANGELISM, AND SOCIAL CONCERN

If there was some division over which other Christians they should associate with and what form that association should take, Presbyterians were united in many other areas, including what they understood to be the purpose of the church. They believed the

Figure 3.2 Women's Missionary Societies port worker with a couple arriving in Canada, c. 1958. Deaconesses, supported by others in the denomination, welcomed immigrants to Canada, offered them assistance, and invited them to attend one of the denomination's congregations.

Presbyterian Church in Canada was a missionary church, called to serve both at home and overseas. They believed in evangelism and calling people to commit their lives to Christ. They believed in building a Christian Canada. They saw themselves as a Reformed denomination in Canada, open to all immigrants and all who wished to join them. While they sometimes spoke of "the mother church" in speaking of the Presbyterian church in Scotland or Ireland, the denomination was distinctly Canadian, deeply aware of their own history. This had been made even more intense given the struggle to continue after the divisions encompassing church union in 1925. While most congregations in Canada worshipped in English, the denomination was very open to communities worshipping in their own language. Active ministry was carried on with Ukrainian, Hungarian, Italian, and Chinese congregations.[14] At the annual General Assembly, which was usually in or near Toronto in the period immediately following World War II, the folk dress one was most likely to see would be worn by those from

Ukrainian or Hungarian congregations. For example, in 1945 the ushers at the opening worship service were from the Hungarian church and appeared in folk dress.[15] Pictures appeared in the denominational magazine celebrating the ethnic communities which were present within the denomination.[16] The church was committed in this period to welcoming all immigrants, specifically immigrants from countries where there were significant Reformed populations. For example, a 1947 report to the General Assembly discussed immigrants arriving from the Netherlands.[17] There are two other illustrations in this period of how the denomination hoped to reach out to Reformed Christians from outside the British Isles and Ireland. Speaking to the Assembly in 1956, the moderator, Finlay Stewart, described the denomination as a Canadian one whose congregations were not "spiritual clubs for expatriate Scottish and Irish" immigrants; instead, "Our doors must be open to men and women of all races."[18] Another indication of attempts to welcome Reformed Christians from a variety of nations was the decision taken by the Committee on Articles of Faith in 1962 to consider other Reformed confessions as equivalent to the Westminster Confession of Faith.[19] The denomination welcomed immigrants from a variety of Europeans countries throughout this period: England, Scotland, Ireland, the Netherlands, France, and Hungary, with immigration from Hungary being particularly significant after the failure of the Hungarian Revolution of 1956.

Presbyterians saw themselves as a missionary church. As a 1964 pamphlet produced by the General Board of Missions put it, "Faithfulness in mission is closely related to the health of the Church. A Church which is strong in mission will be strong. A Church which is weak in mission will be weak. Mission is not a peripheral adjunct of the Church which can be added or subtracted. The Church does not exist where it is not a Church engaged in the mission of its Lord."[20] This statement captured effectively the consensus of the denomination at this time. The sixteenth-century church in Geneva would not have met this definition of being a "missionary church," but the consensus on the centrality of mission to the life of the church was so prevalent that no one seemed to notice. Canadian Presbyterians divided their mission into two distinct spheres: home mission and foreign, or overseas, mission. Home mission involved ministry to Indigenous people in Canada and ethnic communities, other special ministries, and the support of churches who could not pay the complete costs of their minister and congregational expenses.

A Message
of
Welcome

from

The Presbyterian Church in Canada

With an Alphabetical List of Congregations and Preaching Stations

Issued by

The General Board of Missions

Presbyterian Church in Canada

320 Bay Street - - Toronto

Figure 3.3 Welcome pamphlet, General Board of Missions, 1955. One of the resources produced by the denomination to welcome immigrants and those moving communities to the denomination. Note that the General Board of Missions had offices at this time on Bay Street in Toronto.

Foreign mission was directed to the specific mission fields, but the church saw this as well in a particularly broad light:

> Our Church can be faithful not as a Church which *has* Overseas Missions, but as a Church which in the whole of its life is engaged in world mission – in the evangelism which calls men to be the people of God with a mission to the ends of the earth – in Christian Education at every stage training young people for their part in the mission to all the world – in theological education which trains men and women for mission – in congregational life which is outward reaching rather than inward looking – in recruitment of life and raising of money with the urgency of those who are sent as God's messengers to the world – in all of these ways the Church must show its faithfulness in world mission.[21]

What was being articulated here was the clear belief that everything the church did had to focus on mission – and not only mission in Canada but world mission as well. To make this work the church organized its mission work into distinct departments. These departments often functioned independently, even though they were organized under the General Board of Missions. To complicate this tidy picture, the Women's Missionary Societies in the Maritimes (known as the Eastern Division or WMS-ED), and in central Canada and in the West (known as the Western Division or WMS-WD), cooperated but were independent. The WMS raised its own money, paid for its own missionaries and mission projects, and reported independently to the General Assembly.

Mission was considered not only central to the church but an activity that called for sacrifice and devotion. Canadian Presbyterians were expected to know their heroic missionaries, at home and overseas, and emulate them (to whatever degree that was possible). In a 1961 address to the Synod of Toronto and Kingston, Malcolm Mark, the synodical missionary (that is, the person responsible for home missions within the synod), catalogued the heroes of the home mission field. He began with the first individuals who brought Presbyterianism to British North America, telling the story of the Rev. James MacGregor, Dr Thomas McCullough, Dr Alexander Spark, the Rev. Robert McDowell, and the Rev. William Proudfoot, before turning further west to the work of the Rev. John Black at Kildonan, Manitoba; the

Rev. James Nisbett, who began mission work "among the Indians"; the great missionary superintendent of the prairies Dr James Robertson; Dr Andrew Grant, who was a missionary during the Klondike Gold Rush; and the first minister to establish a Presbyterian church in British Columbia, the Rev. John Hall. Each character was lionized for what had been accomplished. Robertson, for example, "thought nothing of exposure, hardship and toil if only he could bring men the Gospel."[22] Mark noted the proud heritage that had been given to Canadians of that year:

> Through their service and sacrifice they have bequeathed to us a great inheritance. This we must regard as a sacred trust, for it was purchased with their very lives. The ministry of these founders of our Church displayed common elements – self-denial, a zeal to evangelize, scorn of personal hardship, emphasis on the importance of education, true patriotism, love for their fellow-men, and above all, love for Jesus Christ with obedience to His commission. Who can stand in the presence of such as these without being humble and acknowledging himself to be a faithless and unprofitable servant?[23]

In contrast, Mark suggested, the church of 1961 was failing in its zeal and its commitment, not only personally (he confessed his own "sense of shame as I see my small service and meagre devotion in contrast to theirs") but also corporately: the General Assembly in 1961 had frozen spending on missions because of the financial crisis. This was clearly inappropriate, the result of a lack of zeal on everyone's part and something that needed to be turned around.[24]

The citation of missionary heroes from the past was a common feature in the denominational magazine and in various publications throughout this period. Many of the same names appeared time and time again. In a WMS pamphlet in 1947 entitled "Our Commission … in Canada … and Overseas" many of the same missionaries (such as John Black and James Robertson) appeared. In addition, however, the WMS added female mission heroes, telling not only of the work of the Rev. James Nisbett among Indigenous Canadians, but of the remarkable missionary activities of Lucy Baker. Stories were told of how Lucy Baker had rowed daily from her home across the Saskatchewan River to the Sioux camp on the other side, learning their language and gradually earning their "confidence" and respect. She was portrayed as a revered missionary among the Sioux and as "the first woman missionary to the Indians in our Church," and this work was portrayed as the beginning (stated positively in this 1947 pamphlet) of "Indian Residential Schools under our Church."[25] Similarly, they celebrated the work of those ministers who, like A.S. Grant, served in the Klondike, but included (and named) the nurses sent out by the women of the Atlin Nurse Committee, Miss Elizabeth Mitchell and Miss Helen Bone.[26] As well as the home mission heroes, there were the foreign missionary heroes: John Geddie, who went to the New Hebrides (Vanuatu); the Rev. John Morton, who went to Trinidad; George Leslie Mackay, who served in Taiwan; Dr and Mrs Buchanan, who served in India; and Jonathan Goforth, who was an evangelist in China. Canadian Presbyterians were surrounded by the memory of mission heroes from the past, both at home and overseas.

Canadian Presbyterians were also expected to know where missionaries were currently serving the church. The church had intentionally rebuilt its mission fields after the loss of so many during the process of church union. In 1947, the denomination had two mission fields in India (the Bhil field and the Jhansi field), a mission in British Guiana (Guyana), and in Taiwan, and was busily attempting to reestablish mission fields in China now that World War II had ended.[27] The results of the Chinese Civil War ended the plans to reengage with mission work in China. Fifteen years later, in 1962, the Presbyterian Church had overseas work in Japan, British Guiana, Taiwan, India, and additionally in Nigeria, a mission that the denomination had shared since 1954 with the Church of Scotland.[28]

Canadian Presbyterians focused on home mission as well as foreign mission. Home mission involved many things, including building congregations on the frontier and in the suburbs (see chapter 2). It also involved work among ethnic communities (Chinese, Hungarian, Ukrainian, and Italian) and among Indigenous peoples. Work among Indigenous Canadians was discussed as an example of the kind of mission work to those who were different from the general congregations (assumed to be British in origin, worshipping in English). For example, in the 1947 General Board of Missions report, a report on "Indians" was included among the reports on "Work Among Non-English Speaking Groups."[29] The "Indian Schools" were discussed later under the WMS-WD report, and again as one aspect of mission work.[30] In the annual summary of home mission work in 1957, one of the two photos was of four Indigenous boys from the Cecilia Jeffrey [Residential]

School. (The other involved work on church extension.) A brief paragraph noted: "The work with the Canadian Indians is more vital than it has been for many years. A new church will open this year at Sioux Village, Manitoba, and much progress has been made in evangelism, education, and health amongst the first Canadians."[31] Another photograph in 1965 showed a group of Indigenous girls from Shoal Lake junior high school enjoying a meal of Chinese food during their first visit to Winnipeg.[32] Residential schools and mission work among Indigenous Canadians received limited attention in these decades, and when it was noted, it was normalized and seen as very much one aspect of the overall successful mission work of the denomination.

Mission was central to the life of the church. It also cost a great deal. Mission was the major expenditure each year within the denomination's national budget. In 1947, for example, the denomination's total expenditure was $376,915, of which $259,479 went to fund mission. This represented 63 per cent of the denomination's budget. Home missions accounted for $145,000, or 39 per cent, of the total budget, while foreign missions accounted for another $91,000, or 24 per cent, of the denomination's expenses. What is remarkable is that this actually underestimates how much was spent on mission: the 1947 budget listed the cost of administering the denomination's mission separately. If this is taken into account, it means that the mission projects of the church took 69 per cent of the budget, leaving the theological colleges, Sunday school and youth programs, publications, administrative expenses, cost of the annual General Assembly, and all other expenses to account for around 31 per cent of expenditures.[33] A decade later the situation had altered, but only slightly. Expenditure for missions now stood at over $680,000, or about 59 per cent, of the national budget of around $1.1 million. One reason for the decline in proportionate share of the national budget was the addition of a new expenditure. One of the largest expenditures outside of those required for missions was contributions to pensions, which was $77,000. If one disregards pensions, the mission board's share of the budget would have been 63 per cent.[34] Eight years later and after considerable administrative and financial rearrangement, missions still accounted for 50 per cent of the denomination's expenditures (or 52 per cent if one again takes pension contributions out of the equation).[35] Two things are clear. First, given the complexity of the national budget and the different accounting decisions made year by year, any comparisons should be made cautiously. Second, home and overseas mission remained the dominant expenditure of the Presbyterian Church in Canada throughout this period. Foreign or overseas expenditures absorbed 19 per cent of the denomination's budget in 1965, while home mission stood at 30 per cent. The mission work of the denomination was not only central, it was costly.

Mission was the central focus of the Presbyterian Church in Canada, but not its only concern. The denomination saw itself very much related to the Canadian nation as a whole, with a responsibility both to evangelize Canadians and to speak to moral and social issues. Throughout this period, these two items were always connected, even though the activities that were recommended might be different. Similar to what Phyllis Airhart has described in the United Church of Canada,[36] Canadian Presbyterians sought to hold evangelism and social concerns together, and housed them in the same committee, the Board of Evangelism and Social Action (known for a period between 1933 and 1945 as the Special Committee on Evangelism and Church Work before returning to its original name).[37] Evangelism was always a concern of this committee. The church followed Billy Graham's 1955 evangelistic meetings in Scotland, the "Tell Scotland" campaign, with interest and favour.[38] The *Presbyterian Record* also spoke enthusiastically about Billy Graham's Toronto Crusade that same year.[39] In 1959 the church was proud to announce a new program of evangelism.[40] Evangelism never ceased to be a focus for Canadian Presbyterians. At the same time, the denomination was not always clear on what was their best and most suitable form of evangelism.

The flip side of evangelism was social concern. Presbyterians were concerned about Canada and were concerned about a variety of issues, yet two things should be stressed. First, Presbyterians were most concerned about issues of personal morality. Second, when Canadian Presbyterians did speak to larger issues, their positions in this period tended to be extremely cautious.

Temperance was one of the moral issues that Canadian Presbyterians continued to focus on. The church continued to advocate temperance, and strongly preferred total abstinence, though they were willing (however reluctantly) to allow members the freedom to be social drinkers.[41] When it came to marriage, Presbyterians were for it. What concerned them most were issues of divorce, something which was an issue in the years immediately following World War II. The war had been a time of crisis, a time when men and women had frequently rushed into marriage. The war and the separation that resulted from men being overseas while their wives stayed in Canada created great strain on many marriages. From our perspective today, the increase in divorces after such experiences is only to be understood. There was not always that kind of understanding at the time. Presbyterians, in common with most other Christians, were opposed to divorce. While admitting that in certain specific cases – primarily adultery – it might occur, it was still not an option that was approved. It was what happened next that troubled Presbyterians. Was remarriage possible? Certainly not for the guilty party in the divorce. But what about the "innocent party"? The denomination explored this in excruciating detail in a 1948 report. In the end, the denomination tied itself in so many philosophical knots it was hard to determine where they actually landed.[42] Despite this, the message was clear – divorce was strongly discouraged and was considered to be a source of shame. Issues of social morality continued to dominate in this period. The one exception was a statement on nuclear weapons in 1962 which attempted to broaden the social concerns of the denomination. It was not approved, but sent back to the committee.[43]

GROWTH AND GROWING PAINS

The Presbyterian Church in Canada entered the post-war period with a membership that was lower than it had been at its peak in 1931. Then it began to grow – and grow rapidly. By 1953 it had surpassed the previous peak and continued to grow. By 1957 it stood at 192,414 members. Growth continued until 1964 when a peak membership of 202,566 was recorded (figure 3.4).

Membership in Church schools was more erratic, but the overall trend of growth was nonetheless clear. Church school membership (figure 3.5) stood at only 72,337 in 1945, and for the next year this declined slightly, but then in 1948 it surged to 83,849. By 1957 there would be over 102,285 children reported as on the rolls of Canadian Presbyterian Church Schools. And again, this continued to grow, until a peak of 112,157 was reached in 1961. The growth in these and other statistics which the denomination collected was remarkable. Most church members would have been encouraged to hear this news. However, denominational officials insisted on comparing the denomination's membership with the overall growth of the Canadian population. This produced a less optimistic picture, one that encouraged them to push harder for the denomination to expand.[44]

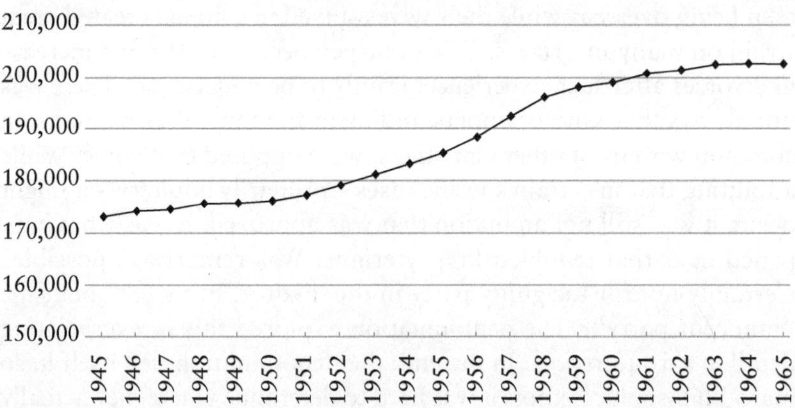

Figure 3.4 Membership in the Presbyterian Church in Canada, 1945–65

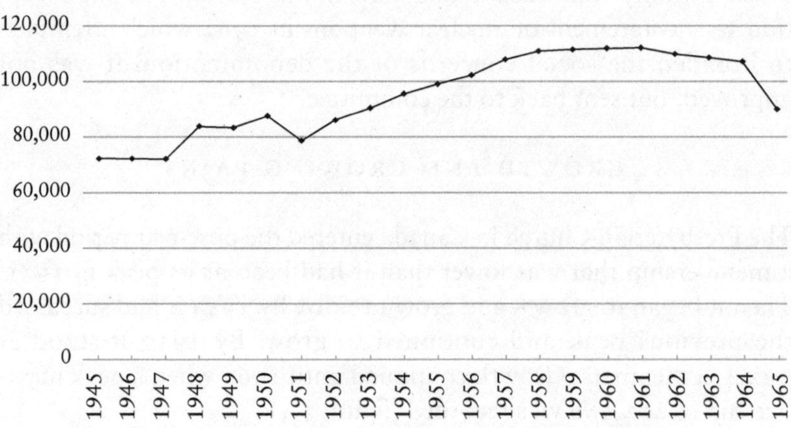

Figure 3.5 Church school membership, 1945–65

Were the structures and administrative systems the denomination had in place capable of handling the growth of the denomination? Church offices were scattered across downtown Toronto. Only in the mid-1950s did the denomination obtain the property at 63 St George Street, immediately next to Knox College, which became the denomination's headquarters. But this stately building was never large enough to house all of the departments of the denomination, let alone the *Presbyterian Record* or the offices of the WMS-WD. Departments were housed in various office buildings across downtown Toronto. This was not an efficient way to operate. There were calls for a national office building to be built.[45] This was finally realized in 1966 when the Walter Gow Memorial Building was opened at 50 Wynford Drive in Don Mills, a subdivision of Toronto (see figure 3.6, figure 3.7).[46]

The scattered nature of various departments being in different buildings was only one challenge. Efficiency and coordination were other issues that arose. The denomination's treasurer was optimistic in 1945 that the financial picture had improved.[47] At the same time there was a concern to require delinquent congregations who had received loans from the church extension fund or the manse fund to actually repay those loans.[48] In 1946 a committee was established to consider the administrative needs of the denomination. The committee reported the following year that revenues being donated to the denomination's general funds were not meeting expenditures. The results were deficits and a growing debt. What was causing this? And what solutions did the committee have to offer? In their summary, the committee stated that "there are many factors in the situation: the problem of the spiritual life of the Church, the financial problem, and constitutional confusion. There is also a 'territorial organization' problem."[49] The report did not provide specifics. It did suggest that the cost of office staff, rent, and the travel and salaries of the various officials at national office was not sustainable. It argued that the 15 per cent of expenditures represented by "administrative costs" (10 per cent for salaries, 5 per cent for rent and other office expenses) was too high. As a "ratio" of the overall expenditures, the committee argued, this could not be increased. This meant no new staff should be added to the national office until the revenue for that position became available through the growth in the overall income of the denomination: "We require an increase in Revenue in excess of $52,000 per annum *to maintain the present ratio in expenditure* before engaging even one new Secretary."[50]

Spending more money than was being received was clearly a financial issue that needed to be addressed. Reorganization, as proposed by the committee, was one strategy to improve efficiency. Even maintaining a clear ratio of administrative costs to program costs has merit, particularly if those in the field doing the work of ministry are not being adequately compensated. The committee recommended that financial statements be produced that were simpler and clearer and showed current expenses and income. While the committee laid out a clear understanding of the structure they believed needed to be in place, the problems in the administration of the church remained unclear. It is also not clear how many of the recommendations were implemented.

The immediate situation related to finance and administration in the late 1940s seems to have been overcome either through the work of the committee, increased revenue, or perhaps both. Yet challenges remained. The incredible capital costs required to build new congregations led to the eventual creation of Synod Corporations (see chapter 2). The balance between revenues and expenditures remained a challenge. In 1955 the *Presbyterian Record* reported that the General Board of Missions had overspent its budget by $115,000, with $93,000 spent on missions in Canada. This was reported within a discussion of the challenges of developing new extension congregations in Canada.[51] Overtures from across the church called for new ways of doing things.[52] A crisis developed after the 1957 General Assembly. In order to balance the budget in 1957, the Administration committee rejected expenditures from the various boards. In response, the General Board of Missions reduced the minimum stipend it would be paying those ministers in new congregations and mission fields who were paid by that board. This was done despite the fact that an increase to the minimum stipend had been approved by the General Assembly in 1957.[53] The reality of a major issue in the denomination's administrative process suddenly snapped into focus. More overtures appeared, addressing both the issue of the denomination's finances and the specific issue of the reduction in minimum stipend. Notably, the Presbytery of Saskatoon sent in two related overtures. In the first they called out the Board of Administration for having more power than other boards, and suggested that the denomination needed both to reorganize its structures and create the office of comptroller.[54] The second reminded the spending boards that in a congregation the first charge on expenditures was the stipend of the minister: in other words, the minister gets paid first and all other expenses are dealt with after this commitment is honoured. You cannot reduce a congregational minister's stipend to balance the budget because the boiler blew up and needed replacing. If this was the case at the congregational level, the presbytery argued, it also needed to be how the denomination functioned. It was a brilliant overture, speaking to the frustration of those (and there would have been many in the Presbytery of Saskatoon) doing ministry on minimum stipend.[55] An overture from the Presbytery of Westminster also raised financial concerns and called for the denomination to hire outside management consultants to look into the "administrative structures and financial policies" of the denomination.[56] This time the issue could not be ignored.

The "Special Committee on the Financial Structure Organization and Procedures of the Presbyterian Church in Canada" was created in 1958. Price Waterhouse was hired as the outside management consultant firm and analyzed the challenges facing the denomination. The committee met over two years, reporting to the General Assembly in 1959 and 1960.[57] In 1959 they suggested that its goals were to "obtain maximum efficiency," to be more business-like in the practices of the administration of the church, and to "eliminate waste, inefficiency and lack of oversight." What were the specific problems? The committee noted that it had consulted the various boards and agencies (for example the individual theological colleges) in preparing its report; it also noted it had not had time to consult with the WMS.[58] After these consultations, it concluded: "The Committee is convinced that a state of emergency exists which fully justifies" immediate action. In justifying its actions, the committee mentioned what it considered "defects in organization and procedures" as noted in Price Waterhouse's report, and argued that the current national staff could not "under the present organization and procedures" carry out what the General Assembly required of them. It further noted the "lack of suitable organizational procedures for the co-ordination and preparation of a balanced budget and a lack of adequate controls to ensure that budget allocations are being adhered to from month to month." This was in addition to confusion between capital funds, reserve funds, and operating revenue, all of which were creating "recurring deficits from year to year and the disturbing increase in the bank indebtedness during recent years."[59] The church was spending more money than it was receiving. This was clear. Some of the technical and accounting challenges – like not managing endowed funds properly – were noted. The solution proposed was the creation of an overarching Church Council. This body, it was believed, would have the authority to oversee all of the different boards and ensure that expenditures did not exceed the budget. The details of this Church Council – which was to be put in place immediately – were laid out within the Interim Act which was appended to the report and provided precise details on how this would work.[60]

Price Waterhouse's report was provided to the denomination to support these recommendations and the actions that had been taken. The consultants argued that there was a "growing demand throughout the Church for tighter control of finances, better administrative practices, and modern accounting and reporting methods."[61] Price Waterhouse noted the "archaic organization and practices" of the denomination and the lack of any "collective action" prior to the 1958 General Assembly to change this. The consultants noted the denomination's polity encouraged joint decision-making and equal authority: "Unfortunately, the pursuit of this principle has resulted in confusion between the legislative prerogatives of governing courts and boards and the administrative needs of the whole Church in the conduct of its day-to-day affairs. The annual meeting of the General Assembly has attempted to solve complex problems of administration in the fields of finance, property management, salary schedules, employee benefits, etc., to the extent that the larger problems of Church policy and long-range planning have been afforded little if any time for serious deliberation and attention."[62] Put more directly, Presbyterians had inherited a church court system that could not manage a modern, bureaucratically organized denomination. Too many trivial matters were coming to General Assembly. Everyone believed they had the right to address all matters. The result was that nothing could be done effectively. Attempts to resolve this had led to the creation of "a multiplicity of interlocking boards and committees," which did not solve the problem but only created confusion and, contrary to intentions, actually concentrated power with a few individuals. Price Waterhouse suggested something completely different needed to be done:

> The challenge of the future can only be met by a major change in the administrative organization of the Church. A plan of organization is needed which will define the major functions of the Church and assign them to responsible groups working in harmony for the overall objective of Christian mission. These groups will require leadership, technical advice and co-ordination. It will not be sufficient to cut the work of the Church into small segments, operating independently of each other, but a co-ordinating, representative body will be needed to effect liaison. Through co-ordination, each group will become aware of the needs, problems and responsibilities of other groups and through mutual understanding and respect, plans for meeting common goals will be achieved.[63]

Central to this was the creation of the proposed Church Council, a central coordinating body that would be responsible for coordination and financial management. The Price Waterhouse report also made additional and very specific recommendations related to the functioning of the denomination.

Most significantly, the report proposed that all of the boards and agencies of the denomination should be consolidated into six departments: Christian Education; Home Mission; Overseas and Inter-Church Relations; Personnel and Training; Administration; and Communications.[64] Responsibilities were assigned to each of these departments. Personnel and Training, for example, would include the two theological colleges, the Missionary and Deaconess Training School, recruitment, and also personnel functions.[65] An even more dramatic change was dividing the General Board of Missions and creating a distinct Home Missions department and a separate Overseas and Inter-Church Relations Department. The rationale provided for the latter was that this made more sense, as overseas mission currently seemed to be involved in "relations with established churches in many parts of the world such as with the Presbyterian Church in Formosa."[66] The consultants' report thus provided an option for a completely different administrative structure for the denomination.

The special committee report in 1959 and its final report to the 1960 General Assembly chose selectively from the recommendations of the consultants. In its 1960 report, it spoke positively of the progress that had been made over the past year, in particular the value of the Church Council. They proposed, and it was agreed, that this body would continue and would be renamed the Administrative Council. Individual recommendations aimed at greater clarity made by the consultants were implemented. The committee added its conviction that the church needed a comptroller and needed this person as soon as possible.[67] What the committee did not attempt to implement, however, was the idea of the consultant that the work of the church be divided into six departments. An Administrative Council was formed, with the representatives of thirteen different boards (including a still united General Board of Missions) and agencies (including the Board of Knox College, the Board of Presbyterian College, and the *Presbyterian Record*). There was now a coordinating function within the administration. The church continued to have a multiplicity of agencies and boards, with the General Board of Missions remaining the largest and most powerful.

CHANGES AND UNCERTAINTY

In the early 1960s, one would continue to be proud to be Presbyterian. One was the member of a growing church, a denomination that was building new churches, expanding into the growing suburbs, and attempting to engage some of the pressing issues of the time. There had been structural issues in terms of the denominational office, with more money being spent than was coming in, but this seems to have been resolved thanks to the work of the Special Committee on the Financial Structural Organizations and Procedures. The denomination was now prepared to continue to grow. Amidst all of this confidence, however, there were signs that things were changing. Growth was slowing. The number of baptisms was declining, down from its peak of 11,380 in 1958. This, one suspects, was due to the fact that the overall birth rate in Canada was declining. There were still over 9,000 baptisms recorded in Presbyterian congregations in each of the years from 1962 to 1964. Over the same period Sunday or church school enrolment decreased slightly from a high of 109,864 to just over 107,000; the fall to 90,000 in 1965, the same year membership began to decline, would have been somewhat of a shock, but the recovery to over 99,000 the next year would have been a relief, and suggested something had gone wrong with how the denomination had recorded church school membership that year. After membership peaked at 202,568 in 1964, a small decline of just over 500 was noted in 1965, and even more so when it dropped again for 1966. One would have been assured by the editorial in the *Presbyterian Record* in November 1967 that addressed this issue directly:

> The decline in church membership in all of Canada's major denominations has been making headlines. Our own statistics show that there were 2,373 fewer Presbyterian members in 1966 than in 1965, a decrease of more than one per cent.
>
> The situation calls for concern but it should not cause alarm. There have always been inactive people on communicants rolls …
>
> The church and its members will never cease to evangelize, but the true strength of the Christian church cannot be measured by numbers. Pruning dead branches from the tree is just as necessary in the congregation as it is in the garden. The quality of witness is what counts in today's world.[68]

Growth was uncertain, and as this had so much to do with the focus of the church's activities since the conclusion of World War II, this was a troubling realization.

The 1960s was a time of change and questioning. This was true both in North American culture as a whole and within Christian denominations. As young Canadians proudly bought houses in the suburbs to give their families places to thrive, critiques of conformity appeared in books, and even in folk songs. In an example of the latter Malvina Reynolds sang of "little boxes on a hillside/little boxes made out of ticky-tacky/little boxes on a hillside/and they all look just the same." Musical plays such as *The Fantasticks* (from which came the popular song "Try to Remember") raised questions about families and relationships. In the United States, John F. Kennedy had been elected president and suggested that his election marked a new era. Change was apparent on many levels, even before Bob Dylan's song "The Times They Are a-Changin'" hit the airwaves in 1963.[69]

One thing which began to change was the relationship between Roman Catholics and Protestant Christians, including Presbyterians. Pope John XXIII called in 1959 for a council of the Roman Catholic Church to meet at the Vatican. The theme he articulated was one of change, of opening the windows of the church. After careful preparation, this council met over three years (from 1962 to 1965) and issued statements making major changes in the Roman Catholic Church. The Latin Mass was replaced by a liturgy in the vernacular language. There was an openness to the broader culture. Canadian Presbyterians followed these developments largely through the general media. Officially, the denomination's Inter-Church Relations Committee made few comments. Given the denomination's extremely cautious approach to ecumenism, even among Protestants, this was not surprising.[70]

Real change was happening. Others voiced concerns that not enough was changing. In the United States, Gibson Winter published *The Suburban Captivity of the Church* and Peter Berger published *The Noise of Solemn Assemblies*, both of which were critical of what they perceived to be the superficiality of religious faith. More criticism appeared. Harvey Cox wrote *The Secular City*. From Great Britain, John Robinson published *Honest to God* in 1963. Not wishing to be left out of this exercise in self-examination, Canadian churches became involved, beginning with the Anglicans who invited a prominent Canadian journalist, Pierre Berton, to critique their denomination. The result was Berton's 1965 book *The Comfortable Pew* which became a Canadian best-seller and focused a critical lens on all of Canada's major churches. Berton shared his own journey from being a devout youth to a more general apathy toward religion as an adult. He discussed how troubled he was by the idea of universal sin, which included children. The book was a challenge to the churches, not only asking if the theology was correct (particularly around sin) but also challenging whether the churches were offering ethical leadership. Berton essentially asked, were the churches Christian enough? Were they applying what they claimed to believe in relation to the ethical issues of the day: nuclear war, racism, poverty, and economic justice? The challenge was for the church to state what it believed and to communicate it effectively, rather than through a "lukewarm pulpit" that produced sermons that were "spiritless, irrelevant, dull and badly delivered."[71] Berton argued that the church needed to free itself from the "institutional chains" in which it found itself and adapt to the modern era and address modern issues.[72] The book created controversy, push-back, and imitation. One volume appeared entitled *Just Think, Mr. Berton (A Little Harder)*.[73] A collection of essays, *The Restless Church: A Response to* The Comfortable Pew, which also had a "rejoinder" by Berton, responded to various points raised.[74] The United Church responded with a collection of essays in *Why the Sea Is Boiling Hot: A Symposium on the Church and the World* in which it invited a variety of outside critics, including Berton, June Callwood, Joan Hollobon, and Arnold Edinborough, to critique what they saw as wrong within the United Church.[75] It remains an odd volume, filled with a variety of quite different (at times seemingly opposing) criticisms. What it clearly demonstrated was a mood of self-criticism (one might go further and suggest self-flagellation) which was emerging in this period in Canada.

Not surprisingly, Canadian Presbyterians joined this movement of self-criticism. With a title that was an obvious play on the United Church of Canada's *Why the Sea is Boiling Hot*, McGill University professor Joseph McLelland's 1966 address to the Synod of Toronto and Kingston "Why Our Pond Is Lukewarm" was published and circulated. The title of the address was not only clever but misleading: the subtitle "Forty Years in the Wilderness" provides a more accurate synopsis of what McLelland was concerned about. In many ways, this address was not speaking to the 1960s but was rehearsing the long debate about ecumenism and what it meant to be a Presbyterian. The first part of the address dealt with this directly, suggesting the denomination needed to abandon its fixation on 1925 and learn to be ecumenical in a new way. McLelland critiqued the veneration of the Westminster Standards within the denomination and the belief that Canadian Presbyterians were unique within the denominational landscape in Canada by being a confessional church: "Our mystique imagines that we are confessional because of the Westminster

Confession, whereas we are confessional only if and insofar as we continue to probe the sole confession of the Apostles and the Prophets."[76] There was a call for the church to move forward, and stop looking backwards; it was also a call to work with other churches ecumenically, not look exclusively inward. In this sense "Why Our Pond" continued the debate that had been fought on and off for twenty years about ecumenism. At the same time, McLelland's rhetoric and his remarkable turns of phrase seemed to capture something, not only of the 1960s, but beyond. A sentence like "I believe we are dangerously close to loving the Presbyterian Church in Canada more than our Lord Jesus Christ" was at one and the same moment timely and timeless.[77] Joseph McLelland would continue to raise such provocative questions the following year in his even more radical address "Blueprint for a New Model" at the national Congress of the Presbyterian Church in Canada (discussed in chapter 6).

SUCCESSFUL YEARS

In the years following World War II the Presbyterian Church in Canada grew. This growth was not unique (other Christian denominations in Canada also experienced growth), but it assured Canadian Presbyterians they had been correct in their decision to remain out of church union in 1925 and encouraged them to believe they had a voice that should be shared with the broader Canadian society. They were a Reformed church. They welcomed all who wished to be part of their denomination, in particular those immigrants who came from Reformed churches in Europe, including Britain. They were also a church deeply committed to mission, both in Canada and overseas. Denominational missionaries of the past and of the present remained heroic figures. The church continued to encourage evangelism and speak to issues of social morality. There was a great deal for which Presbyterians could feel pride. But there were also challenges. Budget shortfalls were a regular reality. Money was always tight. It was hoped that the changes made in the administrative structures and financial arrangements of the church in the late 1950s had remedied that situation. Time would tell. What had not happened was deep and profound change. Proud of their heritage, Canadian Presbyterians continued to stumble along with their church court system to which they added a national office and staff. Efficient? Not always, but it was how things had been done and continued to be done. The

Figure 3.6 Dedication, Walter Gow Memorial Building, 30 November 1967. The dedication of the new office building in the Toronto suburb of Don Mills, where all of the departments were able to be housed in one building.

Figure 3.7 Church offices of the Presbyterian Church in Canada, Walter Gow Memorial Building. A modern office building at 50 Wynford Dr. in the suburb of Don Mills – a source of pride for a denomination that saw itself growing and serving Canadian society.

Presbyterian Church in Canada remained a traditional denomination, looking back to its heritage. This was a strength but also a weakness. In the late 1940s and throughout the 1950s this all worked well. Then things began to change. The mid-1960s were an interesting time. One was still proud to be Presbyterian. One was still a member of a growing denomination, or at least one that had been growing until very recently. Changes were, however, on the horizon. Improved relations with the Roman Catholic Church were welcomed: what might not have been understood was that opposition to the Roman Catholic community reinforced Protestant identity, and vice versa. There was also a growing voice within the church that reflected the general cultural criticism of the decade. What would happen next was unclear.

4

The Changing Place of Women in the Presbyterian Church in Canada, 1945–1966

It is an older black and white photograph of two women, wearing dresses and hats, smiling at the camera (see figure 4.1). The historic nature of what these two women had achieved might not be apparent to viewers today. It is the ribbons they each are wearing which might be the giveaway: these are the ribbons that were worn by commissioners to Presbyterian General Assemblies. And Mary Whale and Addie Forrester were, in 1967, making history as the first women ever to be commissioners – that is, voting members – of a Canadian Presbyterian General Assembly. Women had been present as observers, had spoken on mission nights, and very occasionally addressed the Assembly, but no woman had ever before been a voting member of the General Assembly, charged with determining doctrine, church law, and the processes by which the denomination functioned. This moment came fourteen years after Canadian Presbyterians began a formal discussion about the place of women in the church. The decision of the church to allow women to be ordained as elders and ministers had been made a year previously. To be present at the Assembly in 1967, each of these women would over the last twelve months have had to be elected as an elder in her congregation, then delegated by the presbytery to be one of the elder commissioners to the Assembly. They were now here, and their presence was noted and the picture published in the denominational magazine, the *Presbyterian Record*. The caption stated that "Mrs George Forrester" was from Cardinal, Ontario. Not a great deal is known about her. "Miss Mary Whale," as the caption described her, was not referred to by the congregation of which she was an elder (Erindale Presbyterian Church in the Presbytery of Brampton) but instead it was noted that she was the director of overseas mission for the Women's Missionary Societies Western Division (WMS-WD). She was, in fact, a very prominent member of the denomination who had served the church for many years in various capacities, including as editor of the WMS periodical *Glad Tidings*, as well as in her current position. Yet it was only now that she was able to have a voice and vote within her denomination's yearly national Assembly.[1]

This chapter explores how the Presbyterian Church in Canada arrived at the decision it did in 1966 to ordain women as both elders and ministers. An overture in 1953 began the process. A committee was formed and reported with suggestions. Initial polls of the denomination were not encouraging for those wanting change. The issue gathered momentum in 1960 when a young woman put herself forward as a candidate for the ministry, and the committee, looking at the place of women under a new convenor, adopted a different strategy. That strategy included a study of the Bible called "Putting Woman in Her Place." It was after the publication of this study that a series of votes were held that changed the denomination's position on this issue. This entire process was done carefully and was concerned more about the broad place of women in the denomination than specifically the ordination of women to the ministry. The decision was done based on how the denomination read the Bible. Despite reservations and some opposition, the denomination changed its doctrine and polity in 1966 when it approved the ordination of women as both elders and ministers. It was women elders who made the most immediate change in the denomination. While there was opposition at the time, it did not cause the major divisions that would happen later for the simple reason that those who disagreed believed they could simply ignore the decision.

Women had a limited role in Canadian society in 1945. Things had certainly improved from what they had once been. Women, but only white women as Asian and Indigenous women were not granted this basic right, now could vote, this being granted federally in 1918. Women were also now considered "persons" under Canadian law thanks to the courage of women forcing this issue to the Supreme Court in 1929. These were both positive changes for women and should neither be dismissed nor overestimated in terms of the lives of Canadian women. There was still a great deal of distance to travel to achieve anything close to equality. Women still had limited rights under the law. Women were able to step into and do certain jobs in the workplace – and were encouraged to during times such as World War II – but this was the exception, not the norm. Once peace arrived, women were

Figure 4.1 First female elder commissioners to a General Assembly, 1967. One year after the 1966 decision, Mary Whale and Addie Forrester attend the General Assembly as elder commissioners.

sent back to the domestic sphere. There were few women in politics or in professions. Women might serve as teachers until they were married. Often these rules were unspoken, but nevertheless real. Women were second-class citizens, expected to look after their homes, their husbands, and their children. If this began to be challenged throughout the 1950s and early 1960s, and if women were beginning to move into professions and politics, the pace of these changes was glacial.

What was true in Canadian society was also reflected in Canadian religious denominations. In the Roman Catholic tradition, only men are allowed to be priests. Women are allowed to serve but only as nuns. Despite their differences on so many theological issues, Protestant churches mirrored this arrangement. Men held the major offices and only males were allowed to be ministers. Women who felt called to service were restricted to a secondary role as deaconesses. In the Presbyterian Church in Canada, only men could lead congregations. They were also the only ones allowed to preach. Here there were exceptions, where specific women who were considered exceptionally gifted, or who were needed because there was a shortage of men in a particular circumstance or situation, were allowed to preach under carefully regulated conditions. Yet it is these exceptions that have often attracted our attention. The occasional denominational conversation about whether it was even possible for women to be ordained as ministers or serve as preachers has dominated our conversations about women in the church. "Firsts" often do. And so, various denominations, including the Presbyterian Church in Canada, had considered the question of whether women might be ordained from the late nineteenth century on, and usually answered in the negative.[2] The one exception was the United Church of Canada. In 1936, Lydia Gruchy had succeeded in being ordained as a minister in the United Church.[3] Few other women followed. And ordination for women in the United Church of Canada was only permitted for single women. Indeed, as future moderator Lois Wilson recounts in her autobiography, her decision not to be ordained after completing her theological education in the late 1950s was because the choice at that time was between marrying or being ordained – one had to choose one or the other.[4] Often on the mission fields women were able to do things which they would not have been permitted to do within Canada. Women were allowed to serve in only secondary roles within Canada. In the Presbyterian Church in Canada, as in other denominations, the office of deaconess had emerged (in the denomination's case, beginning in 1908). Deaconesses were trained women, set aside in a particular way, to serve the church in social service, as missionaries, as port workers, in children's education, or in any place where something needed to be done but where there were no male clergy members who might be spared to do it. Decisions, however, were made by men.

The Presbyterian Church in Canada was governed by men at all levels of church life. Sessions (which governed congregations), presbyteries and synods (which governed collections of congregations), and the national General Assembly were all exclusively male. This was the case not only for the clergy, all of whom were male, but for the elders who were also vital parts of these bodies. To be an elder, one needed to be ordained; women, however, could not be ordained. Thus, they were excluded from the governance structures or courts of the church. This was the custom, reinforced by doctrine. Women had, nevertheless, begun to find a way not only to serve but to have a voice and to vote. Women could serve as deaconesses. Women also ran their own organizations. Alongside women in other denominations and in other English-speaking countries, Canadian Presbyterian women began in the nineteenth century to establish Women's Missionary Societies. The Women's Missionary Societies met, studied what missionaries were doing on various mission fields, and raised funds to support those missionaries.[5] At the same time, they chose to do this outside the official courts of the Presbyterian Church. The various WMS bodies were auxiliaries to (that is, they stood alongside) the official work of the denomination. This gave women agency. Women not only raised the money but determined where their money would be spent. Congregational WMS groups sent their funds to the regional groups known as presbyterials. These presbyterials were organized into two regional groups: the Eastern Division, or WMS-ED, which included all of the WMS groups in Atlantic Canada; and the Western Division, or WMS-WD, which represented women in Quebec, Ontario, and the west.[6] The Presbyterian Church in Canada had two structures, unequal and separate. There were the courts of the church – the General Assembly, synods, presbyteries, and sessions – which were exclusively male; and there was the parallel WMS structure – WMS-ED or WMS-WD; synodicals, presbyterials; and congregational WMS groups – which was exclusively female. These structures cooperated, but not without tensions. This was the structure the church had; but was it what the church needed in order to serve Canada in the post-war world?

A CALL TO CONSIDER CHANGE

In 1953 the Synod of Manitoba sent an overture to the General Assembly, asking the Assembly to consider the "Place of Women in the church." The overture began by quoting scripture, noting that "in the Church of Jesus Christ there is no east or west ... neither male nor female" before turning to the major concerns. The overture argued

Presbyterians had "failed to give women equal status and responsibilities in the Church," the result of which was that the full potential of the church had not been realized. The overture then stated that "it is our opinion that the question of the status of women in positions of leadership in The Presbyterian Church in Canada needs clarification, to the end that the Church may recognize the teaching of Scripture, that in Christ there is neither male nor female." The Synod asked the General Assembly to consider this question and to appoint a special committee to report to the next General Assembly.[7] This overture is worth quoting in some detail in order to see what is, and is not, mentioned. The overture presents a clear appeal to scripture. There is a concern regarding women in leadership, with the specific example mentioned being at the congregational level, specifically sessions. What is less clear is whether the synod had women as ministers in mind. What is clearly absent in the overture was the word "ordination." When this overture was presented to the 1953 General Assembly the response was not an unusual one in the Presbyterian Church in Canada: Assembly agreed to the request to form a Committee on the Place of Women.[8]

In 1954 this committee reported to Assembly and raised one key issue: it asked that "if the question of Ordination is to be considered, the Committee be so instructed." If women were to be ordained as elders or as ministers, this would raise questions about doctrine and the committee wanted this noted and wanted clear direction. An attempted amendment to send this matter to the committee that dealt with issues of doctrine (the Committee on Articles of Faith) failed. The Committee on the Place of Women was authorized to consult with "representative women of the Church."[9] The committee was clear about the issues with which it was grappling.[10] Scripture was one issue. The committee recognized the principle of male and female equality in Galatians 3:28 which the Synod of Manitoba raised, but wondered if "this general principle was subject to certain modifications of which I Timothy 2:11, 12 and I Corinthians 14:34, 35 are the extreme examples."[11] The committee also looked at developments in doctrine and history. The committee posed a key question: "How shall we emerge from the confusion of doctrine with custom, and how shall we define doctrine in this matter?" It suggested John Knox's "[First] Blast Against the Monstrous Regiment of Women" was not helpful on this issue and was "of no analogy we may say to the matter of the place of women in the Church, despite much pleading to the contrary."[12] The committee stressed that the denomination should not "proceed on analogy with what has been done in the professions" but needed to focus on "Biblical principles."[13] The committee understood the issues before it to include all aspects of the question of how women were exercising their gifts in the church. The committee suggested, for example, that women could be more effectively used in the work of the church without the denomination changing any of its policies. On the issue of ordination, the committee focused both on ordination to ministry and eldership. It was cautious in seeing either as a solution to what it considered to be the overall problem: "There are many who consider the ordination of women to the Holy Ministry and the Ruling Eldership will automatically solve the problem of the place of women in the Church. The problems are deeper than the matter of ordination. We believe that the Churches that have permitted such ordinations have not the full answer, and have less of an answer than they expected."[14]

The 1955 report addressed the specific issues related to the ordination of women "to the Ruling Eldership or the Ministry or both."[15] It was clear there were two different positions in the church on this issue. The first voice believed that the principle of equality in Christ "should now be put into action." The second voice believed that "equality in Christ" did not "imply equality of function."[16] Recognizing these two different viewpoints, the committee recommended first, that the 1954 and 1955 reports of the committee as well as two papers – one by Professor F. Scott Mackenzie, the other by Professor David Hay – be distributed to the presbyteries, presbyterials, and other "organized Presbytery-wide groups of men or women within Presbytery bounds," for comment; and second, that the two specific questions of whether women could be ordained as elders and whether they could be ordained as ministers be sent down to the presbyteries, presbyterials, and the other groups named, and that the actual number of votes casted be reported back.[17]

The chair of the committee encouraged the denomination to take this matter seriously in an article in the September 1955 *Presbyterian Record*. He noted that the two theologians had each "indicated that the Reformers were absolutely opposed to a ministry of women as ministers or ruling elders, and that the doctrines of our Church in the Confession of Faith, etc., cannot in any way be construed to permit the ordination of women."[18] Identifying whether this would be a change in doctrine was the crucial question the committee had asked the two professors. The professors had explored other matters, including, in Hay's case, making it clear that marriage for him was the central issue: he could agree with ordination of single women but not married women.[19] But that was not what the committee had asked. They wanted to know if ordination would be permitted under the church's current doctrinal standards. The answer to this had been that it could not. As a practical matter, this meant that ordaining women to either the eldership or the ministry would be a change of both doctrine and church law, and thus must ultimately be sent to the presbyteries under the Barrier Act.[20] Louis Fowler, the chair of the committee, encouraged elders, ministers, and WMS members to answer the questions on ordination sent to their respective bodies. The rationale for taking a poll of the church's attitudes was apparent. The committee wanted to get a sense of whether there was a chance of success before taking the time-consuming steps of moving any motion through the Barrier Act.

ATTITUDES AT THE TIME: RESULTS OF THE STRAW POLL

The *Presbyterian Record* provided a series of articles in this period on the topic of women in the church. As well as encouraging those who were entitled to vote in the poll to do so, Fowler expressed his own opinion that the broad issue of women in the church, as well as the specific issues related to ordination, needed to be addressed.[21] Jean Black, a deaconess, argued for women's ordination with a particular focus on women in leadership: "Grant to her equal opportunities for study, equal rights to use her best intelligence in the most demanding theological disciplines."[22] John Johnson argued against women's ordination, rehearsing many of the biblical texts which would limit a woman's role.[23] Frank Morley argued for ordination.[24] While these articles focused on the question of ordination, other articles focused on the broader issues of the place of women in the church.

In March 1958, Helen Scott Sinclair provided an excellent survey of the work of deaconesses within the denomination.[25] Deaconesses had at one time been focused on overseas missions, but in 1958 this had changed and broadened: "Perhaps the greatest demand today is for graduates to be in charge" of Christian education in congregations.[26]

She urged that within the broader discussion of the place of women "the place of deaconesses in the Church deserves a good deal of consideration."[27] News items alerted readers that other denominations were struggling with the same issue.[28] Women's place in the church was an issue before the church throughout the 1950s in the pages of the denominational magazine.[29]

When the results of the informal poll came back to the committee, it was clear that there was limited support for the ordination of women as ministers or elders.[30] As can be seen in table 4.1, in 1956 there was limited support (only 36 per cent) among women for women clergy. This was certainly better than the meagre 17 per cent among male ministers and elders in presbyteries, but the result did not offer much hope for change. Women elders was a different matter. Yes, only 30 per cent of men in presbyteries supported women as elders, but this was considerably more than those who supported women clergy. Even more intriguingly, women were evenly divided on whether they or their sisters should serve as elders. The committee reported these results to the 1956 General Assembly. Margaret MacNaughton, who was a member of the committee, was given permission to speak to the Assembly before various motions from the committee were brought forward. The ordination of women as ruling elders and as ministers was recognized as impassable at the moment. But these results on ordination did not prevent the committee from trying to move forward on its overall agenda of considering the place of women in the church. There were other things which the committee believed it needed to do. One was to consider the question of the ordination of deaconesses.[31] Another was what to do with women who were ordained by other churches while missionaries.[32] The challenge of giving a voice to women remained the main concern of the committee. As they noted in their report to the General Assembly the next year in 1957: "It is now clear to us as a Committee that the matter of ordination for women as Ministers, Ruling Elders or Deaconesses is a minor one compared to the conviction among thoughtful women everywhere that women might well have a more definite voice in the Courts of our Church. The question is, against our centuries' old canonical law, practice and tradition, how shall this be achieved."[33] The committee continued to consider the place of women in the church. Ordination was a barrier. At the same time, granting ordination was not seen as a solution in and of itself to the challenges of the overall place of women in the church.

Table 4.1
Votes on the ordination of women, 1956

	Presbyteries (exclusively male)		*Presbyterials (exclusively female)*	
	Votes	Percentage	Votes	Percentage
In favour of ordaining women as elders	171	30%	826	48%
Opposed to ordaining women as elders	391	70%	908	52%
In favour of ordaining women as ministers	91	17%	638	36%
Opposed to ordaining women as ministers	458	83%	1,113	64%

Source: *A&P*, 1956, 312.

A WAY FORWARD? THE COUNCIL PLAN

It was on the basis of these concerns that the Committee on the Place of Women brought a complex proposal to the 1957 General Assembly. In essence, it argued that if women could not be ordained and thus have their voices heard in the existing church courts, another structure needed to be created so their voices could be heard. The committee proposed the denomination establish presbytery councils, synod councils, and an Assembly council at which women would be able to participate and have a voice. No congregational council was suggested because it was believed that a "Session may call into consultation all groups within the congregation."[34] Under this plan councils (male and female membership) would meet and discuss a wide variety of issues, including doctrine and worship. After this discussion had been completed and agreement was reached, the (exclusively male) requisite church court would then meet "to give formal ratification to the acts and proceedings of the Council."[35] The committee, chaired by Fowler, asked for feedback on the principles of the scheme, knowing that many of the details still needed to be worked out. One of the rationales given for the support of the council idea was the experience of ordination in other churches. Citing the example of the United Church, they estimated there would be "only nine women ministers" across the denomination if the Presbyterian Church in Canada followed the same pattern in proportion to its size; if they followed that of an American denomination, only twenty-eight. It was suggested that this would not give women a voice as ministers, nor would women elders be represented in equal numbers to men, "at least not for a long time," nor would ordaining women as deaconesses solve the issue: "In short on the basis of ordination, women will not come into any practical equality."[36] The practical issue of finding a voice for women – a voice with some degree of equality – had become a greater concern for the committee than had the issue of ordination.

As most of us recoil at the thought of yet another structure or committee, it is perhaps not surprising that the council plan did not receive a great deal of support in the church. The committee reported to the 1958 Assembly the lack of enthusiasm for this plan.[37] Progress stalled. Fowler had done an excellent job of trying to think broadly of how the talents of women might be better used in the church and in his leadership of the committee. As he prepared to step aside from leadership of the committee, he mentioned in a memo to members of the committee in December 1959 that the issue of the ordination of women to ministry was going to be raised in an overture from the Presbytery of Guelph, which was coming to the 1960 General Assembly. The memo also showed that Fowler was thinking broadly about "the place of ALL women in the Church," and how they could be integrated into the various structures of the church.[38] When the General Assembly met in 1960 a new convenor, Eoin Mackay, would be appointed to lead the committee.

TENTATIVE STEPS FORWARD

Shirley MacLeod wanted to be a minister. She believed she was called to this office, and the session of her congregation – Knox Presbyterian Church, Waterloo – agreed and supported her candidacy and forwarded this to the Presbytery of Guelph for their support and approval. As this was not a part of the law of the church, the Synod of Toronto and Kingston overtured General Assembly asking them "to come to the earliest possible decision on the whole question of the ordination of women to the full ministry of the Church."[39] This was the overture Fowler had noted in his memo to the committee. The question of women as elders was not being brought forward, but the issue of women as ministers was being taken directly to Assembly. At the 1960 General Assembly a motion to allow MacLeod to speak was defeated. This lack of courtesy should not obscure how seriously the Assembly took this matter, nor the specific actions they took. The Assembly agreed that "the question of the ordination of women to the ministry" should be sent down to the presbyteries under the Barrier Act and the results would be reported to the next year's General Assembly. They thus agreed to the first step of the process, which allowed for a change of church law and doctrine. The results which came back from the presbyteries should not obscure this action; the 1960 General Assembly was at least open to consider the possibility of women being ordained as ministers.[40]

The remits (changes to church law) sent down under the Barrier Act would have amended church law to permit women to serve as ordained clergy. The various presbyteries were required to vote simply "yes" or "no," and these results were received at the next General Assembly in 1961. Fourteen presbyteries (34 per cent) supported the ordination of women to ministry, but twenty-six (66 per cent) opposed (see table 4.2).[41] The remits failed; however, the Presbytery of Montreal responded with an overture to Assembly noting that the presbyteries had not had sufficient time to consider the issue of ordination of women. They asked that the Assembly withhold any decision "for at least two years" so that a full study could be made "by the Committee on Articles of Faith or such other body as the Assembly shall choose and by the Presbyteries, of the biblical doctrine of woman and of ordination" so that the church could make its decision "on the basis of its own standards."[42]

This call for a serious study of doctrine aligned with the direction the Committee on the Place of Women was already taking under the direction of their new convenor, Eoin Mackay (appointed at the last General Assembly). Mackay opened the 16 November 1960 meeting with a reading from Ephesians and a prayer, "asking for God's direction in the work of the committee and God's blessing on the Church's work within the Church and in the community," and then began the task of clarifying and refocusing the committee's work. This work was cast very broadly, with the task of the committee being "to discover what we conceive to be the real role of women in the Church and the community, and the way in which women can fulfil their role as members of the Church of Christ." The question of place in the "Courts of the Church," including ordination, was clearly central, even though the "evidence based on earlier studies is that women are not clamouring for ordination but they do want a real place in the

Table 4.2
Votes on the ordination of women, 1961, 1965, 1966

	1961 (under Barrier Act)		*1965 (poll by the committee)*		*1966 (under Barrier Act)*	
	Votes	Percentage	Votes	Percentage	Votes	Percentage
In favour of ordaining women as elders	(not asked)		21	64%	31	66%
Opposed to ordaining women as elders			11	36%	16	34%
In favour of ordaining women as ministers	14	34%	18	56%	26	55%
Opposed to ordaining women as ministers	26	66%	14	44%	21	45%

Sources: For 1961 data, *A&P* (1961), 350; for 1965 data, *A&P* (1965), 384; for 1966 data, *A&P* (1966), 456.
Note: The underlined numbers are the only ones mentioned in the denomination's history. Moir, *Enduring Witness*, 255–6.

life and work of the church."[43] A clear statement of the purpose for the committee became part of the report to the 1961 General Assembly: "To define the place of women in the Church in such a way that in the totality and unity of the Church's life and of the Christian life as a whole, women can exercise their gifts to the fullest possible extent as members of the Church of Jesus Christ."[44] The question before the committee flowed from this purpose: "How is the Church to act in obedience to Jesus Christ in relation to the place and contribution of women in the life of the Church?"[45] The committee noted it had "accepted the responsibility of a biblical approach to the matter." In addressing the central question, it stated: "We believe that the matter of the place of women in the Church cannot be rightly dealt with on the basis of considerations of long-accepted custom, traditional or contemporary preferences held more or less strongly, sociological attitudes and pressures of our age with its general acceptance of women in all secular vocations, or isolated scripture texts so often used to justify opposite conclusions to the whole question."[46] The committee was very clear on what it intended to do and how it intended to approach the issue with a focus on what the Bible had to say. The committee was also clear on the challenges it would face. Marriage was one of these barriers. One member noted "his own position as that of being in favour of the ordination of women, but said that for him there was one real theological problem around the commitment required to the ministry in light of a woman's higher calling as a wife and mother."[47] This cultural concern needed to be addressed. The committee was also aware of how the Bible could be interpreted differently. It noted that it wanted to hear "the testimony of the Bible, without falling into the impasse which an uncoordinated use of isolated proof texts inevitably produces on this question."[48]

If the committee had laid out clearly its understanding of its purpose, the question before it, and its intention to look to the Bible as its authority in answering these questions, it also was very concrete in addressing real issues, both large and small. The committee was forthright that it intended to look at "such questions as the ordination of women to the ruling and teaching eldership." The committee was also interested in other ways in which women could "exercise their gifts to the fullest extent as members of the Church of Jesus Christ" not only within the church but within the world. The committee explicitly noted that its task was "to set forth a biblical doctrine of the place of women in the purpose of God."[49]

The overture from the Presbytery of Montreal was directed by the 1961 General Assembly to the Committee on Articles of Faith. Given this subject was before two committees, it was agreed that they should work together. In the months prior to the next General Assembly in 1962, a subcommittee of the Committee on Articles of Faith met with the Committee on the Place of Women to coördinate its work on the doctrine of women.[50] By the May meeting of the joint committee, an outline of an adult study document with some suggested biblical passages for consideration and other content was presented, as well as suggestions for other material.[51] It is not surprising, then, that the report of the Committee on Articles of Faith noted that, in relation to the overture from the Presbytery of Montreal in 1961, it had been working with the Committee on the Place of Women because of its existing and on-going work on "the doctrine of woman."[52] In the end, the Committee on Articles of Faith focused on questions related to ordination in general. The question of the doctrine of woman was handled by the Committee on the Place of Women, and the Committee on Articles of Faith commended the study guide prepared by that committee.[53] Discussions on theology were not restricted to just one committee; this was the work of the entire denomination.

"PUTTING WOMAN IN HER PLACE"

If the denomination was to make its decision on the place of women on the basis of scripture, it was vital that scripture be studied. The Committee on the Place of Women worked with the Committee on Articles of Faith and the Board of Education, and in 1963 produced its important study guide "Putting Woman in Her Place." The title was intended (though we might not necessarily read it this way) as a positive encouragement to the denomination to find the correct place for women within the life of the church. Authorship of the document was ascribed to the committee, with Barbara Sprague as the designer and Robert Carter as the editor. Specific contributions were noted at various places in the sixteen-page booklet.[54] In the introduction to the study guide, convenor Eoin Mackay suggested the committee's hope in terms of how this would be used. He imagined that groups of at least six, each with their own copy, would meet with their ministers to study and discuss the material. Mackay suggested the committee had done their work, not to "present any particular position on the subject," but to focus attention on the relevant passages "in the hope and confidence that if our people will expose themselves to the witness of the Scriptures, God will enable the Church to understand and act according to His will in regard to the function women should fulfill as members of the Body of Christ."[55]

While the committee wanted to expose the denomination to the scriptures, it also wanted to give guidance as to how scripture should be read. The six studies were preceded by three short selections. The first was a summary of an article by Mrs Henrietta Visser't Hooft published in *Theology Today* that looked at the creation stories in Genesis and discussed the origins of sexual differences. The article drew on the insights of theologian Karl Barth and philosopher Martin Buber.[56] This article was followed by a shorter summary of an article which stressed male-female partnership in marriage by Professor Paul Ramsey of Princeton.[57] The final section of the introduction was a summary the committee prepared of a German publication by Johannes Leipoldt, which outlined the latest research on Jewish and Greek attitudes to women around the time of Jesus.[58] These articles in the introduction suggest how the committee was approaching scripture. They wanted to include the latest insights from scholarship with the belief and hope that this would help the average Presbyterian lay person in the 1960s understand the biblical passages in the study guide.

The core of "Putting Woman in Her Place" was the biblical studies themselves. There were six in total and their order was carefully chosen. Texts from Paul which many understood to restrict what women could do within the church were considered, but were not the starting (and thus not the ending) point in this discussion. Instead, these texts were considered within the broader context of scripture. Both creation narratives Genesis 1:26–31 and Genesis 2:18–25 were considered individually in the study on men and women in creation. Each story was considered in terms of how it spoke of the differences between the sexes. In the first creation narrative, it was suggested "mankind, as 'male and female,' is made in 'the image of God.'"[59] Participants were asked to consider, or reconsider, the notion from the second creation narrative that suggested women were derived from, and thus inferior to, men. After looking at how God's good intentions were distorted by the fall in study 2, the guide turned to look at the "redeemed nature of mankind" and how men and women together are called to serve God. Stress was placed on equality in the early church. At the same time one of the tricky Pauline passages, Ephesians 5:22 and its phrase "wives, be subject to your husband, as to the Lord" (RSV) was considered. Questions were raised. Other texts were discussed. Tentative conclusions (plural) were drawn. These tentative conclusions spoke of both men and women in partnership, while also acknowledging differences with wives being "subject to their husbands, in this same sense of walking in love and [they] are to have respect for them" while husbands, though they "are to be the 'head' of the family" and offer leadership, their "headship is [to be] characterized by love and self-giving on the husband's part."[60] These conclusions suggested mutual responsibilities, not equality, between the sexes. On one level, they were quite conservative, not flattening the hierarchy of males over females but only levelling it slightly. Yet, at the same time, this careful discussion avoided having a text like the one in Ephesians be used to merely end the discussion with a clear affirmation that men were superior to women.

This careful interpretation of specific texts within the entire biblical witness continued as the study guide looked at how Jesus viewed women in study 4. Jesus's positive views of women were stressed. The study did not shy away from difficult questions, asking directly for participants to ask themselves why Jesus had not included a woman among the original twelve disciples. At the same time, Jesus's attitude to women was seen as central to the question of the role of women in the church in twentieth-century Canada.[61] "Paul's view of women" and the various texts associated with him were then considered in study 5. Participants were invited to consider the inconsistencies in Paul's teaching, and to compare Paul's writings to what they had already considered in their previous biblical studies. One of the discussion points was direct: "What is your reaction to the proposal that Paul does not seem to have worked out his doctrine about women in the Church as carefully or consistently as he has other matters like circumcision for males, dietary laws and sabbath laws? What would you say to the proposal that the Church today has to work out the place of women in the Church under the guidance of the Holy Spirit, much as the Church had to work out the question of slavery in the nineteenth century?"[62] Finally, study 6, "some practical considerations," looked at a variety of biblical texts addressing very specific questions of the place of women in the church. The committee also asked about customs and how they shaped the place of women in the church, as well as whether the "shortage of men for the 'ministry'" should be a consideration in any discussion.[63] The committee concluded the pamphlet by printing its reports to the General Assembly in 1961, 1962, and 1963, making sure everyone was aware of where the denomination was in this important discussion.[64]

"Putting Woman in Her Place" was an important undertaking. It was published, distributed, and used in the denomination. In calling the church to make important decisions about the place of women in the church, the Committee on the Place of Women looked to the Bible. There was no sociology and no discussion on the equivalent professions which women might be entering in the study guide. The focus was on the Bible. At the same time, the committee had a clear sense of how the Bible should be read. As it had already noted in one of its reports to the General Assembly, it rejected the notion that the church should select specific texts or that a text held the definitive answer. Their intent was to look at the entire scriptural witness, with a particular focus on what Jesus taught through his words and actions. Paul's letters did not trump Jesus's teaching or other verses in scripture. The committee asked the Presbyterian Church in Canada to read texts in their historical contexts and to try to work together corporately to understand their meaning. The influence of neo-orthodoxy is suggested in this approach. What is not evident anywhere in this report is what might be called a "liberal" interpretation, either of scripture itself or in calling individuals to listen to culture and ignore scripture.[65] The committee was very conservative in its approach. Readers today might even suggest it was too conservative, in particular as it continued to argue for males having some superior role to women as the head of the household. It was on this basis of its study and understanding of scripture that the committee asked the denomination to consider the place of women in the church, and specifically whether women could serve as elders, and even as ministers.

One can discern which direction the committee was leaning in its report. If, as it illustrated, women as well as men had received the gifts of the Holy Spirit in the early church, how could one then limit how women might serve? If Jesus has a positive view of women and Paul is understood to still be overly influenced by the rabbinic tradition in which he was educated, the conclusion that we should look to Jesus's approach is obvious. The focus was on women and men working together, equally, in the church. The committee's concern was with the place of women broadly. This was never lost sight of throughout the study. The ordination of women as elders was always a key focus. The committee made the argument for this more effectively than the case for the ordination of women to serve as clergy. While never shutting down the latter, it nevertheless maintained a clear focus on the place of all women in the church.

The Committee on the Place of Women looked to scripture in its study guide "Putting Woman in Her Place." At the same time, those opposed to the ordination of women also looked to scripture but in a considerably different and ultimately nonnegotiable way. In a brief article in *Presbyterian Comment* in June 1961, Everett Bean explored the place of women in the Old and New Testaments. When it came to Galatians 3:28, central to the original overture of 1953 which spoke of there being "neither male nor female" in Christ, Bean declared, "This verse has no bearing on the question of the ordination of women." In the conclusion he continued: "As one considers the role of women in the Old Testament, and as one considers the teaching on the matter of Church Government in the Old and New Testaments, one must conclude that the ordination of women as Teaching or Ruling Elders is not commended in the Bible. In fact it is not permitted. Since the Bible is our 'Church Directory and Statute Book' in doctrine and government, this should settle the matter in the minds of Presbyterians."[66] The study guide "Putting Woman in Her Place" arrived at different conclusions. Both sides were clearly arguing from scripture. They were arguing about theology, including how one read and interpreted the Bible. It was not that one side was rejecting tradition and scripture and one side was holding on to these things; rather, both sides were interpreting tradition and scripture in different ways. What we should recognize is that, in 1966, these divisions were between the neo-orthodox, who seem to have been the majority, and the confessional orthodox and other conservative theologies.

But what happened to Shirley MacLeod, the young woman who had helped to push the denomination to consider this issue? DeCourcey Rayner, the editor of the *Presbyterian Record,* gave an update to the readers of the denominational magazine in 1964. He reported that MacLeod had graduated from her arts degree with honours and began studies at Knox College, but then after a few weeks asked for "permission to withdraw": "The reason? To accept an invitation to holy matrimony, extended by a young minister whom she had met on a student mission field the previous summer." The editor noted this, indicating he was in no way criticizing her actions, "for she has been called to another high office, that of wife and mother and mistress of the manse," before turning his attention to the issue that would be coming before the Assembly again in 1964. He referenced the study guide "Putting Woman in Her Place," perhaps as an encouragement for readers to consult it. While the church had said "no" to women as ministers a few years before, Rayner suggested the committee had done some "hard thinking" on the matter and the study guide needed to be considered carefully by all members of the denomination. The process might seem slow, he suggested, but this careful deliberation had its values. The matter was still before the denomination.[67]

THE CHURCH DECIDES

When the Committee on the Place of Women reported to the General Assembly in 1964, it began by noting that the study "Putting Woman in Her Place" had been widely distributed, used, and generally well received.[68] It had received considerable feedback and input from the church in relation to its work. To those who responded that they believed "the material was slanted a bit in a particular direction," the committee members noted that this had not been their intent, "however well we succeeded." The committee then laid out what it believed were its main affirmations. The first was that "genus man" (humanity) was to be a partnership of male and female, and that men and women were created to live in harmony. The second was that when the Bible speaks of "man" it was referring to "this partnership of male and female."

One of the implications of this, which the report noted, was that when this was forgotten, "when we think and act as if only the male is called to know and serve God and His purpose for the world and as if only the male is endowed with the Holy Spirit to fulfil such a calling we are unbiblical."[69] A third affirmation was that challenges in living this out related to the challenges of biblical interpretation. The committee again argued that an impasse was reached when "isolated proof-texts" were chosen. The church needed to look more broadly: "The prophetic-apostolic Word of God of which the incarnate form and content is Jesus Christ is not to be identified in any mechanical way with the individual words of Scripture. To put it bluntly, a verse we may read in Leviticus or in a pauline epistle must be judged and, if necessary modified or corrected in the light of Jesus Christ and the essential message of the gospel. The confession that both Church and Bible stand under the final authority of the Word of God is a cardinal tenet of reformed theology."[70]

Based on these affirmations, the committee then went on to state its conclusions and make recommendations. The committee concluded that there "can be no distinction in the status accorded men and women as members of the Body of Christ." The church, it was argued, should serve as an example to the world in this regard. The committee next concluded that women could be ordained as ministers. As they put it, "we believe that women should not be barred as women from taking their place in the pulpits of the Church."[71] The committee remained cautious, suggesting that while there might be differences between men and women, they were no spiritual difference that would prevent women from serving. The committee did note the challenge that marriage was said to present to women being ordained. They acknowledged there might need to be some (unspecified) adjustments, but again suggested this was not a "fundamental difficulty."[72] When it came to ruling elders, the committee was more direct: "We believe that women in whom the Church discerns the necessary gifts and calls to exercise them should be free to take their place in all the courts of the Church."[73] Marriage was not noted in relation to elders. These conclusions were followed by a series of six recommendations. The central ones dealt with women as ministers and elders respectively and requested that these be sent down to the church for study, essentially a poll, "with a view to issue an action at the 1965 Assembly."[74] Perhaps because it was not clear who was to issue such an action or deal with what was reported back, the committee's motions were amended. The amended motion specified the committee would continue and would be responsible for communicating the responses and for proposing the actions which needed to be taken.[75]

The committee reported the findings from the poll to the next General Assembly in 1965: of the forty-nine presbyteries, thirty-two had reported (leaving seventeen who had not responded for whatever reason). Of those, when it came to ordaining women as elders, twenty-one presbyteries (64 per cent) were in favour with eleven presbyteries (36 per cent) opposed. When it came to women as ministers, those in favour were three fewer: eighteen (56 per cent) were in favour with fourteen (44 per cent) opposed. As can be seen in table 4.2, this presents a marked shift from the results just a few years before.[76] The positive results on women as elders (a question not asked in 1961) were also notable. The committee reported these findings and then noted: "Thus, while we have by no means reached a common mind in these matters, when compared with the responses made in past years the returns indicate a definite trend towards the acceptance of women into full partnership in the life and work of the Church. The conclusions of your committee as reported a year ago remain substantially the same."[77] The 1965 General Assembly considered the motions dealing respectively with the ordination of women to the ministry and eldership.[78] The Assembly approved sending these to the presbyteries: "That the substance of recommendations 3 and 4 be sent down to the presbyteries of the Church under the Barrier Act in the form and terms required by the said Act."[79] Sending these down under the Barrier Act moved the discussion from the theoretical (affirming a right) one step closer to implementation (this could become the law of the denomination). This motion to send this down to the presbyteries formally under the Barrier Act, as well as an additional motion to have the committee continue, were passed without any recorded dissents.[80] It is important to pause and note this. For whatever reason, even those opposed to this direction did not signal this at the 1965 General Assembly.

The 1966 General Assembly was thus set to make a decision on the ordination of women, both as elders and as ministers. The responses to the remits were reported. In relation to women as elders, thirty-one presbyteries (66 per cent) said yes, while sixteen presbyteries (34 per cent) said no. The support for women as ministers was notably lower, with twenty-six presbyteries (55 per cent) agreeing with the remit, and twenty-one presbyteries (45 per cent) disagreeing.[81] These results (see table 4.2) were very similar to the results of the simple poll the committee had reported in 1965. A majority of the church was now supporting women being ordained to each of these offices. It was now a case of debating what the final decision would look like. The two remits that had been sent down under the Barrier Act were presented to Assembly, and in later sederunts their wording was debated. In each case, the text noted that "women are eligible" to serve in the respective offices, and made it clear that all of the sections of the relevant *Book of Forms* would now apply to women as well as men.[82]

The motion to approve the ordination of women to the eldership came first. The motion passed. Although there was clearly opposition, the debate was brief. Twenty-four dissents were recorded.[83] When the motion pertaining to the ordination of women as ministers was presented to a later session, more significant opposition appeared. It was agreed to record the vote: 133 in favour, 72 opposed. More dissents were recorded. The reason given by those thirty-two who dissented from the ordination of women to the ministry was straightforward: "We can find no authority in the Scriptures that would require or permit women to be ordained to the teaching eldership."[84] The Assembly took the unusual step of appointing a committee to reply to the dissents related to women as elders. The committee met and produced the following response, which was approved by the Assembly: "By the adoption of this Report and the approval of the recommendation on the ordination of women to the ruling eldership the General Assembly has affirmed its conviction that such action is 'in obedience to Jesus Christ who is the Word of God as His Will is made known through the witness of the Holy Scriptures, as the Spirit attests the essential content of that witness to the Truth' on this matter and is in keeping with a true understanding of the faith of our Church, *reformata et semper reformanda* [reformed and always reforming]."[85] The 1966 Assembly was clearly divided on this issue. At the same time, the Assembly affirmed in no uncertain terms that it believed its decision was scripturally and doctrinally sound. The results of the decisions of the Assembly were clear that women could now be ordained as elders and ministers.

AFTER THE DECISION: RESPONSES AND IMPLEMENTATION

The 1966 decision was reported in the news, notably in the Canadian edition of *Time* magazine. *Time* noted that the Presbyterian Church in Canada, the third largest Protestant denomination in Canada, was now the second to "allow women pastors." The magazine's reporting of the decision focused on Marion Webster, who had recently graduated from Knox and had not been eligible for ordination, and now was able to serve as a minister.[86] Notably absent from *Time*'s coverage was the reality that the denomination had also decided to allow women to serve as elders. And it was here that changes began almost immediately. Two women, Wynn Thomas at Fallingbrook in Scarborough and Joan MacInnes at St Andrews, Arthur, were ordained as elders within the month following the decision.[87] In the subsequent months and years more and more sessions, as they held elections, elected women to serve as ruling elders. As noted in the introduction to this chapter, at the next General Assembly in 1967, Mary Whale and Addie Forrester appeared for the first time as elder commissioners with a voice and vote. Whale spoke at the General Assembly, with one commissioner asking that it be noted that this was "the first time in history that a lady elder" had spoken at Assembly, and another commissioner adding, "It certainly won't be the last time."[88] The historic achievement was noted, but also mocked. While being aware of the reality (whether welcomed or otherwise) of women elders, the church seemed oblivious to the possibility of women clergy. At the very same Assembly in 1967, the Commission on Recruitment and Vocations continued to wring its hands over the lack of suitable candidates for the ministry. Nowhere in that report, nor in the report a few years later titled "Ministry of the Presbyterian Church in Canada" (commonly called the Ross Report), is there any indication that, by its actions in 1966, the General Assembly had doubled the pool of potential recruits for the ordained ministry.[89] As women continued to be elected as elders to sessions across Canada, the first woman minister, Shirley Jeffrey, was ordained in 1968. This was marked with considerable fanfare in the denominational magazine as well in the Knox College *Bulletin*.[90] Anne Wightman followed, with much less fanfare, in 1969. No women were ordained as ministers in the next two years.[91] As the Presbyterian Church in Canada moved out of the 1960s and into the 1970s, the decision made in 1966 had its greatest impact at the level of women elders.

Over a period of thirteen years, the Presbyterian Church in Canada wrestled with the question of the place of women in the church. It is important to recognize the concern was for the place of women within all aspects of the life of the denomination. Early on it was recognized that ordination was an issue that needed to be dealt with; however, when Canadian Presbyterians used this term, they were referencing not only ordination to the ministry as a teaching elder, but also ordination as an elder within a congregation, or ruling elder. In considering the question of whether women might be ordained, the church was clearly dealing with very practical issues. At the same time, it was dealing with both cultural issues and theological issues, the latter derived from interpretations of scripture. In considering the decision, Canadian Presbyterians took the Bible seriously. They made this decision based upon what they considered to be the biblical witness. Where they differed from other denominations – and among themselves– was in how they chose to read and interpret scripture. This problem of different ways in which scripture could be read was noted from the beginning. Canadian Presbyterians were very aware that they had different understandings, and could (and did) point to different specific passages of scripture in seeking to resolve the question. Was it a matter, as the original overture suggested in 1953, that in Christ there was no difference between the sexes? Or did verses from Paul's letters limiting what women could do prohibit women from being ordained and holding office in the church? The denomination wrestled with its inherited theological understandings and with what it found in the Bible. In the important study guide "Putting Woman in Her Place," the position was argued that the entire witness of scripture spoke of both men and women working and serving together equally. This, it was proposed, was God's original intention and what Jesus affirmed in his ministry. It was on this understanding of scripture that the Committee on the Place of Women made its recommendations that women could serve as both elders and Ministers of Word and Sacrament.

What role did culture play in all of this? The debate about the place of women in the church took place at the same time that these issues were being debated in the broader society. But society did not speak with one voice. Nor by 1953 – or even 1966 – had the broader culture accepted clearly our current conception of the fundamental equality of men and women. This was true in terms of both voice within organizations and employment within the professions. Women doctors, engineers, and lawyers were still a rarity in this period. The contest in society was reflected, in some ways, within the church. As the role of women changed in the culture, the church did experience pressure, from without and within, to consider what women were allowed to do within its structures.[92] At the same time, caution should be exercised so as not to ascribe to the "traditional" position a biblical mandate, and not to assume that it was only those wishing to change the status quo who were affected by culture. The existing understandings within the church of what women could and could not do had already been shaped by culture. The entire issue of marriage was one of cultural value which we clearly see in these discussions, one that some Presbyterians in this period saw as a barrier to women being in leadership in the church. One would be naive to assume culture had no impact on the church's decision or on its consideration of the place of women in the church. But one would be equally naive, and incorrect, to argue that the status quo of the church in 1953 was purely biblical, unpolluted by any cultural influence. This was clearly not the case. Both those arguing for reconsidering the place of women and those arguing for the status quo were shaped by culture, just as they each looked to scripture as they made their case.

Looking back on the events of 1966 from our perspective, the question emerges: Why did those opposed to the decision taken in 1966 to ordain women as elders as well as ministers not take more dramatic action? Why did they not leave the denomination? Why did they not insist on being allowed some kind of exemption to this change when it was decided? This latter idea has recently led some Canadian Presbyterians to insist that, indeed, those opposed insisted on and were granted "liberty of conscience" on the issue in 1966.[93] This did not happen. No provision was made for tender male consciences in 1966, nor did anyone request this at the time. The question remains: Why not? Donald MacLeod has suggested several reasons why those opposed failed to organize, in a manner similar to what they would later do (see chapter 8).[94] At the same time, it is clear that the decision on the ordination of women was only one of many points of contention, not only during this period but specifically at the 1966 General Assembly. As MacLeod has noted, the emerging issue of the Vietnam War, the softening of opposition to communism (particularly related to mission and China), and the proposed new confession of faith (see chapter 5) were all seen as more pressing issues in 1966.[95] The decision to ordain women was only one of many decisions made at the General Assembly in 1966 on which confessional conservatives and evangelical Presbyterians disagreed. The September 1966 issue of *Presbyterian Comment* focused its opposition to what had happened at the General Assembly on the proposed "Draft Statement of Faith."[96] *Presbyterian Comment* did not support the ordination of women, but there were other issues they considered more important.

The question remains: Why was there not greater opposition in the late 1960s among those who did not accept the denomination's decision to ordain women? The answer may be simply that, while they were opposed, they believed they would never be affected. Even those who supported the ordination of women seem to have imagined that this decision would only result in a few exceptional (single?) women moving into ministry. As noted, the committee responsible for recruitment did not in 1967 suggest that the shortage of ministers had been resolved by opening the position of minister to women. The members of that committee would generally have been considered supporters of the ordination of women. If those who supported women as Ministers of Word and Sacrament were limited in their vision as to how many women might choose this path, it is perhaps understandable that those opposed might think that this was something they would be able to avoid. If they served as an interim moderator while a congregation was searching for a new minister, they could quietly ignore any female applicants. The presbytery in which they served might simply refuse to process a call to any woman candidate. If they were in a presbytery where this would be impossible to prevent, they might develop other strategies. Women ministers, as much as one might oppose them, were not the serious priority, and would not have the immediate impact that something like a new doctrinal statement would. When it came to women elders, the solution was even simpler: do not allow them to be elected. Within Canadian Presbyterian polity, sessions had considerable power over who might be elected as an elder. (It is best to consider them as a self-perpetuating oligarchy, rather than an example of democracy.) If the minister voiced his opposition, the likelihood of a woman being elected was dramatically reduced. If powerful elders opposed electing women elders, this, similarly, could prevent any women being ordained within that specific congregation. The Presbyterian Church in Canada had decided women were eligible to serve as elders and ministers. The church, however, did not require – or even in the early years following this decision actively encourage – individual congregations to elect women as elders. This was left up to each local congregation. Those who were opposed to the 1966 decision simply acted as if nothing had changed. And this largely worked. Until it didn't.

5

Preserving the Past

Theology and Worship

Predestination is the doctrine most associated with Presbyterians. Those inside Presbyterian churches know this but for very few Presbyterians is this doctrine central to their worship or how they live their faith. Nor did Canadian Presbyterians generally argue amongst themselves about the expression of predestination found in the Westminster Confession. What troubled and divided them was something else entirely. Disagreements over the relationship between church and state had splintered Presbyterians into various competing denominations.[1] In order to reunite, they had granted "liberty of conscience" on the specific sections of the Westminster Confession that dealt with relations between government and church. Calling this a disagreement over "church and state" may be somewhat misleading in the early twenty-first century. We imagine that this would be a disagreement about the political or economic issues to which the church could speak. This might be an issue facing the church today. Historically, however, it was a completely different debate and it centred on money and power: what money should the church expect from the state, and what power should the state have over the church. Presbyterians managed to divide into three major positions on this issue, with the dominant tradition (the Free Church tradition) expecting some financial support from the state, while denying the state any ability to interfere in the church. While this was the dominant theological position, in practice the church relied on member's monetary contributions (one of the other positions) and the state had no financial obligations to the church. But the question "What are the obligations of the state to the church, and the church to the state?" remained an open question, one they had agreed to disagree on.

The crisis of World War II raised the question of whether agreeing to disagree on church and state matters was enough. Did the church ultimately have no position? And, if this was the case, how could it speak to certain issues? Or was the position clear: the church could tell the state what to do, but the state had no business interfering in worship services? These were the questions Canadian Presbyterians began to grapple with during World War II. As we noted in the discussion on church union and rebuilding after union, the Presbyterian Church in Canada was more closely tied to the Westminster Standards (the Westminster Confession of Faith, the Larger and Shorter Catechisms, the Directory of Public Worship, and the Form of Church Government) after 1925 than had been the case prior to the disruption. Ephraim Scott notably argued that the one thing the continuing denomination did not need was a committee responsible for doctrine as there was nothing that should be changed.[2] The crisis of World War II challenged this notion, and the denomination created a committee to look at doctrine. This chapter will explore why this committee was created and how it attempted but failed to create a contemporary statement of faith. It did address the issue of church and state relations and created a statement, the "Declaration of Faith Concerning Church and Nation." The creation of a revised *Book of Common Order* also proved remarkably contentious. Canadian Presbyterians had tied themselves more tightly to their traditions. Looking back to these standards gave them great strength. It also proved a challenge as they attempted to adapt and move forward. On what basis would any changes be made? Who got to determine what needed to be changed? These were all questions that confronted Canadian Presbyterians in this period. This chapter will argue they were ultimately not able to resolve these in the immediate post-war period. The church remained very traditional.

THE PARIS DELIVERANCE

As conflict loomed in Europe in 1939, the Presbytery of Paris, Ontario (just west of Brantford) made an "official statement" about the world situation. What became known as the Paris Deliverance arose out of the worsening international situation "particularly in view of the possibility of war," and was read in all congregations in the Presbytery of Paris on Sunday, 23 April 1939.[3] It was then given to the press, as well as forwarded as a memorial to both the Synod of Hamilton and London and the General Assembly. This statement has become central to the way Canadian Presbyterians have told the story of how they began to rethink their understanding of church and state relations during World War II.[4] The emerging situation in Europe was clearly the driving force in the production of this statement. In mind was the rise of the National Socialist Party (Nazis) and Adolph Hitler, who "erected a totalitarian claim" on the lives of all German society, including the church in Germany. The Paris Deliverance was direct and stark in terms of what it saw happening:

> the truth of the Gospel has been publicly attacked by the leaders of the German State, and a pagan philosophy and religion has been officially sponsored and taught in the schools, in youth organizations and in universities and by radio, press and public platform. The "Confessional" Church in Germany has boldly condemned these errors both within and without the Church. And because of her witness to the truth her ministers have been imprisoned or removed from their pastorates or otherwise intimidated. Seminaries have been closed by the State Secret Police, printing presses seized and Christian literature banned.
>
> German National Socialism means the dictatorship founded upon the conscious lie and the blind power of the myth of the anti-Christ, with the inevitable consequences of inhumanity, loss of freedom and lawlessness in the sphere of all national, social and cultural life. Hence, the expansion of this power constitutes not only a political and moral problem, but also a theological problem.[5]

Those in the Presbytery of Paris who authored this document (Gordon Peddie is generally considered a key figure) were clearly responding to what they considered a grave crisis. The Paris Deliverance was forwarded to, and received by, the General Assembly as a memorial; nevertheless, the text was not printed as part of the official proceedings of the denomination. [6] The committee established by the General Assembly recommended that this statement be distributed to the presbyteries for their consideration; however, this motion was tabled and nothing further seems to have happened with this statement.[7]

CRISIS DURING WORLD WAR II

Three years later, two overtures and a different memorial that had limited, if any, connection to the Paris Deliverance came before the General Assembly. In 1942 the Presbytery of Paris sent another memorial to the General Assembly, again asking that it consider issues of church and state. The text of this memorial (which again was not printed in the *Acts and Proceedings*) bears little resemblance to the Paris Deliverance. The two overtures, one from the Synod of Hamilton and London (overture 18) and one from the Presbytery of Toronto (overture 24) were sent, alongside this new memorial, to one special committee as they all related to issues of church and state. Their differences from each other, and from the 1939 Paris Deliverance, need to be recognized.

The memorial from the Presbytery of Paris was entitled "A Petition for a Declaration on the Doctrine of Liberty of Conscience and on the Lordship of Christ over the State" (1942).[8] The 1942 memorial argued that there was "confusion" around issues of church and state in the Presbyterian Church in Canada because of the way the denomination was created. As the document noted, at the time the Presbyterian Church in Canada was formed in 1875, it was agreed in this Basis of Union (1875) that "nothing contained in the Westminster Confession or Catechisms regarding the power and duty of the civil magistrate shall be held to sanction any principle or views inconsistent with full liberty of conscience in matters of religion." "Liberty of conscience" had been agreed to during the negotiations on this union. The memorial suggested that this understanding of liberty of conscience created an "intolerable situation" for all ministers. They had to accept the Westminster Confession in such a way that "a man is asked to vow that which liberty of conscience in turn disavows."[9] Why this mattered, Gordon Peddie argued in the pamphlet "King of Kings," was that it undermined the idea that Christ was sovereign and Lord over all nations: "What *had been decided* in 1875 was that on the question of the Lordship of Christ over the State, including specifically, the practical application of such a doctrine, there must be NO decision!"[10] Therefore, he suggested, the church found itself – at all levels – unable to speak to issues confronting it in the present crisis. He suggested this was a problem because "at this very moment" the church faced "problems of papacy, problems of propaganda and education, problems of civil and religious rights – *world problems now*" which no court could address.[11] This was what the pamphlet argued; it is not clear that all Canadian Presbyterians in 1942, let alone today, would agree with this interpretation. The church needed to change this, Peddie argued passionately, or it could not speak to any of these issues. With this background in mind, the suggested remedy of the petition becomes clearer. The church, it was argued, needed to rectify what the memorial understood was a "confusion."

Overture 18 from the Synod of Hamilton and London echoed the 1942 memorial from the Presbytery of Paris in suggesting there was a lack of clarity around church and state relations in how one accepted the Westminster Confession of Faith. This was, it suggested, a challenge for many to "affirm their loyalty to the State; and the State on its part is left without assured knowledge of its powers and duties, under the Lord Jesus Christ, towards the Church."[12] The redress that the overture recommended, echoing the memorial, was that the General Assembly "take steps to provide for a Confession of Faith with respect to the powers and duties of the Civil Magistrate and the relation which exists, under the Lord Jesus Christ, between the Church and the State."[13] Overture 24 from the Presbytery of Toronto was much longer and different in substance. The complaint was that the state was calling its own worship services. Ministers were finding themselves in a bind – services of worship were being called by civil leaders and voluntary civic committees, with no previous consent from or consultation with the denomination, and with the expectation that ministers would participate. There was also a concern that officials in the denomination were involved in these committees, but without the authorization of the denomination. If these challenges were not enough, the content of the services was deemed to be problematic for Presbyterians as "the forms of religious worship prepared for these services, and the prayers suggested for use in them, which are prepared with a view to including Protestant and Catholic, Jew and Gentile in one 'religious' act, and which, therefore do not confess Jesus Christ, but are notable for the omission of all references to His Name."[14] The drafters of the overture raised the question of whether the state could call the church to such services, what role these national committees had, the responsibility of the church to the state, and the approval of services which were "notable in their failure to confess Jesus Christ."[15]

These overtures and the memorial from the Presbytery of Paris were combined and a special committee was sent away to come up with a suggestion as to what the church should do in response to the issues raised.[16] The committee responded in detail to all of the points raised in overture 24 before turning to consider together overture 18 and the memorial from the Presbytery of Paris. The committee recognized that each overture asked for a "Confession of Faith" dealing with issues related to the mutual duties and responsibilities of church and state, but argued against this as "no issue as to the relations of Church and State exists in this land"; further, the relations that do exist were "founded upon mutual respect and goodwill" so there was no need for a declaration other than the one found in chapter 23 of the Westminster Confession of Faith; and finally, that any statement would cause needless controversy within the church and possibly between the church and civic authorities.[17] General Assembly disagreed. Instead, it created a committee "to take this matter into consideration and bring in a finding at next Assembly."[18] As a result of this action by the General Assembly in 1942, a special committee was struck to look at the continually thorny issue for Canadian Presbyterians of the relationship between church and state.

The "Special Committee Re Overtures Nos. 18, 24 and Petition of Presbytery of Paris" reported to the next General Assembly. In its report the committee continued the model that had already been established of dividing these concerns and dealing first with overture 24 (the state calling worship services), and then dealing with overture 18 and the concerns of the Presbytery of Paris (could the denomination speak to issues of church and state). In relation to the former, the moderator, Dr Norman MacLeod, reported on a meeting that he and the leaders from three other Protestant denominations had with the Prime Minister Mackenzie King in Ottawa. MacLeod wrote:

> They were very cordially received by the Prime Minister, and assurance was given by him that, while in the past there have been sent out forms [of worship] for special services which were admittedly unsatisfactory, the name of Jesus Christ having been nowhere mentioned in at least one of them, the same thing would not happen again, and that Church leaders would be consulted when such forms were being prepared in the future. The Prime Minister said he fully recognized the place of the Church in the national life.[19]

The report also states that "considerable discussion" on church and state relations took place, including the position the church might find itself in "if at any time a government unfriendly to the Church might arise in Canada," given that the church considered Christians to have "dual citizenship" as citizens of the state as well as members of the church; however, no resolution was recorded. Instead, the committee turned after lunch to consider the other overture and the petition, and how this related to the Westminster Confession of Faith. The committee agreed on three things: first, it was not the time to look at church and state issues, as any "pronouncements" would lead to "misunderstanding and confusion"; second, that these issues needed to be looked at in terms of all of the theological issues which required study; third, the special committee therefore recommended the establishment of "a larger committee, comprised of the ablest men in the Church" who would be given the task of "re-examining our whole confessional position as a church, with a view to eventually stating what we believe, as a Reformed Church, in language and concepts relevant to our own day and situation."[20] Other churches, including the Church of Scotland, were working on these "larger issues."[21] With seemingly little debate, the recommendations of the special committee were adopted, and continuing Presbyterians found themselves with a committee mandated to broadly consider the denomination's doctrine.[22]

TOWARDS A CONTEMPORARY CONFESSION

This committee set to work and reported their progress to the Assembly over the coming years. One task the committee somewhat tentatively suggested be undertaken was the preparation of a brief statement of faith, based on both scripture and the Westminster Confession.[23] They began this project by presenting to the next year's General Assembly (1945) a seven-page statement outlining key doctrines. The statement was divided into headings that described various theological doctrines – the Doctrine of the Knowledge of God; the Doctrine of the Grace of God; the Christian Doctrine of Man; the Doctrine of the Person of Christ; the Doctrine of the Church; and the Social Order – and the committee began the task of exploring each of these stated themes.[24] This was not an attempt to put the Westminster Confession into more understandable language, or offer a commentary on various passages, but to address these theological themes in relation to the issues of the day. This can be seen in the section that explored the doctrine of humanity. (As was the custom at the time, the statement used the word "man" to speak of all humanity, men and women.) The statement began by affirming traditional Christian beliefs before moving on to state objections to what it considered to be contemporary misunderstandings. For example, in opposition to ideas about evolution, the statement declared: "We reject all purely naturalistic doctrines of the origin of man. We believe that man was created a 'living soul,' with a capacity to hold communion with God and with a purpose to rule, under God, over all other orders of God's creation."[25] Something similar was done in the next section, where the committee turned to their understanding of the doctrine of Christ. This fourth section was the first to directly refer to the Westminster Confession of Faith, with a brief note of the confession's understanding of the full divinity of Jesus Christ. Of greater interest were contemporary views of Christ, which the committee protested against and suggested should be condemned and even labelled as "heresy."[26]

The intention through the statement was to address current issues. This was evident not only in the general theological affirmations but when the committee turned to address issues of church and state. The parallel section of the Westminster Confession of Faith was chapter 23, "Of the Civil Magistrate," which stated that while the civil magistrate (the state) should not become involved in worship or interfere with the church in its functions, the civil magistrate did have the "authority, and it is his duty, to take order that unity and peace be preserved in the Church, that the truth of God be kept pure and entire, that all blasphemies and heresies be suppressed, all corruptions and abuses in worship and discipline prevented, or reformed, and all the ordinances of God duly settled, administered and observed." This section went on, allowing the civil magistrate to "call synods, to be present at them and to provide that whatsoever is transacted in them be according to the mind of God."[27] This was one of the sections within this confession with which Canadian Presbyterians had historically struggled. In their statement, the special committee spoke to issues of the twentieth century and tried to resolve some of the disagreements Canadian Presbyterians might have previously had. The sovereignty of God over the state, and all institutions, was reaffirmed. Civil states were part of God's plan and had rights, such as the "power of the sword for its defence against menace from without," as well as responsibilities.[28] In relation to the church, the statement directly rejected "the conception of a State-Church, in which the Church becomes the agent of the State's will." At the same time, the special committee also rejected the "common conception of a Free Church, in which it is assumed that the respective interests of Church and State can be absolutely separated and dissociated":

> We believe the functions of the State to be fundamentally protective and temporal, i.e., to guard the proper interests of the true faith, to restrain the public and social consequences of Sin, to eradicate temporary evils, to initiate and maintain just laws, and to foster such conditions as contribute to the public welfare. We believe the functions of the Church to be fundamentally redemptive and of eternal significance, i.e., to save, deliver and release the souls of men from the bondage of sin and death.[29]

The statement went on to recognize that these functions could never be entirely distinct. This was not a call for the church to abandon its commitment to society; indeed, in the next section, the statement detailed how the church should continue to be engaged in issues within the social order. What this represented, rather, was an attempt to resolve the historic differences within Canadian Presbyterianism that had led to "liberty of conscience" being granted on this issue. The discussion on Christian liberty of conscience addressed this directly. The special committee made clear their disagreement with the Presbytery of Paris' contention that granting liberty of conscience on the issue of church and state meant liberty of conscience had been granted on all issues, thus leaving the denomination on all matters – not just church and state issues – "confession-less."[30]

Creating a contemporary statement of faith everyone can agree upon is a difficult task. The committee quickly discovered this. The process they followed was rather simple and quite participatory. The committee would bring, as it did in 1945, draft statements to the General Assembly. Those draft statements would then be distributed to the church for comment. Those comments would be received and the committee would revise its statement or add a topic for consideration. This took considerable time. In 1947 the committee presented an updated version of the discussion on the Knowledge of God in response to feedback it had received. It also provided in 1947 a section on the Doctrine of the Holy Spirit, something which the church noted had been omitted. This section continued the pattern of speaking to contemporary issues, arguing against specific modern understandings such as universalism and "Pentecostalism." The committee – now known as the Articles of Faith Committee – rejected both the tendencies "to identify the Holy Spirit either with a rational principle or with an emotional experience."[31] That year it also provided a section on its understanding of scripture, "Holy Scripture, or the Written Word."[32] While it worked on the contemporary statement of faith, the special committee was also asked to comment on other theological issues.[33] Progress was slow. This was, in part, as the committee noted, due to the divergence of opinions expressed. It may have also been connected to the committee's statements not always being concise or clear. The section outlining the doctrine of church and state (including the section on liberty of conscience) in their 1945 statement was not only long, but dense and confusing. The section in 1945 dealing with the doctrine of election was brief and understandable. The committee returned to this doctrine in 1948, deciding that it should be one of three headings under the doctrine of God. Not only was the resulting discussion of predestination much more confusing, it also divided the committee.

The section on "Election and Predestination" started well. The special committee noted its understanding that this was a concern for members of the denomination, and assured them that those responsible for the Westminster Confession (the "Westminster divines") had been stressed "salvation is entirely the work of God's free grace" as they wrote about what they themselves considered a "high mystery."[34] The authors then veered into obscurity and raised the question of whether "the Confession has consistently understood God's free grace as the 'grace of our Lord Jesus Christ;' that is, whether election and predestination have been understood as being in Christ alone."[35] The committee continued in this vein with statements such as, "in an evangelical doctrine of predestination, any reference to rejection must be subordinated to the doctrine of election" and "We believe, therefore, that a great weakness of the [Westminster] Confession of Faith is its entire lack of a doctrine of God's election of Jesus Christ."[36] For many Presbyterians, then and now, the understanding of double predestination articulated in the Westminster Confession (that God chooses both those who will be saved, and those who will be damned) is one they struggle with. Over the six and a half pages the committee took to explore this issue, not only was it unclear what the solution to this struggle might be, it was unclear whether this was in fact the question the special committee was addressing. The section was not only obscure but controversial. One of the members of the committee, Dr William Stanford Reid, dissented from this section. His dissent, brief and to the point, was included with the committee's report. Stanford Reid argued this statement went "beyond the scope of the work of the committee" as the committee had not been given the power to revise the doctrine of the church but only to express it more clearly, and that what was in the report was "definitely not the doctrine held by the Westminster Confession of Faith." More than this, he argued that the positions being taken were opposed to those in the Westminster Confession, and what was being suggested was "anti-Reformed, and rejects the historic position of Presbyterianism." He further noted: "This doctrine is set forth in such paradoxical forms, and with the term 'elect' being used in so many different connotations, that it is much more obscure and difficult to understand, than the doctrine which it is supposed to clarify."[37] The committee forged on but the divisions within it were clear. The report to the 1949 General Assembly saw the committee proposing two different articles relating to the doctrine of the church.[38] The work on a contemporary statement of faith faced considerable challenges.

The overture from the Presbytery of Montreal – overture 18 "Re Church and State" – that appeared before the 1949 General Assembly created a major course correction to the committee's work. Instead of looking at the broad confessional position of the church, the overture asked the Assembly to narrow the committee's focus to this one area. The overture, as all overtures do, began by offering a rationale for the need for a statement defining the relationship between church and state. It spoke of the world situation which caused "grave concern" to Christians in terms of church and state relations. The overture also affirmed that the lack of clarity around this issue within the Presbyterian Church in Canada was a problem rather than a strength. It noted "the doctrine of the relationship of Church and State is nowhere unambiguously set forth" by the denomination, and referenced the fact that the Committee on Articles of Faith itself had noted this ambiguity in terms of chapter 23 of the Westminster Confession of Faith in its 1945 report, arguing that it was "vital to the life and witness of our Church that our confessional position be clearly set forth for all men to see."[39] A clear solution to this urgent issue was also suggested, namely for the committee to return to the work it had done in its 1945 report and either produce a "declaratory clause" to resolve the "ambiguity" or "otherwise, to clarify, as may seem best to the Venerable the General Assembly, our teaching and our faith in this most urgent matter."[40] It was a brilliant overture; it suggested the committee's work had gone too far afield and it needed to focus on this one precise task. The notes in the overture, which was supported by the presbytery, indicate that its seconder was the Rev. Dr W. Stanford Reid.[41] The result of this overture was significant. Beginning in 1950 and continuing over the next few years, the work of the Committee on Articles of Faith on a contemporary statement of faith was essentially put on hold. Instead, a joint committee comprised of members of the Committee on Articles of Faith and a subcommittee of the Board of Evangelism and Social Action was formed to undertake the task of devising such a statement. It was the joint committee that worked on the section relating to church and state relations that eventually became a doctrinal statement.

THE WORK OF THE JOINT COMMITTEE: PREAMBLE, ARTICLES, AND DECLARATION

In 1951 the joint committee gave its first substantial report to the General Assembly. From this point until the vote on one of the documents it produced, the "Declaration of Faith Concerning Church and Nation," the joint committee worked strenuously to resolve what it mentioned in 1951 was an urgent issue: that the church had no position on church and state. It also suggested that the church had inappropriately used the concept of liberty of conscience.[42] In its work, the committee sent study documents to presbyteries, received feedback and commented on it, and produced three documents: the Declaration, a Preamble to the Article of Faith, and Articles of Faith Concerning Church and Nation. All three documents were presented to the 1951 General Assembly.[43] The joint committee was working to create a "Declaratory Clause." As it had indicated to the Assembly in 1950, its intent was not to produce a "mere interpretative statement to be added" but one that would replace the section on church and state within the Westminster Confession. In the committee's words:

> What your Committee proposes is a *Declaration* which will, if and when adopted by the Church under the Barrier Act, supersede chapter XXIII of the Westminster Confession *and* that rider in the Basis of Union which at present exempts the chapter from the doctrinal standards of our Church. It would then be incumbent upon the Church to replace the words, "as adopted … in the Basis of Union," in the subscription questions, with words signifying the new form of adoption.[44]

The committee believed its work was important and urged the church to "move slowly in so decisive a matter." It suggested that the church not rush to approve the Declaration but carefully study it alongside the Articles of Faith which it had drafted, as the Declaration "purports to be the distilled essence of the larger work, in a form which, we trust, will be readily comprehensible."[45] The Declaration was thus intended to be the doctrinal statement that replaced chapter 23 in the Westminster Confession of Faith.[46] The deeper exposition of the issues was to be found in the Article of Faith Concerning Church and Nation and its Preamble.

THE "DECLARATION OF FAITH CONCERNING CHURCH AND NATION"

The culmination of the joint committee's work over the next two years came when a revised text of the "Declaration of Faith Concerning Church and Nation" was presented to the 1954 Assembly. This was a major source of debate at the General Assembly that year. Changes to the text were made during debates at the Assembly, and the final vote was not without opposition or dissent. The Declaration nevertheless passed at the Assembly; indeed, the Declaration was passed as an interim statement, which means it came into force in 1954, even while the result of the votes under the Barrier Act were being awaited.[47] In 1955 the report on the votes under the Barrier Act were reported (28 presbyteries approved, 8 disapproved), and the Assembly voted again to approve the "Declaration of Faith Concerning Church and Nation."[48]

But what had the denomination done? Despite the intentions of the joint committee clearly stated in its report in 1951, the Declaration did not replace chapter 23 or end the discussion on church and state relations. The joint committee had been very clear: the Declaration was to replace chapter 23 of the Westminster Confession of Faith, and thus there would be no need for any reference to "liberty of conscience," yet somehow along the way this had been lost. Three overtures in 1955 related to issues of church and state. The Presbytery of London noted that the world situation made the relationship between church and state a matter of "grave concern"; yet, while acknowledging the work already done, the presbytery suggested that the church take steps to "ensure the further study and revision of the 'Declaration on Church and Nation' thus keeping the matter before the Church."[49] Of greatest significance was the overture from the

Presbytery of East Toronto. While recognizing the validity of the Declaration, the presbytery raised the issue of its status, specifically challenging whether it should be considered a subordinate standard and suggested it be considered a "comment upon Chapters XX, XXIII and XXXI of the Westminster Confession of Faith."[50] The presbytery questioned whether the Assembly's decision had gone too far as it "contains no affirmation of its relative character but purports to be a definitive statement of doctrine to be subscribed in the letter." The overture contended that this infringed on "the Christian liberty now enjoyed."[51] The overture also asked that the Committee on Articles of Faith return to its task of developing a "complete Declaration of Faith" with the idea that this would be incorporated into it.[52] The status of the Declaration thus emerged as an issue, something not lost at the time: one member of the Presbytery of East Toronto, Stuart Coles (who had been a member of the Committee on Articles of Faith), dissented from the overture as it "constitutes a misunderstanding of the 1954 Assembly's action."[53]

WHAT DO PRESBYTERIANS BELIEVE?

With the passage of the "Declaration of Faith Concerning Church and Nation," the Committee on Articles of Faith did not, for whatever reasons, return to the task of creating a contemporary statement of faith. The task of helping people understand what it was they believed was left to others in the denomination. In 1957 the editor of the Presbyterian Record, John McNab, published a booklet entitled "What Do Presbyterians Believe?" John McNab had commissioned a series of articles that were published over several months exploring various theological topics for the magazine. He chose ministers from across the denomination's churches and theological colleges that represented the different perspectives known to exist in the church. The response was very positive and included requests from individuals and from church sessions that this be published.[54] McNab complied. The book was organized around the themes addressed in the Apostles' Creed and helpfully provided a copy of the creed for the reader. McNab voiced his hope in the preface that this book would be used by all in the church, including youth. Mariano Di Gangi addressed the topic of evangelism: "This may be done formally, through visitation evangelism. Or it may be carried on informally, in the course of our social contacts. But we are under obligation to speak with conviction, with conviction flowing from a true understanding of the Bible and a real experience of the grace of God."[55] Ideas were expressed clearly and practically. Even the very challenging doctrine of predestination was explored, with Scott Mackenzie arguing this was "not only a Presbyterian but a Scriptural doctrine" that all Christians should embrace. Mackenzie noted the scriptures where this doctrine could be found, even noting the Greek verbs used, yet still managed to explain clearly the idea that salvation came from God:

> When all is said, the truth contained in the doctrine of predestination can only be fully appreciated when it is set against its proper background, which is the unsearchable riches of Divine grace. This is what lay behind all Calvin's thinking on the subject, as it lay behind the thought of Paul, from whose testimony the doctrine directly springs. This testimony of Paul flows right out of his own overwhelming religious experience, and it is a testimony which has been confirmed in the experience of believers in every generation since. They all unite to testify that from first to last, man's salvation is the work of God.[56]

He argued this should not lead to fatalism, but to conviction and working for God in one's life; thus, pride is "utterly excluded, because of the overwhelming conviction that it is all of Divine grace."[57] This was a publication that sought to, and succeeded in, helping Canadian Presbyterians in the late 1950s understand what their tradition believed.

REVISING THE *BOOK OF COMMON ORDER*

Doctrine unites a denomination. So does worship. A denomination's worship style is often laid out in a prayer book that includes the various services of worship that are commonly used. Canadian Presbyterians called this compilation of worship services the *Book of Common Order*. After union they used the 1922 *Book of Common Order*. The denomination then revised this twice, once in 1939, and a second and more minor revision in 1948.[58] The prefaces to these two revisions show the tensions present in the denomination. On the one hand, there was the desire to have a single form of worship used across all congregations in the denomination. On the other hand, there was the desire to allow individual ministers to adapt the services to the circumstances and preferences of the congregation. The advantage of the former was that Presbyterians would recognize the worship service wherever they travelled or if they moved to a new community – something more and more common in many parts of Canada as the twentieth century progressed. This tension was evident in the prefaces to the *Book of Common Order* itself. In the first revision in 1939 it was argued that "a Common Order in regular Church Worship and Office, without rigid uniformity, is correspondingly desirable, in so far as it is practicable." At the same time, the preface argued for "freedom of the Spirit" and suggested that the services that were offered were not intended to "restrict the exercise of such freedom."[59] The second revision, while agreeing to both principles, nevertheless included only one morning and one evening order of worship so that "there might be more uniformity throughout the Church."[60] In 1953, the Presbytery of East Toronto suggested further revisions needed to be done. One reason it offered was that "many ministers [were] using Books of Common Order other than our own." It noted failings of the current book and some changes – more rubrics, more prayers – that it believed could be made. It also argued that "recent studies on the meaning and practice of Reformed worship indicate the need of a revision of our present Book, with a view of incorporating the fruits of these studies."[61] Even a suggested membership for the committee was proposed, with Mackenzie and other professors from the theological colleges playing a key role alongside those who served in the various boards and agencies of the church.[62] Assembly agreed to the formation of this special committee to start revising the denomination's book of services.

Over the next ten years, the committee did what the Assembly had asked it to do. As a special committee assigned to do one task, it worked closely with the existing Committee on Worship. Indeed, the work on this project became the main task of the Committee on Worship throughout this period, with only limited time to work on possible revisions to the hymn book (*Book of Praise*) and the planning of special services to mark anniversaries related to the Reformation.[63] In 1955 the special committee informed the General Assembly that the only way to meet the request of the overture was to create a new *Book of Common Order*. This is what it set out to do, each year updating the church on its progress. It circulated drafts of its work for comment. It surveyed the church and reported its findings as to how Presbyterians conducted various elements of the worship service in 1957. For example, it was noted that only 12 per cent of Presbyterian congregations regularly used the Apostles' Creed in their regular services. The Apostles' Creed, if used, was most likely to be used (68 per cent of congregations) during the communion service. When it came to music, the vast majority of congregations (84 per cent) used four hymns and a psalm at morning worship, with some using less (10 per cent), and only 6 per cent using five hymns and a psalm during this service.[64] This was valuable information for committee members to have at hand as they went about their task. They were clear about that task, intending to produce a service book "that will contain our Reformed traditions interpreted in the light of the most modern Reform studies and findings" and also produce a book "that will be of definite value in meeting the many demands for new services that are being made upon us."[65] The committee continued in its tasks, circulating draft services, revising, and circulating again. A draft book had been produced by 1959 and was sent to the presbyteries for comment and approval. The members were proud of their work, noting it was "the most advanced of any Book now in use in any Reformed Church."[66] Delays in publishing the draft meant that more time was needed to receive comment and approval. The committee was open to responding to feedback and criticism and made adjustments to the final product. This was a lengthy process – one that the committee both participated in and at times seemed frustrated by. Eventually, a *Book of Common Order* was presented to and approved by the General Assembly in 1964. The committee continued to oversee its production. Five hundred copies sold in the two months following publication, something the committee considered a notable success. It also noted favourable comments had been received from scholars in the United States and Great Britain.[67]

The new *Book of Common Order* (1964) noted that it had been approved by the General Assembly "for voluntary use." The book offered a variety of alternative morning and evening services. There were four services for morning worship, as well as a distinct service – The Order of Word and Sacrament – which the committee suggested should be the "normative pattern" for Presbyterian worship. This, the committee argued, had been part of its mandate all along, to bring the best of contemporary Reformed scholarship to bear on current practices. It argued that this scholarship suggested the "main services of worship includes Word and Sacrament together. It follows, whether Holy Communion is celebrated frequently or infrequently, that worship should have this basic structure."[68] While thoroughly convinced of this, the book nevertheless included the other models for morning worship in order to link to the previous worship books and "to offer a form for ministers and sessions who prefer a different order."[69] The first service was thus taken directly from the 1922 version of the *Book of Common Order*. As well as the regular services, the 1964 *Book of Common Order* included services for the sacraments and special services. There was a baptismal service for infants, one for adults, a confirmation service for those who had been baptized as infants, and a confirmation service followed by baptism, for someone who had not previously been baptized. There were various communion services in addition to the Order of Word and Sacrament. There were marriage services, funeral services, services for special days (Family Day, Remembrance Day), and services for the special activities of the church, from the dedication of an organ to the dedication of a missionary. The book also included "A Treasury of Prayers" and a very brief lectionary.[70]

Despite the voluntary nature of this *Book of Common Order*, as well as the committee's willingness to make adjustments and accommodations, controversy dogged both the committee's work and the final acceptance. Where should the sermon be in relation to the morning offering? Presbyterian congregations had developed different customs and understandings. If the service entitled the Order of Word and Sacrament was to be considered the norm even for services without communion, then the answer was clear: the sermon came first, with the offering being a response to the sermon as well as a response to all other gifts from God. For those who disagreed, the committee included the 1922 order, where the sermon came after the offering. The variety of options offered in the book and the stress on its voluntary use, both as the committee was doing its work as well as on the actual cover of the book itself, raised the question: Why did this take as long as it did? And what was at the core of this opposition?

At one level, disagreement over something as central as how one conducts worship should not surprise us. Presbyterians remained in the Presbyterian Church in Canada for a variety of different, sometimes competing, reasons – they had been unified in their opposition to church union and not necessarily much else.[71] John Moir correctly notes these divisions in his discussion of the debate on the *Book of Common Order* in *Enduring Witness*.[72] But there were themes that emerged in the reports of the committee and in the debates that suggest more specific reasons for the objections to the work of the committee. Despite the fact that the mandate to look at the most recent scholarly understandings of the Reformed tradition was in the original overture and was constantly referred to by the committee as central to its work, this approach was not universally accepted. The decision to advocate that the normal morning worship service should include communion as well as preaching was strongly challenged. In its 1961 report to the denomination, the committee noted that only one presbytery had approved its understanding of this as the "norm" of worship, where four had said "no," four more seem to have been "unclear," and the rest offered no comment. The revised book as a whole had greater support: nine presbyteries approved, five offered qualified approval, thirteen offered disapproval, and four offered no comment. The denomination as a whole clearly had differences with the committee, and these were detailed thoroughly in the committee's report in 1961.[73] The difference on this one aspect – what the norm of worship should be – is worth noting. Also worth noting was what seemed to be, from some, a lack of trust in the committee. This is seen particularly in the motions passed in relation to the *Book of Common Order* by Stanford Reid at the Assemblies he attended. At the 1958 Assembly he asked that the "criticisms of the order of service also be printed in order that a full discussion might be ensured."[74] Two years later he offered an amendment to the committee's report that asked it provide all the responses from presbyteries to the committee received by a certain date "summarized and mimeographed" and then shared with all of the presbyteries. This was a very unusual request. Not surprisingly, the amendment was defeated. Stanford Reid then dissented on a technicality – "the names of the members of the Committee" had not been included (as they should have been) in their report.[75] When the draft was ready to be distributed to the denomination in 1962, Stanford Reid seconded a motion to delete the preface and replace it with a simple statement that it was approved for voluntary use.[76] Others also objected to the *Book of Common Order* along the way. Dissents were recorded when the denomination approved it in 1964. One of the core reasons noted in these dissents was the belief that the new service book departed too much from the theology of the Westminster Confession of Faith.[77]

Who should interpret the Reformed tradition? How should that tradition be interpreted? These were clearly points of disagreement that existed, not only in relation to creating a contemporary statement of faith but also in how worship was to be understood and conducted. The members of the committee working on the new service book were clear in their conviction that modern scholarship (particularly as it related to worship) needed to be part of the denomination's deliberations. Others in the denomination disagreed. Their vision of the Reformed tradition was the one they adhered to. For some this was a belief that the Westminster Confession was the first and final word, and that nothing should be changed, even if it were demonstrated that John Calvin, one of the great theologians of the Reformed tradition, had been misunderstood by those creating the documents around the Westminster Assembly. For others it was more selective, but they rejected certain interpretations of the Reformation and the tradition. William Stanford Reid's biographer, A. Donald MacLeod, has argued that Stanford Reid was opposed, not only to David Hay (who is primarily associated with the 1964 *Book of Common Order*) personally, but also to the "Barthians" and the neo-orthodox movement in general, including their understanding of the doctrine of election.[78] This was a contest as to who should interpret the Reformed tradition. It was also a reflection of the evangelical tradition at work in the denomination. Stanford Reid is referred to as an "evangelical" frequently in this biography.[79] This is appropriate. The evangelical tradition of spontaneous worship services and an informal liturgy had been grafted on to the worship of Canadian Presbyterians. Among the other criticisms the *Book of Common Order* received was that it departed too far from what people were used to. Indeed, in 1963 an attempt was made to have the book include two "orders of service in conformity with Canadian present practices."[80]

LIMITED CHANGE

Canadian Presbyterians established the Committee on Articles of Faith to consider changes in doctrine. Issues of church and state were central to this action. The committee recommended that a contemporary statement of faith be written and set out to do this; however, this was unsuccessful. The Committee on Articles of Faith refocused its work and, as part of a joint committee, produced in 1954 the "Declaration of Faith Concerning Church and Nation" – a document that dealt with issues of church and state. This major achievement was undermined by the denomination being unable to agree on the status of this document. Despite having produced a doctrinal statement, the denomination continued the tradition of allowing for "liberty of conscience" on this issue in ordination and induction services. The committee continued to deal with theological issues of various kinds, including a great deal of consideration of how one subscribed to the Westminster Standards. In terms of worship, greater success was seemingly achieved in updating the *Book of Common Order*, yet the long contentious debate took its toll. There was no agreement on how the denomination was to update its worship and doctrine, nor which voices should be given the greater authority in these discussions. Having tied themselves so tightly to their tradition during the church union debates, Canadian Presbyterians now found themselves struggling to adapt as they moved forward.

6

Adrift in a Sea of Change

Presbyterian Identity in a Changing Canada

Was it the spirit of the times?[1] Or was it something they saw within their own denomination? The answer is not clear. What is clear is that in the mid-1960s Presbyterians who had seemed confident, indeed proud of their heritage and accomplishments, began questioning all that they were and all that they had done. There were early glimpses of this. Presbyterians always compared their growth to the growth of the population as a whole and knew they were not keeping pace. This generally seemed to increase their resolve. The nature of the criticisms began to change. The denomination held a Congress during 1967, Canada's centennial year. The theme of the Congress was "Man in God's world," a direct play on Expo '67's theme of "Man and his world." Joseph McLelland's address at the 1967 Congress amped up and broadened his earlier critique. We were no longer speaking of the response to church union and its continuing impact on ecumenism. We were now talking about multiple facets of the church's life. The address was published verbatim in the September issue of the denomination's magazine.[2] This address meant to provoke – even shock – and it succeeded. Despite the title, what it did not provide was either a model for change or even a blueprint for a potential model. Instead, there was a scattergun of criticisms of the church. This was noted in a letter to the *Presbyterian Record* by William Stanford Reid.[3] Though a long-time opponent of McLelland's position in terms of ecumenism, Stanford Reid seemed more puzzled by the address than angered. And he was correct. It was hard to see anything like a plan in this address. What there was were various calls for change.

This chapter will explore this changing mood beginning with the crucial early years from 1967 to 1971 when the denomination produced notable reports attempting to deal with what it understood to be happening in Canadian society. These reports demonstrated contrasting visions for what the Presbyterian Church in Canada should do, with some arguing for more change and others arguing that too much had already changed. Despite all of this questioning that was such a feature of the times, the denomination continued to go about its work. In 1975 the denomination celebrated its centennial year. The denomination was also continuing to experience dramatic loss in membership and participation. A concern for church growth which would address this decline emerged in the late 1970s. In 1979 a new committee, created outside of the normal structures of the church, was empowered to assist the church to grow. The Committee on Church Growth to Double in the Eighties attempted to do what its title suggested. The concern to address the membership decline was appropriate and demonstrated Canadian Presbyterians took this issue seriously. But the denomination was divided between those who wanted to adapt to changes in society and those who argued the church needed to reject these changes. These divisions were evident when the denomination returned to its quarrel on ecumenism, this time focused on the World Council of Churches Program to Combat Racism. Change in Canadian society and the world was evident. Canadian Presbyterians could not agree on how they should respond.

A LOSS OF CERTAINTY: 1967–71

The four years from 1967–71 were a time of critical self-examination for Canadian Presbyterians. There were two congresses – an official one in 1967 and an unofficial "Congress of Concern" in 1968 – and three major reports (the LAMP report, Ross report, and report on membership decline). The denomination was aware that things were changing, but uncertain how to respond. Deep in the background was an awareness that the denomination, like many others in Canada at the time, had stopped growing and was beginning to decline. Some reports dealt with this directly, others indirectly. All three reports began as fairly routine requests to do something.

For example, what eventually resulted in the Life and Mission Project, or LAMP, began in 1965 when the Administrative Council, the body in charge of finances, was informed "that the work of the several boards and Committees of the Church requires $545,530.00 more than the total income for 1964" – a 25 per cent increase over

Figure 6.1 Joe McClelland, one of the speakers at the 1967 Congress, sits in a lounge at Queen's University for an informal discussion. Notable is the relative youth of those participating and the number of women. This made Congress gatherings very different from the General Assembly in this period.

the current received income of nearly $2,000,000.[4] After the financial challenges the denomination had so recently overcome, the call for some sort of prioritization made sense. "The Special Committee Re Administrative Council Recommendation 10" was created to conduct "a thorough study of the vocation, work and mission of The Presbyterian Church in Canada in the changing life of Canada and other nations."[5] This work would eventually morph into LAMP, a year-long project whose reporting on all aspects of the denomination's work would become known as the LAMP report (1969).

What is commonly called the Ross Report (1970), arose out of the work of the Committee on Recruitment.[6] Concern for declining church membership led the Synod Corporations (responsible for financing new congregations) to ask in 1968 for a study and action to reverse these trends. Instead of being produced the next year, a report was finally completed in 1971 as part of the work of the Board of Evangelism and Social Action.[7] Each of these reports arose from routine concerns, but responded with a broad critique of what the church was actually doing and offered different suggestions as to what the church should do.

Joseph McLelland called for change in his 1967 Congress presentation "Blueprint for a new model." An even more dramatic critique appeared in an article "Crisis = Danger + Opportunity" written by Stuart Coles and published in the May 1968 issue of the *Presbyterian Record*. Coles was the national secretary for Lay Ministry in the Board of Education. The article argued the denomination suffered from a series of crises: "*If this is a time of crisis, and since crisis means a moment of dangerous opportunity, let us help one another gather the courage to try an experiment.*"[8] Exactly what that experiment might look like was not detailed; the various crises the church was currently in ("crisis of identity," "crisis of purpose," "crisis of conviction and faith," "crisis of transmission," "crisis of church government," "crisis of ministry," "crisis of church education," and "crisis of discipleship") were stated as existing and self-evident. For example, when it came to ministry in the church, Coles wrote:

> Not in all our pastors, but in most of them there is a mounting sense of desolation and debilitation, a loss of confidence in one's own calling, role, effectiveness. We do not behave with dynamic freedom, freedom to be a living, human kind of human, one who can really laugh, really cry, really curse, really bless, really communicate. *There is a crisis of ministry*. Our pastors are traditionally said to be "the teaching elders" but few of them have much feeling of achievement in communicating to the other men and women and youth of the church a sense of ministry and participation. The task of Christian education is not taken seriously in our seminaries. Our attitudes towards deaconesses is barbaric.[9]

Congregations were failures in multiple ways: "We can whip up our enthusiasms and talents for building buildings and buying new pieces of real estate; but we do not know so much about communicating Christ. We can construct 'Christian education wings;' but we are not so good at putting them into use." The litany of failures in what was a powerful jeremiad was expansive. Yet no information was provided to support any of these claims. Some of them were patently false: whatever one might think about "Christian education wings," the full Sunday school classrooms in this period would suggest they were still very much in use. This was powerful rhetoric: "Our salt has lost its zing. If Presbyterianism were to disappear from our Canadian and overseas communities, how many of them would notice the loss?"[10]

The provocative questions and statements seem to have hit a nerve. Colleagues suggested they should gather and talk further, and on very short notice a Congress of Concern – meeting outside the official sanction of the denominational offices – was planned to gather just prior to the 1968 Assembly.[11] Coles prepared a manifesto, and invitations were sent to all of the delegates who had attended the 1967 Congress, as well as other interested individuals. The plan was to meet at North Park Church on 4 June and 5 June 1968, with the Assembly to begin later on 5 June.[12] The plan was to have people arrive and discuss the ideas laid out in the draft manifesto, hear responses from invited speakers, and then break into one of seven task force groups to explore these ideas further and suggest practical additions.[13] The music chosen was "contemporary hymns" led by Warren McKinnon and musicians from the Teen and Twenty Chapel (a Presbyterian Christian band that used rock music instruments).[14] Invitations were sent out along with copies of Coles's article in the May 1968 *Presbyterian Record* and the Draft Manifesto.[15] Those gathered were a broad group, with firm ties to the denomination. Two of the three nominees for moderator in 1968 attended the gathering, as did prominent officials from the national office.

Discussion at the Congress of Concern seems to have been wide-ranging and engaged. "A Declaration of Concern" signed by the delegates was one result.[16] At the 1968 General Assembly the impact from the Congress of Concern was felt, as the gathering helped to promote and gather support for change. Delegates from Montreal came to the General Assembly with suggestions for altering how Assembly conducted its business. It was agreed that this new format be implemented the next year. Support for the work being done by the "Special Committee Re Administrative Council Recommendation 10" resulted in approval of a recommendation that a "full report with recommendations for action" be presented to the next General Assembly.[17] This was the origins of the Life and Mission Project (LAMP) report. Finally, the recruitment committee received approval for its recommendation that an outside consultant be hired to look at the challenges of ministry within the denomination. The results two years later were recorded in the Ross Report. The energy created at the Congress of Concern, as well as the continuing excitement and the provocative questions addressed at the 1967 Congress, contributed to these crucial decisions at the 1968 Assembly.

THE LIFE AND MISSION PROJECT (LAMP) REPORT

Having set the daunting goal of producing a report within a year, those charged with the task set about their work. Staff were reassigned to work on the project, notably Robert Carter, John C. (Jack) Cooper, and Wayne Smith. Month by month, readers of the denominational magazine were kept informed and their opinions were solicited. The work of the LAMP committee and the challenges it faced was summarized by the committee's convenor, Charles Cochrane, in the *Presbyterian Record* in April 1969. Cochrane suggested two different views of the church and its role had emerged. On one view, God was interested in the church and "if you wanted to find God you went to the church, or to the minister, or perhaps to a Sunday school teacher." He noted, however, that "more recently we tend to hear quite the reverse." On the other view, God was interested in society at large and present there, to the extent that "ours is a day of the 'secular' God who is not in church but in protest; he is not in creed but in the civil rights struggle; he is not in worship but in trying to ban the bomb – he is somewhere 'out there, where the action is.'" Cochrane noted that these were both "caricatures of the truth." He stated: "The view that the church should preserve its God within the seclusion of her own walls, safely embalmed, ready to be passed on to the next generation, is a form of blasphemy. Conversely, the thesis that the church should march in step with the spirit of the times and in accordance with the world's standard of values, is a sell-out."[18] Rejecting both of these positions, Cochrane suggested that the work the committee was doing was assisting the church in renewal and repentance. The repentance would include recognition of "our sorry record of adaptation and adjustment to the pattern and spirit of the age, to society's judgments of both people and issues." Put more directly, the church had betrayed its own values, had gone along to get along, on issues Cochrane identified as "race, war, poverty, and social problems."

Cochrane suggested that the church needed to begin by repenting for allowing the society to "domesticate" it and "blunt what should be the cutting edge of the church's message."[19] He suggested the committee was not interested in "revolution" but "orderly, if radical, change" so that the church would be renewed in order to fulfill its mission. In how he expressed these ideas Cochrane conveyed his awareness of the issues and terms being used in this period, including the focus on openness and participation stressed by the Second Vatican Council. He also offered a response to Pierre Berton's biting critique on the church's social ethic (the church mouthing words about following Jesus, but allowing itself to be domesticated), agreeing this might be the case but suggesting there was a way forward.

The potential for division on that way forward, however, was noted. In May, the article "Can We Face these Explosive issues?" appeared in the *Presbyterian Record* and laid out what it saw as two views, the "distinct divisions" in the denomination between those who believed "worship and witness are the only valid work of the church" and those who believed that the church had greater social responsibilities in "the affairs of the community, the nation and the world." It suggested these divisions existed at all levels of church life. While acknowledging that these views shared a "common allegiance of Jesus Christ," it was noted that "lurking just under the surface lies this deep and troublesome division. It does more to disrupt and immobilize our Presbyterian mission than most of us are prepared to admit. Must we opt for one view or the other, and agree to go our separate ways? Or can we agree to serve Christ, each in our own style, with deeper honesty and mutual trust towards one another, and remain open to the further guidance of the Holy Spirit?"[20]

After a year of considerable energy and a great deal of work, the recommendations of the LAMP committee were presented to the 1969 General Assembly in a report titled "Into the '70s in Life and Mission" that would become known as the LAMP report. The Assembly itself, as noted, was already unusual. The schedule was a distinct break from the past, with the Assembly beginning on a Sunday with worship, holding two days of informal information sessions, and then moving into the formal debates. Even more change was in the air. The moderator, E.H. Johnson, "broke with tradition and refused to wear the usual ruffles and lace that signify the office" of moderator. His picture on the cover of the Assembly issue of the *Presbyterian Record* saw him in the regular clergy gown worn at the time by almost all ministers of the denomination.[21] The Assembly also featured Young Adult Observers who, as the name suggested, were young people who were present to observe the work of the Assembly. The LAMP report itself was extensive – spanning twenty-two pages in the *Acts and Proceedings* – and included thirty-two recommendations.[22] The sheer scale of the report makes assessing its impact challenging. The report was debated and motions were adopted, with many of them being moved to various committees for further implementation.

Subsequent to the General Assembly, the LAMP report was published and widely distributed. The first 4,000 copies sold out, and another 5,000 copies had been printed by December for distribution.[23] The LAMP report included the report of the committee, the recommendations made and how they had been received by the General Assembly, alongside photographs intended to illustrate the various points being made. The structure of the report – beginning with the changing context in Canadian society and the world, and then turning to the specific ways of addressing these issues – is noteworthy. The photos scattered throughout illustrate the themes in interesting ways, intermingling pictures of the world and pictures of the church.[24] The context was seen as changing, sometimes dramatically. For example, the report stated, "we live in a world where one half of the total population has moved out of colonialism into post-colonial nationalism in a short span of years. So mission patterns related to the colonial era are being adjusted to fit the movements towards nationalism."[25] The report detailed what it believed was required, including "new eyes that see the world as a place where God is at work in and through all that is happening."[26] It detailed multiple issues and suggested a variety of different responses. The first part of the report ended with a section bringing many of these themes together and posed the question "what is our goal?" Pointing to John Calvin's focus on worship, fellowship, education, and concern for the society (which they redefined as "outreach, mission, evangelism, and social action"), the committee advocated a balanced and wholistic approach to ministry. It recognized "this balanced view of the church's goal is not shared by all people." Some, it suggested, wanted to focus on evangelism, while others focus on social action. While recognizing the diversity of views, the committee pointed to the importance of "obedience to Christ" and suggested the starting point was Jesus. For all of the discussion about change, the LAMP report maintained a fairly traditional understanding of the goals of the church: "Our priorities and the strategies we employ may change, but the mission of God remains the same. God's mission in our world remains the same. God's mission in our world is to save us and our world from sin and death." This meant that the church needed to "share what we have received from

God – not what we are in ourselves." The committee also suggested the importance of repentance, worship, and service in the world. Outreach was not to become "mere social dabbling, without motivation, purpose or effectiveness."[27] The language used was not traditional and at times vague, but there were no new theological ideas expressed. The church was not being called to move in a completely new direction. Instead, the committee was calling the denomination to express its faith in ways that were more contemporary.

It was the section arguing for a new way of organizing congregations that would be one of the most remembered aspects of the project. The LAMP report argued that the work of each congregation should be organized around the session. Session was to be the hub. Four standing committees of session were to be created and include members from the congregation at large: worship and nurture; finance and maintenance; mission and outreach; and policy and planning. The most radical change was the creation of a finance and maintenance committee, which, the LAMP report suggested, would assume the "functions of the Board of Managers as described in *The Book of Forms*."[28] There were other practical accomplishments of the LAMP report: "study leave" was introduced which gave ministers structured time off and an allowance to take various forms of continuing education;[29] personnel committees were established; and, a call was made to establish a national conference centre.[30]

The work of the LAMP committee was a major undertaking of the Presbyterian Church in Canada in 1968 and 1969. Even if not all its proposals were implemented – many congregations chose not to replace the board of managers with a finance committee responsible to session – a different model was proposed for how congregations should function. This model was designed to improve the effectiveness of each congregation's ministry. At the same time, this model required a massive level of participation. Indeed, the call for greater participation was one that rings throughout this period. In responding, the LAMP committee suggested structures that required many people. It was simply assumed that each congregation would have enough people to participate in each of these committees. Four committees at eight people per committee meant thirty-two volunteers were needed each year for the committees alone. The reality of how much time was spent in meetings, as opposed to actually doing some of these tasks, was something not given adequate consideration. Would congregations not have been better off with adult education event with people participating, rather than a dozen people participating in monthly meetings that might (or might not) plan such an event? In some ways the committee was replicating structures from the business world of the time. The congregation now had a clear organizational chart. Everyone knew what each committee was responsible for. There was greater participation and greater clarity. What should be noted is that the mission itself had not changed. Congregations still existed to worship, raise money for mission, and serve in their communities. These functions did not change: what was being suggested was a better way to achieve the same goals.

The LAMP report is notable for a subtle shift in confidence. In the immediate post-war years Canadian Presbyterians were confident that they had a product (their understanding of the Reformed Christian tradition) that they believed in and that they believed Canadians needed. They also trusted that Canadians, if given the chance, would respond positively. In the years immediately prior to the LAMP report, there was a loss of confidence. Rather than the church having the answers for the world, the idea emerged that the world might have the answers for the churches. Throughout the report there is a general sense that things are not working. Data on specific weaknesses was never provided, yet there was a pervasive sense that change was needed in order to respond effectively.

What is also notable is what was missed. There was not a clear section on evangelism. There was not a clear section on Christian education. There was not a clear section on work with youth. Youth were to be represented more in the programs of the church – but what about programming for youth? What about a focus on helping them understand the faith more effectively? It almost seems to be assumed that by letting a few youth observe the General Assembly, all issues related to youth would resolve themselves. What was also missed was the needs of congregations. The concerns were with participation and structures within congregations. Nowhere in the report was there a sense of the importance of supporting congregations in their ministry. The denomination had spent all of this energy and enormous financial resources establishing new congregations. They did not appear as a central concern in the report. Congregations were taken for granted. The focus was instead on experimental ministries and the challenges of urban ministry. While each of these were important, it is noteworthy what this important report did not address.

Figure 6.2 Young Adult Observers began to attend General Assembly in the 1970s, representing young Presbyterians across Canada. They were able to observe – but for many years could not vote, nor could they speak without special permission.

TWO DIFFERENT VOICES: THE ROSS REPORT (1970) AND THE REPORT ON DECLINING CHURCH MEMBERSHIP (1971)

The LAMP process had noted divisions within the denomination. The two subsequent major reports demonstrated these divisions. The Ross Report argued that there was a crisis in ministry. As a result, a significant number of ministers were leaving the church for what they considered more meaningful work. This was a damning critique of the state of ministry. The report went on to suggest that recruitment and retention of ministers would be challenging unless there are "ministries that are relevant."[31] When the Ross Report was released it made headlines in the press: "Presbyterians aren't with it"; "Presbyterians Called 'Rigid and Inflexible'"; "Presbyterians told they face extinction"; and, "'We're Stodgy, Too Slow to Change,' Says Report."[32] At the 1970 Assembly itself, the report was presented along with various proposals. Many of these recommendations were adopted. However, the majority of the recommendations were forwarded to various committees for implementation. Given the expansiveness of the recommendations, which included not just recruitment but all areas of church life, this was perhaps not surprising.[33]

Two things need to be noted about this report. The first is that nowhere in the Ross Report was it considered that women, who had recently been allowed to be ordained in the denomination, might be a solution to the shortage of ministers. There were no initiatives to reach out to women and encourage them to enter the ministry. Women are largely absent from the final report. This is true as potential ministers and also as deaconesses. Where women do appear in the report is as wives of ministers whose dissatisfaction (reported by their husbands) may lead their husbands to leave ministry.[34] The second thing to note is that no data was ever provided to support the conclusion of the Ross Report that there was a crisis in ministry. The belief that there was a crisis in ministry bordered on being an operational principle, shaping the questions asked and the interpretations given to the responses. Outside consultants may have been hired, but findings of satisfaction among many clergy were ignored, as voices inside the committee continued to insist there was a crisis.

One group in particular played a prominent role, and appeared in the Final Ross Report with their own section, "Reformers." The reformers were not a surveyed group, yet their comments, received largely outside of the formal process of the survey or interview groups, received prominent coverage.[35] The section began by noting that within the generally traditional Presbyterian Church in Canada there was a different group: "There is today, however, a dedicated minority that sincerely believes that the reforming process within the Presbyterian Church in Canada has virtually ceased. These members believe that the church is stagnating, has become irrelevant, and will surely die unless the church 'gets with it' and becomes relevant again."[36] The group was depicted as on the whole younger and the 1968 Congress of Concern was seen as a vital place where the concerns of this group were voiced. Indeed, twenty-three comments from the Congress are included in the report (these did not emerge from the process conducted by the P.S. Ross company) in a format similar to earlier comments gained through the surveys. The report went further, citing large sections of its conclusions from Stuart Coles's article "Crisis = Danger + Opportunity." Within the report the reformers were portrayed as the voice of wisdom in contrast to the traditional and static. As a final section of the report states: "The Presbyterian Church, because of its conservatism and traditions, is not likely to accept the views of these reformers in their entirety, but if one thing is certain, it is that the church needs reformers and will be a more vital institution because of them."[37] While an interesting sentiment, it is worth noting that there was nothing provided in the data gathered to produce this report which would necessarily support such a conclusion. It was also not evident – again from the data gathered in the surveys – that the crisis in ministry was of the severity being claimed. The data actually showed greater satisfaction in congregational ministry as it existed than was portrayed in the report.[38] The Ross Report reflected the voice of those calling for dramatic change.

The voice of those suggesting too much had already changed was captured effectively in the report "Declining Church Membership" that appeared as one section of the Board of Evangelism and Social Action Report in 1971. The report began with dramatic graphs showing the trends from 1956 to 1968 in terms of the number of baptisms, communicant membership, number of households, and church school enrolment.[39] These graphs demonstrated growth followed by decline. The commentary was even more stark as it compared the situation – "*a continuing decline in many significant areas*" – to broader trends: "the rate of Church membership has never increased proportionately with population growth since World War II."[40] Hard data was provided to the church, but never seriously analyzed. The committee even noted, "the quantification of Christianity is a questionable measurement in and of itself."[41] Instead, the committee focused on the "Rapid Cultural Change" in Canadian society. It recognized these changes as real but understood them as primarily hostile. The report suggested that negative voices inside the church were one part of the problem. What was needed was "devoted discipleship":

> Reversing the trend in declining membership will not be accomplished by any simple administrative techniques. We have been dealing with an erosion of faith. If our problem is unknowingness in relation to the Gospel, then what is needed is a deeper understanding of the Gospel by both the ministry and people. A relevant proclamation of the Gospel, supported by an authoritative teaching ministry, militantly oriented for Christ's sake, and a strong, courageous and well-instructed laity will retard the erosion process. The Presbyterian Church in Canada will have a distinctive witness only in so far as it becomes a community of believers able to articulate its faith and declare God's Word.[42]

As much as the changing context in Canadian society was acknowledged, the committee rejected the notion that the denomination needed to listen to society or that God was more active in society than the church. God was active in the church! Congregations were, it was argued, "the key to power" and were "neither obsolete nor irrelevant."[43] But were they working? The report suggested that they were not nearly as effective as they should be, and one weakness highlighted was the clergy. Clergy members have lacked "conviction." They have been too cold. They have not communicated effectively. Even more troubling, they have not been committed to evangelism. Preaching needed to "return to Biblical expository preaching" – indeed it was suggested that the move back to this would improve the situation in terms of membership.[44] Clergy did not have a strong enough devotional life, and their theological education needed to be improved.[45] The litany of failures among the clergy seemed endless. Yet the harshest critiques in the report were reserved for Christian education and how the denomination had done church extension.[46] The critiques were harsh. But were they true? Similar to the Ross Report, the conclusions seem to have been operating principles. No data was provided to show that clergy sermons were atrocious, or that it was the curriculum in Church schools that was the issue. Voice was given, however, to those who believed the church had listened too much to culture and changed too much in response.

Everyone agreed that change was happening within Canadian society. Everyone agreed that the church needed to communicate effectively. Everyone agreed that evangelism and social action were both needed (though the balance between the two might vary). No radical new theological ideas emerged. Where the LAMP report and Ross Report were most radical was their focus on new and experimental ministries and their lack of attention (apart from administrative reorganization) to congregations. In contrast, the report on church membership in 1971 saw congregations as crucial but inept, largely (though not exclusively) due to weak clergy. This report was a call to return to basics, to recognize the world as hostile, and to reject the changes that were emerging. Change was being taken seriously. The Presbyterian Church in Canada was aware of, and trying to respond to, declining membership, the loss of youth in church programs, and cultural challenges affecting the church. Canadian Presbyterians were not united in what they saw as either the problem or the solution. Different solutions to what were understood to be different problems were proposed. The church debated these, and implemented some (though not all) of the ideas. The challenges were noted. The denomination was, however, unable to agree on a coherent response.

MINISTRY AND CELEBRATION

It is important to remember that alongside all of the angst, self-doubt, criticism, and the various reports presented in the late 1960s and early 1970s, many aspects of church life continued as usual. Congregations worshipped. Children attended Church schools.[47] Presbyterian congregations remained active and the denomination continued to offer programs. Regional Presbyterian Young People's Societies (PYPS) held conferences and events. Presbyterians continued to believe in and support foreign missions. What was it like to be a Canadian Presbyterian in this period? Answering that question is challenging as the sources that might provide answers (interviews, diaries, letters) are much more challenging to access than are the reports to committees or official minutes of the denomination provided in the annual *Acts and Proceedings*. What seems clear is that while the General Assembly debated various issues those who were members of the denomination went about their work, worshipping in congregations, educating their children in faith, and serving their communities. They wrote to the committee involved in revising the hymnbook, making various suggestions.[48] They attended gatherings together. One of the interesting features in this period was the number of Congresses that brought together Presbyterians from across Canada. Following the more famous 1967 Congress, Congresses were held in 1971, 1975, and 1979.[49] These events featured noteworthy speakers. They were also well attended, including by significant numbers of younger Presbyterians. At the 1971 Congress, for example, one-third of the 589 delegates were reported to be under the age of 30. Music at these and other events attempted to blend not only traditional hymns on pipe organs but folk hymns and music on more contemporary instruments.[50] Various examples across the country were provided in the pages of the denominational magazine. Students from Knox College toured Nova Scotia churches in 1972, complete with guitars and folk songs.[51] In 1974, a group called "Messiah's Minstrels" toured various churches providing music and experimenting with new forms of evangelism.[52] Presbyterians also camped. Summer camps and programs were one of

Figure 6.3 Teen and Twenty Chapel was a Presbyterian rock band that played throughout the Toronto area, one of many groups in the late 1960s and early 1970s playing contemporary music in an effort to reach young people. This is part of the group, with the minister leading the service. A companion photograph from the stage shows a full church with many young people in attendance.

the major areas where faith was nurtured, specifically of children and youth. In 1972 the first Presbyterian music camp was held, a family camp intended to develop a variety of forms of music within congregations.[53] Experiences varied from province to province, from individual to individual. What the denominational magazine provided was a series of snapshots of those experiences, including the debates (pro and con) on the Christian Pavilion at Expo '67 and the importance of evangelism, be that a back cover promoting friendship evangelism in 1961 or news from later conferences focused on evangelism.[54] The denomination was engaged with the culture, whether providing a youth hostel for those coming to Expo '67, creating youth drop-ins in the summer month in church basements (see figure 6.4), creating a children's television show on cable TV, as the Rev. Gordon Fish did with *Nut 'n Bolts'n Things*, or reflecting on the growing charismatic movement in the 1970s.[55]

One gradual change was an increasing concern for support for relief work throughout the world. The increased activity in the Committee of Inter-Church Aid, Refugee, and World Service in the mid-1970s reflected this concern. In 1980 this agency was renamed Presbyterian

Figure 6.4 Painting a poster at a youth drop-in, Carpenter Shop coffee house, Port Carling, Ontario, 1970. Attempts to reach young people included coffee houses, either in the summer or at other times in the year. Self-expression and posters were one of the features of these gatherings.

World Service and Development (PWS&D).[56] The denomination continued to support home missions as well, with the budget of the Board of World Mission remaining the major component of the national budget. Presbyterians continued to promote evangelism. Church school curricula continued to be developed. Social concerns continued to be voiced. This was one area where a person can see an expansion of concern. Where moral issues had once dominated, issues of a more economic and political nature gradually began to be discussed. Presbyterians continued to be opposed to abortion, but this did not become a major cause or source of division within the denomination, despite one moderator highlighting this in the early 1980s.[57] Canadian Presbyterians did produce study documents on nuclear weapons and social issues such as euthanasia.[58] They also disagreed in the early 1980s, vocally, on American social policy in Central America, an area where the denomination had recently appointed a missionary.[59] It is important to pause and remember this. The denomination evolved in this period in some of its concerns, but it remained very much what it had long been – a very traditional Christian denomination.

In the mid-1970s Canadian Presbyterians began to prepare for the celebration of the 100th year of their denomination. The centennial celebration of the 1875 founding of the Presbyterian Church in Canada was crucial to the denomination's continuing sense of identity, as it was clearly stating that the denomination founded that year did not disappear into the United Church of Canada in 1925. That message was important. At the same time, the focus was less on what had happened in 1925 and replaying past conflicts, and more on where the church was at the moment, celebrating what had been achieved, and preparing for the future. As the centennial year approached, plans were made, committees established, and articles appeared in the *Presbyterian Record* in preparation for the upcoming celebrations. Heritage and history were naturally celebrated. The importance of Presbyterian identity and the denomination's roots in the Reformed tradition were stressed.[60] The denomination was pleased to announce in November 1974 the publication of a new history of the denomination, *Enduring Witness*.[61] Four years previously, Dr John S. Moir, an adherent of a Presbyterian congregation and a "professional church historian," had been approached and persuaded to take on this project. Moir began serious work on the project in 1972 and as the editor of the *Presbyterian Record* remarked, "produced a remarkable volume in a short period." The challenge, as Moir recounted to the editor, was that while there was a great deal written on the nineteenth century that needed only minor work, "the real challenge was the past century where virtually no history had been written." The book was intended to make the story of the denomination accessible to all in the denomination, provide a critical assessment ("for there are bound to be warts on human beings"), and create a renewed interest in the denomination's history within as well as outside the denomination.[62] DeCourcy Rayner, the editor, noted in particular his appreciation of the chapters related to church union, which he found less partisan than previous writing and presented "an objective view" of those crucial years.[63] Throughout 1974 four articles written by Brian Fraser appeared. Fraser was introduced as not only a student at Knox College but someone who had assisted Moir in the "research for the centennial history of our church."[64] These articles shifted the focus from brave pioneers who established the first churches or first missions, to the important work of those who sought to assist the church in being faithful in their particular circumstances, something certainly relevant to where the church found itself in the mid-1970s. Some of those featured had also later entered the United Church of Canada. The articles also underscored what had been a traditionally strong link between evangelism and social response and the centrality of each of them within the denomination.

As noted in the introduction to this book, Canadian Presbyterians celebrated the centennial of their denomination in 1975 with great enthusiasm. Finlay Stewart called the denomination to reflection but also action and renewal. There were to be exchanges between congregations. There was a hymn competition. There was a banner competition. There would be choirs, including a choir from the Korean church in Japan that would be coming to Canada. Congregations were encouraged to celebrate and do this positively and ecumenically. The events of 1925 were to be remembered but not in a resentful way: "Issues that were conflicts to our fathers need not be conflicts to us if we mature in the full sense of the ecumenical movement."[65] The high point of the year was to be the General Assembly held in Montreal, the same city where the denomination was established a century before, followed by a Congress held in Hamilton at McMaster University.[66]

Throughout the following year the *Presbyterian Record* kept readers informed of what was happening throughout the denomination. There were centennial bus tours (Eastern Canada, Western Canada, or Ontario and Quebec) designed to bring Presbyterians together, meet Presbyterians in other parts of the country, and see areas of current and former mission.[67] There were exchanges between congregations in different parts of the country. The winners of the hymn competition were announced, and it was noted that the winning hymns would be published in the songbook *Praiseways*.[68] Photographs of Presbyterians in historic costumes celebrating the denomination appeared alongside news items. The winners of the banner competition – worship banners were welcomed from various age groups, young and old – were announced as were the opportunities Presbyterians across Canada would have to see these banners.[69] The 1975 General Assembly and the subsequent Congress were reported on. The Centennial Choir was featured in one article that detailed its origins and all that it had done from its first presentation at the 1974 General Assembly. Their participation at various concerts was described, including the 1975 Assembly and the denomination's centennial service celebration broadcasted on CBC.[70] It was an active year where the church celebrated and shared.

NO LONGER GROWING: DENOMINATIONAL STATISTICS

Canadian Presbyterians celebrated. They also counted. Each year they published detailed information related to their membership, the number of congregations, the number of children in Church schools, the number of baptisms, and a myriad of other statistics. Some years it was discussed. What the numbers in this period – and through to the end of 1985 – clearly show was that the Presbyterian Church in Canada was shrinking. What had been hoped was a temporary correction of congregational rolls when membership first declined in 1965 was clearly much more serious (see figure 6.5). Membership kept going down; indeed, in 1976 it dropped below what membership had been in 1945. Membership was not the only indication of decline: baptisms were down, the number of children in church schools was down (see figure 6.6), and the number of people joining the church was down. Presbyterians knew they were not alone in this. Other large Canadian denominations were experiencing a similar reality.[71] Presbyterians found little comfort in this situation. Throughout this entire period since World War II, their preferred comparison was between their membership and the total Canadian population. This was a misleading comparison. Presbyterians had declined in relation to the total population but that had been because of the growth of the Roman Catholic population as a proportion of the Canadian population, not a reflection of their situation.[72] The result was that they never appreciated how much they had expanded in the 1950s. What they were experiencing in the period after 1965 was a new problem not simply the continuation of an ongoing one. They had moved from considerable growth to significant decline in their membership. Because of their preference for a comparison of their membership to the total population, this was obscured. Canadian Presbyterians also continued to believe there was something unique about their situation. They knew others were experiencing similar trends, yet there was a tendency to see their denomination as uniquely failing, even when this was not true. Behind many of the events and decisions taken in this period, there was always the awareness that things were not going well.

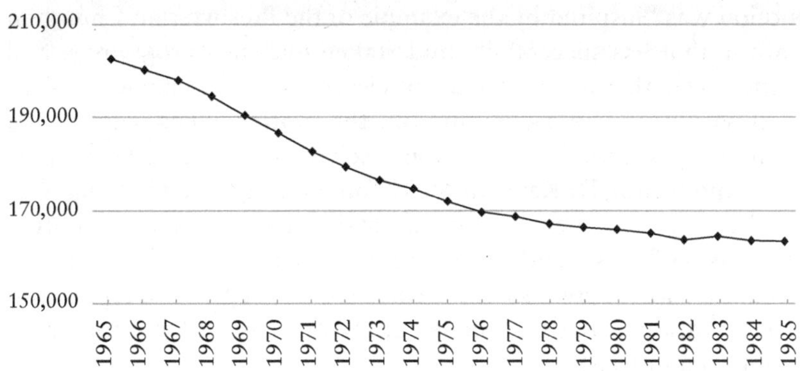

Figure 6.5 Membership in the Presbyterian Church in Canada, 1965–85

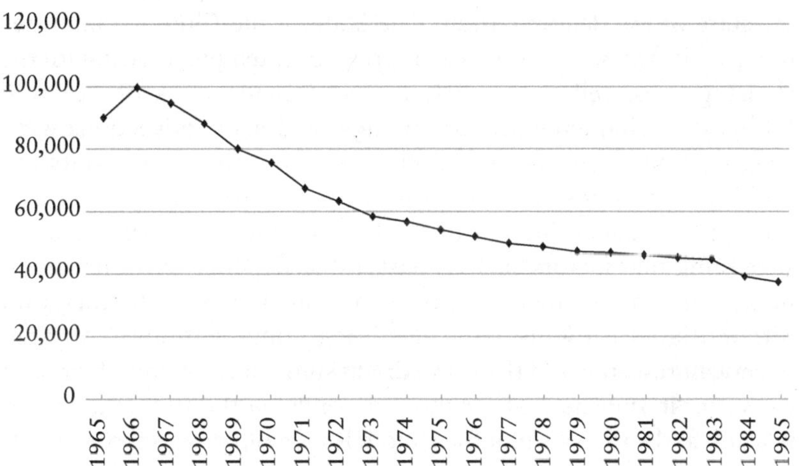

Figure 6.6 Church school membership, 1965–85

CHURCH GROWTH

The Presbyterian Church in Canada responded to their dramatic loss of church members by focusing on church growth. As Canadian Presbyterians remember the story, at the 1979 General Assembly, a minister from Duncan, BC, James Stratham, proposed a motion from the floor "that the 105th General Assembly of the Presbyterian Church in Canada commit ourselves to double our membership in ten years as a realistic goal."[73] The *Presbyterian Record* noted this as the "most enthusiastically received proposal adopted" by the Assembly. This motion was "inspired by the example of the Presbyterian Church in Taiwan that has successfully undertaken one such programme and launched another, and motivated by eleven years of declining membership within our own communion, the motion when put carried without opposition." The motion received the enthusiastic support of the moderator, Dr Kenneth McMillan. He suggested that what was needed was "not a new strategy of mission, but for a new inspiration for mission." [74] A standing ovation followed his remarks. A special committee was appointed with Dennis Oliver as chair, and representatives of various boards, the colleges, and members at large appointed to the committee.[75]

What this narrative neglects is that the denomination was already taking action on issues of church growth. A committee had already been created, because of the concern for membership decline, to look into the state of the denomination. The State of the Church committee reported in 1978. It was aware of previous attempts to deal with the challenges, as well as the early Project Canada work of Reginald Bibby. One characteristic that it suggested distinguished growing congregations from those in decline was that they were "outward looking" as opposed to focused only inward. Findings from a Presbyterian denomination in the United States were then shared, suggesting that factors such as pastoral leadership, active programming, and involvement in social action had been factors that differentiated growing from declining congregations.[76] It cited American research and then stated: "In summary, for church growth to occur, 'it appears that far more depends on the strength, clarity, warmth and enthusiasm of the church leadership program than on its theological orientation.'"[77] After noting the strengths and weaknesses of the Presbyterian Church in Canada, the committee suggested there were clear implications for the denomination, which it set out to list. The report made specific recommendations related to church growth and renewal.[78] The State of the Church report (1978) called the denomination to focus on mission, social action, and work for renewal and church growth.

The Boards of Congregational Life and World Mission began to work in these areas. A study guide on church growth was widely distributed within the denomination. Special funds had been provided for consultants in church growth. A workshop "Church Growth – A Presbyterian Perspective" had been designed and was being tested before being used more extensively in the church. Work was underway to develop a national strategy for church growth. These and other steps were carefully laid out in the report. There was also a focus on mission with youth, including encouraging the participation of Canadian youth in a major Presbyterian youth event held in the United States every three years.[79] Real plans were being made and actively engaged by those involved through the Board of Congregational Life.

Why then did the Presbyterian Church in Canada feel the need to create a second, independent, committee working on church growth when an existing committee was already working in this area? The *Presbyterian Record* noted that the "naming of a committee that would act independently" had consequences for the Board of Congregational Life who had already begun work in this area. The convenor of the Board of Congregational Life noted it understood this as an "implicit criticism" of their work.[80] Dennis Oliver, in a paper presented to the Canadian Evangelical Theological Society, stressed the spontaneous nature of what happened at the 1979 General Assembly. It came in response to the address given by the moderator of the Presbyterian Church in Taiwan, the Rev. John Lee. Oliver noted that this was done "without prior study or overture, and apart from the work of any established board or committee." [81] Oliver was aware of the work already being done in church growth but argued that what happened in 1979 was similar to the actions that had led to the creation of the State of the Church committee itself. What he argued was a pattern where "the grass roots" of the church had proven in both cases ready to "run ahead of her official boards." The actions in 1978 and 1979 suggested "that Presbyterian commissioners [to General Assembly] were capable of a greater vision than their servant structures."[82]

Following the 1979 General Assembly those "servant structures" had two separate committees dealing with church growth, one under the Board of Congregational Life and the other, known as "The Committee on Doubling Membership," functioning independently. The 1980 Assembly received reports from each of these committees. The former reported through the Board of Congregational Life and detailed the work that had been done throughout the year in promoting church growth. Workshops had been conducted and 250 copies of the congregational workshop guide "Church Growth – A Presbyterian Perspective" had been distributed. A task force had been established which developed a detailed strategy for church growth in the denomination, with a focus on what needed to happen at the congregational level, the presbytery level, the synod level, and the national level through the General Assembly. The issue of evangelism was addressed directly:

> There is no Church Growth without evangelism in the widest and best sense of the word. While Church Growth is more than just another term for the latter, it is of paramount importance that the Church be constantly conscious of the necessity to reach out to the unconverted and lapsed – the "outsider." This attitude and emphasis must prevail in all our activity in Church Growth. We will need to explore and develop new ways and new language if we are to reach these persons with the Good News of Jesus Christ. The making of disciples to engage in this ministry is a necessity in fulfilling our commission. This is not something that can be left to the "professional"; it is the work of the whole Church.[83]

The brief report of the Committee on Doubling the Membership was quite different. There had been health and workload challenges which had led Oliver to step aside as chair, though he remained on the committee. Another minister, Chuck Congram, took over the responsibilities as chair.[84] The joint work of the task force on church growth was noted. At the same time, the committee made its own perspective clear. It saw its work as "actionary" as opposed to reactionary and noted its belief that "the Lord Jesus Christ is calling the Presbyterian Church in Canada to a ministry of growth and outreach that will result in increasing numbers of unchurched Canadians being led into Christian faith and fellowship. In a calling to numerical growth, Christ also summoned us to a renewal of discipleship, worship, and every other aspect of our life and calling."[85] Scripture was quoted to demonstrate the centrality of witness and outreach. The committee ended by noting that "the doubling of our Church is a realistic goal" for the denomination, if not for every congregation. Rather than seeing this as a "burdensome legalistic obligation" the committee invited people to see it as "joyful aspiration."[86]

A concern for church growth had thus become a renewed concern for Canadian Presbyterians as the 1980s began. This work was deemed so important that it was not to be done through the normal channels or by an existing board or agency, but by a newly created committee that functioned with remarkable independence, even as it understandably saw all of church life relating in one way, shape, or form with either a growing or declining church. The concern was clearly driven by the reality that the denomination had seen its membership decrease for over fifteen years, beginning slowly but now reaching significant proportions. This could not be understood any longer as just removing inactive members from congregational membership rolls. The committee continued to insist that doubling the denomination's membership during the 1980s was a realistic goal. The choice of a name "The Church Growth to Double in the Eighties" reaffirmed the belief that this was possible. In 1981, in its first significant report to the General Assembly, the motion passed at the 1979 Assembly was italicized and included as central to what the committee was doing: "The 1980s is the decade the Presbyterian Church in Canada has committed to the doubling of her membership. Inspired by our sister Church overseas, aware of the opportunities before us in Canada, and acknowledging both the abundance of our God-given resources and Christ's Commission to reachout [*sic*] to all people, the 105th General Assembly enthusiastically and humbly agreed that: *The Presbyterian Church in Canada commit ourselves to doubling our membership in ten years as a realistic goal.*"[87]

Repeating something, even adding italics, does not make it true. Was this a realistic goal? Not all in the denomination believed it was. The committee continued to insist, without ever providing any proof, that this was possible. Indeed, the multiple twists and turns that the committee took (discussed below) suggest that no one was clear as to either what specifically was impeding growth or what in practical terms could be done to address it. The fresh start that those involved in the committee believed they had made with the creation of the committee blinded them to the reality that the church had been struggling for over a decade – admittedly going in different, and at times opposing, directions – to respond to the changes in Canadian society. The church had not had its head in the sand. It may have tried the wrong solutions. But it had tried. And then tried something different. Did those on the committee take seriously enough the challenges in Canadian society? Many of the resources cited came from the very different religious context in the United States. Aspirational titles inspire many; they also can lead many to raise questions. Those questions were not always welcomed. In 1984 the committee proudly announced that "for the first time in twenty years, our denomination increased its communicant membership in 1983 by approximately seven hundred and fifty members." The committee went on to note that there had also been an "increase in communion attendance (2%) and adherents (9%)" which were "signs that the Church is now growing."[88] The good news even made it in the *Christian Century*, where it was noted that the denomination "is among the first of Canadian mainline churches to show appreciable growth since the onset of the general decline in the 1960s."[89] Unfortunately, at the next year's Assembly the committee needed to report that this trend had not continued and in 1984 membership had again declined.[90] Midway through the decade, the news was not good. Despite all their hard work and some noble efforts, membership losses may have been slowed, but no consistent progress had been made in reversing these trends, let alone doubling the membership. This was not the fault of the committee or its staff; however, aspirational goals can become very sour, very quickly.

The Committee on Church Growth to Double in the Eighties was remarkably independent from the normal structures and at times seemed to revel in its maverick status. But was this independence ultimately a positive or negative feature? Most of us have a bias, either conscious or unconscious, towards bureaucracy and structure and how effective they are in dealing with significant challenges. There is no question that by the early 1980s the Presbyterian Church in Canada was highly structured and had a national staff and bureaucracy. If one believes that bureaucracy *is the problem,* the creation of a committee without the checks, balances, and protocols of the Board of World Mission or the Board of Congregational Life would have been the correct approach to take. What was needed was an independent committee. Alongside this perspective there exists a different one: for long-term effective change to happen one has to engage and work with the structures that exist. Indeed, these structures fulfil a purpose. What seems clear is that those involved in the Committee on Church Growth to Double in the Eighties leaned more to the first position: bureaucracy was ineffective and a problem to be overcome. The committee seemed to pride itself on its creation arising from a spontaneous movement of the Spirit at the 1979 General Assembly and worked to maintain its autonomy. There were benefits to this. There were also challenges, and challenges beyond the normal bureaucratic infighting between committees and departments that one sees in any human organization, including religious denominations. The greatest loss may have been momentum. Considerable – and good! – work had already been done by previous bodies in the Presbyterian Church in Canada in terms of ideas regarding church growth. Too much of that work was ignored.

What made the situation particularly challenging was that the Committee on Church Growth had ideas – a lot of ideas – but no clear focus as to what should be done. In 1981 the committee provided the denomination with ten objectives for growth, ranging from a "renewal of evangelism" to "secure maximum participation of as many members and adherents as possible in church growth according to their gifts and abilities"; from helping ministers and congregations see the possibilities of growth to providing a "strategy to renew declining or stagnant congregations."[91] Everyone was to be involved in church growth. The next year the focus shifted, and shifted dramatically, to only one of the ten recommendations. In 1982, the committee reported its discovery of the importance of building new congregations to overall denominational growth. Church extension (or the failure to do it effectively over the previous decade) was seen as both a problem in the past and the major solution for the future. The committee signalled a narrowed focus on new church development. It suggested the goal of the denomination should be to establish ten new congregations each year. Growth, it seems, was not what all congregations could be involved in, but something that required the establishing of extension congregations. (This theme will be explored further in chapter 7.) In 1983, however, church extension was only one of four foci of the committee.[92] The next year, in 1984, the committee focused on the work of the evangelism task force and the lay ministry task force.[93] These were all vital areas of church life and the comprehensive concern of the committee was commendable. There was not one clear focus. Midway through the decade, it was still unclear what precisely the denomination needed to do in order to staunch the bleeding of members, let alone reverse that trend and double the membership.

ECUMENISM AND THE WORLD COUNCIL OF CHURCHES

The relations with other churches had been a major issue for Canadian Presbyterians in the late 1940s and early 1950s, in particular the relationship with the Roman Catholic Church. At one level, the issues of the relationship with Roman Catholicism had been resolved with the very positive outcomes that grew out of the Second Vatican Council. Cooperation developed from the congregational level through to the theological colleges. The creation of the Toronto School of Theology in 1969–70 meant that students at Knox College in Toronto now shared classes and instructors not only with Anglican, United

Church, and other Protestant students, but with those in the Roman Catholic tradition as well. Where Protestant-Catholic marriages had been seen as a serious problem previously, one document produced by the Presbyterian Church in Canada described them as a practical experiment in ecumenism.[94] Alongside these positive and obvious examples of a thaw in relations, there were more subtle but important consequences in the life of the church. Presbyterian worship had often been defined by what it was not, namely Roman Catholic or Anglican. Now that it was no longer necessary to have worship that was intentionally opposed to anything in the Roman Catholic tradition, a variety of options opened. Presbyterians found themselves gradually (and this trend would only continue in the years following 1985) following the traditional church year and using a lectionary of common scripture texts in worship. Not all Presbyterians supported these changes, but they are notable nonetheless. Presbyterians would never have considered marking Lent in the late 1950s; by the mid-1980s, a significant (and increasing) minority found themselves marking this season of the church year. Advent, again not something Presbyterians had traditionally marked, was even more popular, with advent candles and readings becoming a part of the yearly preparations for Christmas. The paranoia about any potential union largely disappeared and many Presbyterians worked to improve relationships with the United Church of Canada and to engage on co-operative ventures.[95]

If relations with the Roman Catholic Church improved, support for the World Council of Churches and other ecumenical agencies became less automatic. As we have seen, there had always been voices in the Presbyterian Church in Canada suspicious of the ecumenical movement in general, including the World Council of Churches. In the late 1970s this opposition grew and found a particular focus in opposition to the World Council of Churches' Program to Combat Racism. The Program to Combat Racism provided humanitarian aid to rebel groups fighting against regimes in Africa, in particular Rhodesia (Zimbabwe) and South Africa, that practiced different forms of racial discrimination including apartheid. Opposition to the Program to Combat Racism came from various corners of the globe, from both inside and outside the church.

In Canada, opposition to the Program to Combat Racism became a major story in 1978 thanks to a segment on the Canadian Television Network (CTV)'s public affairs show *W5*. In an episode entitled

"A House Divided," voices in the Anglican church sharply criticized their denomination's support for not only this program of the World Council of Churches but the World Council of Churches itself. Archbishop Edward (Ted) Scott came in for strong criticism on camera, to the point that he and the Anglican church filed a complaint about the professionalism of the program with the Canadian Radio-Television and Telecommunications Commission (CRTC).[96] Canadian Presbyterians had clearly been watching this program. The Board of World Mission had, over the years, noted its support for the Program to Combat Racism and faced some criticism for this at the yearly General Assembly. Opposition was now on a completely different scale. It came from across Canada and used a new tactic – a flood of overtures all dealing with the same topic. James Ross Dickey, the editor of the *Presbyterian Record*, noted, "No less than TEN Overtures were directed to this Assembly" on this one issue and that "as far as can be determined the accumulation of ten overtures all addressed to the same subject was unprecedented, at least in recent Presbyterian history."[97] The ten overtures all complained in various ways about the Program to Combat Racism. For example, the Presbytery of Niagara noted the "considerable discontent" among congregations that church funds were given to this World Council of Churches program and asks that the General Assembly "critically review the present attitude" towards this program in order to better understand the denomination's "relationship to the whole question of political involvement and violent upheaval."[98] Among the other nine overtures there were several calls for the Presbyterian Church in Canada to suspend its membership in the World Council of Churches and cease all financial support immediately. This was clearly an issue that had mobilized Presbyterians in all regions of the country. Some of the common details in these overtures suggest communication between these congregations and presbyteries. The wording of the various overtures and the sharpness of debate suggest that this was about far more than one program. Canadian Presbyterians were also voicing their disagreement with the choice of ecumenical partners as well as an understanding of what mission might involve. What had once been more of a minority voice, opposing the denomination's support for the World Council of Churches and associated bodies, now seemed to be not only a stronger voice but one suggesting other forms of ecumenical connections.

DIFFERENT VISIONS

From the mid-1960s on, Canadian Presbyterians found themselves struggling to adjust to the changes they discerned in Canadian society. In the background throughout was the awareness that their denomination was no longer growing but was actually shrinking. Canadian Presbyterians responded in a variety of ways. They created committees, studied and issued reports, and then took the actions they believed were necessary. The LAMP report consumed a vast amount of energy and called the church to find more effective ways of communicating its message. This project also noted two different voices in the denomination: one that looked more to the world than the church and called for radical change, and another that believed the church had already changed too much and needed to return to fundamental beliefs. Each of these voices found expression respectively in the Ross Report and the Declining Church Membership reports. Canadian Presbyterians celebrated their centennial in 1975, but then returned to consider the challenges they faced. The focus in the early 1980s became church growth. What was remarkable was that the committee and staff responsible for this work functioned independent of the normal structures of the denomination. Work that had already been done on church growth was ignored. At the same time, the committee had no clear plan nor a consistent focus for its own work. The denomination did not double membership in the 1980s. Membership continued to decline. As this happened, Canadian Presbyterians seemed less confident in their ability to work together. Outside voices, as noted in the debate on the Program to Combat Racism, seemed to carry greater weight. It was no longer clear that there was a denominational consensus as there had been earlier in terms of what Canadian Presbyterians stood for and what they had to offer – collectively – to Canadian society.

7

Coordination and Planning

The Challenges of Starting New Congregations in a Changing Environment

A new modern office building in the Don Mills area of Toronto was a powerful symbol of how the Presbyterian Church in Canada thought of itself and its future (see figure 3.7). It also spoke to its belief that centralization, coordination, and planning were crucial to how a modern Christian church should function. One of the places where this became clear was in the area of church extension or new church development. The denomination had depended on decentralized church extension, relying on each presbytery to be responsible for this work with only limited input from the national office. That changed in 1963 when church extension became a function of the national denomination. Whether a direct result of the challenges of finances, or as an attempt to better coordinate the important work of building new congregations, the denomination appointed a full-time director of church extension in 1963. The Rev. J.C. (Jack) Cooper, who was already at the national office working for the mission board, assumed this role. Mission work had been frozen at existing levels in 1961.[1] A freeze on new church development was in place in the years 1963 and 1964. This freeze meant that no new work could be started, although existing work continued. Indeed, in a report to the General Assembly in 1965, Cooper reported that fourteen new congregations had been organized in 1964; the concern was that there was no money for any new congregations in 1966.[2] Cooper's appointment in 1963 coincided with a clear national mandate for church extension, one that spoke of the "evangelization of the unchurched" and providing worship services for Christians who moved. Together it was hoped that these groups would become involved in "Jesus Christ's Ministry of reconciliation at home and abroad."[3] Presbyteries and synods were to support this work and be responsible for certain aspects of it but the main direction would now come from the national church.

This chapter explores this second phase of church extension in the denomination where the national denomination, at the level of the General Assembly and the board responsible for mission in Canada, was crucial in planning and the execution of these projects. This second phase has dominated the memory of the denomination. This, many suggest, is how church extension was always done. As we have already seen in chapter 2, church extension was locally driven in the period immediately after World War II. This chapter will detail this second phase, noting the theology and policies that shaped church extension, and exploring some of the careful planning that went into starting new churches in different parts of Canada. Church extension became part of the normal operations of the denomination as one more aspect of its ministry. The importance of starting new churches was stressed by the Committee on Church Growth to Double in the Eighties. This led to ambitious plans in the early 1980s and a revitalization of church extension. Costs, however, continued to be a major challenge. Canadian Presbyterians did not find a way to successfully fund this venture, which became increasingly expensive as the cost of land, buildings, and servicing mortgages increased. Centralization may have been necessary in order to continue establishing new congregations in this period, but central planning was not able to resolve these issues. What was never taken adequately into account was the religious environment in which those congregations were being established had changed dramatically since the 1950s. Canada was no longer in a period of religious revival. Canadian Presbyterians failed to notice.

CENTRALIZING CHURCH EXTENSION

The appointment of Jack Cooper to the position of director of church extension for the denomination highlighted the importance of new church development. It also allowed the denomination to state why it believed it should be starting new congregations. Early in his tenure, Cooper addressed a workshop on church extension and offered a theology of church extension. Jesus had established the church. This was a primary conviction and something which he argued more recent theology had recaptured from the errors that arose as a result of "19th century liberalism." He was critical of those "who in my view, have an old-fashioned theological position with regard to the church who say that the church is not essential to Christianity."[4] The church was established by Jesus, and it was important that it "confess its faith."[5] It followed logically that building communities for believers was a natural extension of, and a vital part of, Jesus' own ministry. This was not about merely institutional survival. Instead, it was through the institution that, Cooper argued, the gospel was shared and people's lives transformed: "church extension is for the sake of others and not for the sake of the church. The church does not derive its strength from the addition of members, but from the spirit of Christ which animates it. It is we who need what the church dispenses."[6] Congregations were places of evangelism: "My contention is that the church has something precious to share with others, a ministry and a mission. We seek to bring as many people into the kingdom as possible because it the kindest thing we can do for any man."[7] Why build new congregations? Because in the mid-twentieth century this was an effective way of reaching out to Canadians and sharing the gospel. The conviction here – as it would have been in other denominations – was that most Canadians had a general Christian belief; what they needed was a fellowship of others that would deepen their belief. It was through that kind of congregational fellowship that people were reached by the gospel and their lives transformed.

Those involved in church extension had a purpose and a theological rationale. They had an awareness of the challenges they faced. They also had clear ideas about how church extension might best be done. The issue of challenges was addressed in September 1967 by the immediate former moderator, the Rev. Deane Johnston. Johnston noted with concern that the Canadian population was growing while the church's membership had "shown a decline." He proposed that presbyteries might be too small to oversee the work of church extension and suggested synods might be more effective. He also drew on his recent tour of the United Kingdom to suggest that a different model of pastoral oversight, similar to one used in Ireland and Scotland whereby ministers in extension charges served on an appointment rather than being called by the congregation, might be more effective. He also argued strongly that one of the challenges was the "urgent matter of the relocation of congregations – the closing out of some and the disposal of their property."[8] This was urgent and something presbyteries found difficult to implement. Yet it needed to be done in order to reallocate the resources of the church: "we simply have neither the men [*sic*] nor the money to subsidize sentiment."[9] The issue of resources was one that many considered vital. The establishment of a national director of church extension allowed for the consideration of these challenges and for proposals to change how new churches were being established.

Policies and procedures could also be coordinated. National grants and regulations around funding had been in place before 1963. What the coordination of church extension at the national level ensured was that there would be consistency across the synods and presbyteries. By 1966 the funding was fairly straightforward. For the first two years, new congregations received "full grants" for their ministers' stipends (salaries), housing, and travel costs. After two years these grants were reduced and congregations were expected to take on an increasing share of the ministers' stipends. The land for each new congregation was donated by the denomination. This was a generous donation; it also allowed the denomination to determine where a congregation would be situated. The next task was the construction of a building for worship and other activities. In 1966 congregations received a grant of $10,000 towards their new buildings. They also had access to loans of $25,000 with generous terms (five years interest free, 4 per cent interest for the next five years, and 6 per cent for the next, and hopefully final, four years). There was also an incentive built into this schedule to encourage congregations to construct a building as soon as possible. Once buildings were dedicated, the congregations received a special $3,000 grant that could be applied directly to the principal and reduce the interest payments.[10] Congregations received $2,000 in the second year and $1,000 in the third. After this, as the plan noted, "the congregation then settles down to the twin tasks of paying for their building and reducing their annual deficit grants" from the national church.[11] Put more directly, congregations were expected to pay an increasing share of their way in terms of both their personnel and the buildings they had constructed. On paper this worked well. Those involved in church extension were aware this did not always work out as smoothly in every situation. One of the crucial challenges was that the congregations bore the entire responsibility for the debt required to construct buildings: the challenges this posed in terms of welcoming new members, limiting the development of programs (all the money was going to the mortgage), and morale of ministers and people were known. Suggestions for new and different ways of doing things came from both inside and outside the department and the committee responsible for church extension. In 1966 Cooper wondered if the denomination might be wiser to build fewer but more regional congregations, as opposed to churches within neighbourhoods, as had often been the case when presbyteries bore the primary responsibility for church extension:

> Reduction in the rate of establishing new charges has given impetus to the growing conviction that as a church we should aim to establish regional congregations. If we cannot establish charges in every new neighbourhood, we ought then to locate new and relocate old congregations in areas where they can serve a large population in several neighbourhoods. Such a policy would tend towards a better use of the Church's resources of money and manpower. It undoubtedly will mean expensive sites near important crossroads, but it may be much cheaper than three or four "cheaper" sites for projects of smaller potential each of which may have to keep a minister occupied at or near the minimum stipend.[12]

This was one of many proposals aimed to try to deal with the challenges of church extension, in particular the ongoing costs of establishing a new congregation. Those costs were born both by the denomination (personnel costs to get the congregation established, cost of the land for each congregation, and the need for a capital reserve in order to provide lower-than-prime interest rates to assist congregations in constructing their building) and by those who joined these new congregations (personnel costs for an organist, other staff, and an increasing share of the salary for the minister, and the payments for the mortgage on the newly constructed building). One reality that the centralization of church extension in the national offices brought was more consistent and clear policies.

PLANNING FOR GROWTH

One of the presumed benefits of centralized planning of church extension was expertise. The director of church extension, working at the national office, could pull on a range of statistics, standardize the questions asked in planning work, and make difficult recommendations that might be a challenge for someone at the synod or presbytery level. One of the tasks of the director was to write reports for the

National Church Extension Committee for specific presbyteries. A report was prepared for the national committee in September 1965 on church extension in London, Ontario, that illustrated this well. Using the census tracts in the city of London, a table was provided which broke down the city showing the number and percentage of Presbyterians, Anglicans, Roman Catholics, United Church members, and "all others" in each tract, as well as the earnings of the head of the family. One clearly could see which areas had the highest and lowest concentrations of census Presbyterians. Another table outlined the membership of the nine congregations the denomination currently had in the city of London. The two congregations with membership under 100, Byron and St Lawrence, were singled out for concern. With the Chalmers congregation already in the process of relocating, it was suggested that St Lawrence needed to do the same, and that a new site in a strategic area be bought to allow this to happen. Byron, on the other hand, was in an area that was geographically cut off from surrounding parts of London, and with a relatively low percentage of census Presbyterians. This congregation, it was suggested, should be incorporated into one of the four proposed new congregations. It was suggested that sites be purchased in designated areas: "The new sites are quite widely spaced one from the other and from existing churches. It is felt that statistics indicated that this should be so in order to create strong congregations in the new areas and avoid unnecessary relocations at a later date."[13] Two additional sites were also noted as possibilities. One final table was added, noting the population in 1965, the projected population in 1990, the projected census Presbyterians in that area, and the estimated number of communicant members for each of these congregations. It was all carefully planned, with the statistics giving weight to the recommendations.

The same approach was evident the next year in a report to the Presbytery of Westminster in British Columbia that looked at eleven churches in Vancouver. In addition to considering trends in Vancouver population growth and the distribution of census Presbyterians, more information was provided in this report on the congregations that were being studied, including their trends in membership since 1939. These congregations were explored in detail, with information on the history, building, and current situation all provided. Recommendations for each congregation followed. These recommendations were made in light of the principles of planning that were articulated earlier in the report. The centrality of location, the importance of visibility, and a mission spirit were all held up as essential for growth. The good news, the report suggested, was that with "the advent of town planning" it could now be "predicted with reasonable accuracy if a congregation started at point 'A' will have a constituency to serve, say twenty years hence."[14] This was crucial to success: "new work should be located where there is a present and future need, and where there can be missionary outreach. This is a more basic factor than leadership in the establishment of a congregation, and fortunately, one over which the church can exercise considerable control."[15] Build it in the right location and they will come. This was the central message of the report. Even a theological rationale was provided: "For the Church to ignore this great new factor in its planning would be a reckless kind of stewardship of the resources God has entrusted to the church for His Mission."[16] Many of the congregations in the study were in the wrong locations; others lacked another key feature, visibility. The lack of a "Missionary Spirit" in those congregations that were declining was also noted. The recommendations made by the report to the presbytery on what it should do with the older congregations that were not growing were all derived from these principles.

The same confidence in the value of careful planning was evident in a report provided the next year (1967) to the Presbytery of Assiniboia. Regina was a rapidly growing city and the expansion was going to continue in areas to the north and west. The report focused on three congregations in this vicinity. There was a particular challenge in Regina – there were few census Presbyterians. As a percentage of the total Protestant population, Regina shared with Winnipeg and Saskatoon a very low ratio of 5 per cent which compared, the report noted, unfavourably to places like Guelph, where it was over 20 per cent.[17] What this meant was that the denomination "can afford mistakes less in Regina than most places. To put it another way, a Presbyterian congregation in Regina has to have everything going for it in order to be a viable unit carrying its weight, and supporting the mission of the Church on the frontiers of Canada and the world."[18] The problem was that there were already congregations in this part of Regina, and they were not, on the whole, doing well. Walter Martin was small and in the wrong area and the region around it was becoming more industrialized. Northside was the congregation created in 1925 from those in the north of Regina who had wished to continue as Presbyterian; the report suggests this was an issue as it had more of a "remnant" mentality than one focused on "outreach and mission."[19]

Calvin, begun as an extension congregation in the 1950s, had never advanced beyond the first small building constructed in 1957. There was still debt from that earlier build. After laying out the challenges, the report recommended that the three congregations merge and move to a new location. It was recognized that this would be challenging, but a centrally located new site – based on all of the planning principles and the information provided in the report – was what was recommended. This merged congregation could then be designated an extension congregation and receive the benefits of support from the presbytery and the denomination nationally.[20] The solution to the challenges in Regina was clear; it was just a matter of executing this carefully laid out plan. What was never considered was why, if there were so few Presbyterians in Regina, the denomination was committing significant resources to build congregations where they were not obviously needed. Believing they were a national denomination, this question was not one Canadian Presbyterians seriously considered.

CONTINUING THE WORK

The Presbyterian Church in Canada continued to invest in church extension. It saw it as one aspect of its mission and of being a Reformed church within Canada. It recognized that many of these newer congregations were vibrant. It also saw them as a possible answer to what it saw as a real issue – the population of Canada was growing rapidly, and the Presbyterian share of that population was not keeping pace. This was how the issue was often framed within denominational discussions: the membership in Presbyterian congregations was compared as a percentage to the growth in the overall population. Tables calculating these percentages appeared in many different studies. Presbyterians worried about this. In his report in 1967, Jack Cooper addressed the issue directly and suggested that establishing new congregations was one part of the solution: "The long-term post-war population trend reveals an increase in Presbyterian Church membership of 1.3% annually, whereas the adult Protestant population of the country has been growing by 2.3% annually. This gap can be closed within the next ten years if Church Extension, i.e. outreach to the community, becomes the concern of all congregations and not just new congregations. New work in strategic areas under competent leaders will also be essential during this period. Both of these forms of outreach should be the concern of the

Church Extension Committee."[21] This was important work. To make that work more effective, Cooper was granted a sabbatical in 1968 in order to do "a concentrated study on modern methods of church extension among other churches in the United States and Canada" that he could then bring to bear on his own context.[22]

On his return from sabbatical, Cooper provided a workshop to church extension ministers. He organized and summarized his thoughts on both the trends within North American society that were affecting the church and how the church might respond. He noted the increasing mobility of the population, the challenges that new communications (especially television) posed, and the increasing role that government was playing. He noted that planning had become an essential aspect of modern life and argued this needed to become even more a part of church extension. Congregations needed to have a statement of purpose. They needed a financial plan and an accurate description of "the mission field" (i.e., their neighbourhood). The minister needed a job description. The mission of the congregation needed clear objectives. Planning was crucial to success. At the same time, success was not, Cooper argued, paying off the mortgage of a congregation or becoming self-sufficient. The goal was not any of these things because the purpose in church extension was to bring people into the church and "communicate the gospel": "Bringing people in to the church is the best thing you can do for them."[23] Despite the challenges, congregations remained vital institutions needed for the mission. As he commented to the General Assembly on his study of the experiences of the American churches: "The American Churches are great experimenters. They have tried and discarded experiments we haven't even commenced. Fully aware of the many voices that are critical, they have found that the congregation is here to stay. They realize that in some areas there is a place for special ministries. The primary question is what is the purpose of the congregation? We must make it that the Church is the Church, and outreach must be the permanent activity of the congregation. There must be a spirituality which the world cannot give."[24]

In its report to the 1970 General Assembly, the General Board of Missions provided a surprisingly negative assessment of the Presbyterian Church in Canada's experience in establishing new congregations. The National Church Extension Committee shared data which Cooper had presented to the March meeting of the board: "Mr. Cooper surveyed the progress of new congregations started in the 50's and 60's. In the decade of the 50's, the Presbyterian Church in Canada started 111 new congregations. Of these 40 have become self-supporting, 18 were ultimately closed, and 52 are aid-receiving. Eighteen have been linked with other charges. In the decade of the 60's the church started 41 new congregations. Of these, nine have been closed and 32 are aid-receiving, of which six are linked with other points."[25] The committee then noted there were thirty-six situations where new work was possible and that it was anticipated that between 1970 and 1975 sixteen congregations would be involved in building projects.[26] The dissonance between their optimism for future projects and the negativity of the numbers presented in the report is jarring. The report was stating, in essence, that the Presbyterian Church in Canada had failed. Certainly this was how John Moir, who quoted these statistics in *Enduring Witness*, understood the message. Moir noted it was a "discouraging record" and spoke of the "failure of many of the new postwar congregations to develop as viable entities."[27] This brief report, through its inclusion in the denominational history, has shaped how Canadian Presbyterians have viewed their work in establishing new congregations. Ultimately, it is believed, they failed. But is this true? As we saw in our exploration of church extension in the period when it was under presbytery control (chapter 2) this was not what was believed. Indeed, new congregations were established and existing congregations were revitalized in this period. So, what was going on in this report? Cooper had been seconded to work on the LAMP project during this year. This may have been a factor. It is also worth noting that the report did not provide the source of the information that was used to arrive at these conclusions. Which 111 congregations were they? Where were they located? And in particular, where were the eighteen congregations that failed? Of the forty-one congregations started in the 1960s, where were the nine that closed? A 20 per cent failure rate should have set alarm bells ringing. Instead, the report simply continued, noting what was planned next. The message was: we have failed in the past but we are continuing on the same path. These numbers and how they were reported remains puzzling. It has not been possible to determine which congregations these were, or whether this analysis was accurate. Nor was the report to the denomination completely accurate: what the minutes of the meeting of the General Board of Missions (11 March 1970) record is that "Mr. Cooper called attention to the list of congregations organized in the 50's and 60's."[28] The details on the number of congregations established in each of these decades, let alone the fate of these congregations (self-supporting, failed, aid-receiving), may have been provided as part of the list, but they are not recorded in the minutes. What the minutes record was the average congregations per annum, both for the entire twenty-year period (5.9 per annum) and for the 1960s (3.1 per annum), with the suggestion that "it is anticipated that it will be a little more for the 70's."[29] The rest of the report went into the normal work of the department and how it was operating, including suggestions that flexibility in new church buildings was essential and the assurance to the board that a method to control the cost of new buildings had been implemented.[30] The impression given by this report, as it was published in the *Acts and Proceedings*, however, remains clear. In memory, it has come to represent a massive failure for the project of establishing new congregations. What it might indicate was the challenge of the model of church extension adopted by the Presbyterian Church in Canada: too many new congregations were started with too little resources. This is possible. What is not clear, however, is whether this analysis was true. Despite these damning statistics, no significant changes in how Canadian Presbyterians established new congregations were being proposed.

The resignation of Cooper as Director of Church Extension in 1972 did not end the denomination's work in church extension. The responsibilities were shifted to another staff person at the national office. Church extension was no longer a separate, prioritized piece of work. Instead, it was one aspect of the overall mission work of the denomination, specifically what the denomination was doing in home missions. This was how work in this area was reported to the denomination year after year, with the work in new congregations scattered across the various field reports from the synods. There was no major articulation of goals. Those responsible for home missions continued to do the planning, follow the processes, and implement the program as it had previously existed. The program remained largely as it had become at the time of national coordination: a planned approach to church extension that relied on national expertise and the support and cooperation of the presbyteries. What had changed was the circumstances under which this was taking place. One reality, not always recognized but a reality nonetheless, was that growth of each individual congregation was slower as the Canadian population gradually became less and less interested in joining a church. Another reality was the increasing cost to build new congregations. This was due to increasing construction costs and the costs of mortgages, which from 1973 to 1979 ranged from 9 to 11 per cent. Land had also become very expensive. In 1970, a report had been presented on the campus idea, whereby various denominations would cooperate and purchase land together, even potentially sharing building space.[31] While never the ideal, this was always noted as one possibility given the cost of land. This remained a major concern, especially in expanding urban areas where the cost of land was particularly prohibitive. Nevertheless, new congregations were established. In 1978, for example, the report on church extension noted that new congregations had been established in Waterloo, Ontario, and Langley, British Columbia. New work was beginning in Brampton, Ontario, and Hamilton, Ontario, and reports were given on four other places where congregations had recently been established. The work went on. The report also noted the challenges. The high cost of purchasing land was particularly noted.[32]

Establishing new congregations was now part of the routine work of the Board of World Mission. The Home Missions division was actively involved in church extension, establishing around three congregations each year. In its report to the 1979 General Assembly, it noted that the work of church extension was the "most hopeful, exciting, satisfying and frustrating areas" of the mission board's work. It noted that ten new congregations had been established across Canada over the past five years. They also listed them (something that was not usually done): Sackville, Nova Scotia; Trinity-Kanata, Ottawa; Malvern, Toronto; Brant Hills, Burlington; White Oak, Mississauga; Glenbrook, Mississauga; Waterloo North, Waterloo; St Mark's, Malton; Centennial, Calgary; and, Langley, British Columbia. Work had begun on four more potential congregations (Toronto, Hamilton, Saskatoon, Vancouver Island) and someone had just been appointed to begin another church in Brampton. The number of these churches in suburban areas surrounding major cities is noteworthy, but so too is the fact that they were scattered across the country. Opportunities existed in other parts of Canada, according to the report, but "resources are not available." The individual presbytery played a key role in this process:

> When a proposed site is approved by the presbytery and the Board of World Mission, there begins the long and often discouraging process of seeking a suitable site to be purchased for the new congregation. Often there is consultation with

> other denominations interested in the same area, and occasionally, because of the inflated cost of land in many areas, the only possible alternative is to purchase a site jointly for shared use. When sufficient housing units are occupied in the area to justify a start, a minister interested in and suitable for this type of assignment is appointed. The work generally begins in rented facilities, frequently a public school. The emphasis in every case is the development of a worshipping, Biblically-knowledgeable community. Communicants classes, eldership training courses, etc. follow naturally, as well as outreach to the neighbourhood through evangelism and service programs.[33]

This was the carefully structured process of developing a new congregation that the Board of World Mission had developed by the late 1970s. Increasing costs meant that the church was working to make sure that every project succeeded. Those costs were laid out and included the cost of accommodation for "the minister and his [*sic*] family," which frequently meant purchasing a manse as soon as possible. The report stressed the need for "capital funds" to purchase the land, which was what the denomination provided "as a gift to the new congregation," as well as a house for the manse. These were the capital costs assumed by the national church; there was also the need, through mission funds, to provide the operational costs such as the basic stipend for the minister for the first five years.[34] It is only fair to restate that after the first five years the new congregation would assume the responsibility for paying the minister, as well as the cost of building a new church and facilities on the land the denomination had purchased. Church extension was a costly venture for all involved. It is worth noting in passing that in this report it was assumed that the minister would be male ("his family"). Thirteen years after the ordination of women to the ministry had been approved by the denomination, this reflected the culture of the mission board as it related to women in ministry. (This will be explored further in chapter 8.)

These challenges were explored further in the next report given to the General Assembly in 1980. On the one hand, there was the "need and opportunity for establishing new congregations" (growth in parts of Alberta and BC was cited) while on the other hand there was "the inevitable escalation in the cost of real estate for manse and church sites."[35] Finding appropriate church sites was a problem, and this had led the denomination to cooperate with other denominations in dealing with land developers and in planning for where land for churches might be made available. It also led, in some cases, to the denomination sharing land "with two or more denominations" to save money. Given some confusion as to "the intent of these church campus projects," it was felt necessary to clarify that cooperation was important in planning for land purchases, but the goal was, wherever possible, to "secure single sites for the erection of our own buildings." Campus projects where several denominations shared the same property (land or land and buildings) were to be used "where circumstances warrant." Cost was clearly the determining factor in this second option. In fact, cost was a major challenge for all projects. The committee stated bluntly: "Despite the various provisions for assisting congregations, the escalating costs of construction are creating almost insurmountable difficulties for new congregations. One undesirable tendency is to plan a building too small for any but the immediate needs of the congregation. The result is that a second unit is required before the first is paid for, and growth is impeded."[36] Despite these challenges, the Church Extension Committee that worked under the Board of World Mission continued its work of planning for and establishing new congregations throughout Canada.

THE CHURCH GROWTH MOVEMENT AND CHURCH EXTENSION

The creation of a committee at the denominational level committed to doubling the membership of the Presbyterian Church in Canada (see chapter 6) during the 1980s had a significant impact on the work of church extension. Church extension was happening, if at a careful pace and not in any way that would challenge the denomination financially or excite it institutionally. It was one of many interests of those charged with the oversight of the mission work of the church. The challenges of high land costs for both a manse for the minister to live in and for the church were real. Despite this, the denomination had managed to create three new congregations annually from 1973 to 1981. In 1981 it reported that there were seventy potential sites it was aware of but the challenges of finances, and the issue of the economic slow-down in Canada at the time, meant the denomination could not move forward with these potential projects.[37]

This changed dramatically the next year in 1982, as the Committee on Church Growth to Double in the Eighties turned its attention to the issue of church extension. At the time of the church growth committee's report in 1981, a supplemental motion had been moved from the floor asking the committee to, "in consultation with the Board of World Mission, study the relationship between new church site development and numerical growth and report to the next General Assembly."[38] Report it did. It seems the Committee on Church Growth to Double in the Eighties had discovered the solution. In all-capital letters it declared to the 1982 General Assembly:

> After a study of existing research and research of the extension experience of the Presbyterian Church in Canada, we conclude that there is a direct, positive and significant correlation between new church site development and numerical growth, a correlation which has profound implications for a national strategy for church growth.[39]

The report shared the research the committee had consulted. The committee suggested that denominations that were growing also had an increasing number of congregations; similarly, denominations that had an increasing number of congregations had a growing membership. The opposite was also true: denominations with a decrease in membership reported fewer congregations, and "every denomination reporting a decrease in the total number of its congregations reports a decrease in numbers." The committee was quick to note this did not "prove a 'cause and effect' relationship" but it was nevertheless excited by this finding and suggested "that new congregational development is an essential component in the growth and decline of denominations."[40] (One can almost hear the cries of "Hallelujah! We're saved.") The committee cited findings from the United Presbyterian Church in the United States in support of its argument. It then noted that over the past five years, fifteen denominations (it did not mention which denominations, or whether any of these were from Canada; one assumes the majority were from the United States) had initiated church growth programs. Four had resulted in "significant growth" while two had stopped the loss of members and stabilized: "Of the four reporting significant gains, church growth was linked to new congregational development."[41] For those who wondered if the five-year time span was too short to evaluate success, the committee concurred but noted that the experience of the Korean Presbyterian Church over a longer time frame had been similar. It concluded: "Thus the available North American Research leads to the conclusion that growing denominations are planting new congregations in very great number and that strategically placed, new congregations grow. So overwhelming is the evidence that Schaller, Hunter, and Hurn, among others, agree that church growth in terms of numerical gains in membership is related to the rapid, intentional planting of new congregations and this effort forms the foundation of a viable denominational strategy for growth. But is our Canadian Presbyterian experience compatible with this data?" The committee made clear that it was. It cited evidence from the last twenty years (1960–81). According to the committee, the denomination had started sixty new congregations in this period, over half of them during the 1960s. It noted that higher costs had been one of the factors which led to a decrease in new congregations after 1965. It also hastened to note that from 1956 to 1965 "the church was forming new congregations faster than it was closing congregations, numerical membership was growing at an annual rate of 1.2 percent." However, in the following decade when fewer churches were being established and more were closing, "numerical strength declined at an annual rate of 1.5 percent." The committee then zoomed out to look at the period from 1965 to 1981 and suggested that while the denomination as a whole declined 18 per cent, "membership in new congregations grew some 71 percent."[42] Only a careful reader would pause to note that two different things were being referenced in this sentence – on the one hand, the decline in the denomination as a whole, and on the other, how individual congregations were faring. It was not surprising at one level that these new congregations had grown over 70 per cent, as they had started from a base line of zero. Certainly the question should have been, how have they contributed to the overall growth of the denomination? One could even answer this by subtracting the membership of the sixty congregations from the overall membership of the denomination and stating the difference. This might have made a compelling case. But this was not done. Nor did the committee provide a list of which specific congregations it was referring to in this statistic or in its statement that "of the sixty new congregations, two are closed, and only four can be classed as declining, based on the period, 1976–1981" or its statement that of these new congregations "all but a dozen could be classified as rapidly growing congregations."[43] All of these statements might be true. But as was so frequently the case in reports of this nature created by Presbyterian committees, they did not "show their work."

No one outside the committee could look at the data and challenge it or ask slightly different questions. Instead, the case was made with the statistics reported. And in this situation the case was made compellingly that what the church needed to do was build more congregations.

The committee went on to extoll the other virtues of extension congregations. Rather than being failures – as suggested by the Board of World Mission's report in 1970 – the denomination's extension program had been a remarkable success. The failure was in allowing the admitted financial challenges to slow down this vital element of the denomination's life. Graphs. Tables. More statistics. All were included to make the case:

> The research into the relationship of new congregations to growth in the church is significant. These signs point to one or two alternatives for the Presbyterian Church in Canada in the 1980s as we move forward in our goal of growth; either there will be a substantial decline in the number and comparative size of Presbyterian congregations with a consequent decline or at best plateauing of membership; or there will be a fresh, new wave of new church development particularly in growing metropolitan centres. No existing congregations can grow large enough or fast enough to make a significant impact upon the present population, let alone adequately minister to a growing one.[44]

Planting new churches was provided as the only way the denomination could double its membership or grow. Without realizing it, the Committee on Church Growth to Double in the Eighties had returned to the rationale – we must build churches to minister to Canadians – that had driven the initial phases of post-war church extension work.

The report provided not only a solution to the challenge of decline (build new churches) but also a detailed plan as to how to make this happen. The committee suggested that the existing plans for three, or even six, new congregations per year was inadequate: "If the church expects significant numerical growth in this decade no less than ten and more favourably, fifteen new congregations per year must be planned for and given highest priority."[45] The committee turned to the challenges, beginning with the challenge of funding such an ambitious expansion. The committee argued that "an increasing body of evidence" had developed which suggested that the costs might not be as "high as it has been in most denominational families, including our own." The healthiest congregations, it was suggested, needed "only modest financial subsidy" according to the research, and that larger support might "not even be compatible with church growth for new mission congregations or existing ones."[46] While somewhat reassuring, exactly how much these even modest subsidies might be was not specified. The committee then turned to the question of ministers. These new congregations needed ministers to serve – not just any ministers, but the right ministers who would assist the newly established congregations grow. The committee noted this was a challenge, one that might begin to be addressed by encouraging graduating students for ministry to consider working in this area. The weakness of their training in this area was noted, with suggestions on how this might be improved. Finally, the committee noted the potential issue of existing congregations feeling threatened by the competition that new congregations posed, suggesting that "many existing congregations are not only reluctant, but refuse to help with the establishment of new congregations." The committee suggested instead that the "new energy" produced by establishing a new congregation might actually benefit existing congregations. The committee noted these challenges but nevertheless concluded that the denomination needed to move urgently in this direction, adding italics to its statement to reinforce its seriousness: "*Therefore, we conclude that numerical growth is positively related to new church development and that increased new congregational development will require a significant re-ordering of the priorities in the church, particularly in terms of the resources spent in Canada. National resources alone are not sufficient to meet the needs for new congregational development.*"[47] The specific recommendations called on the denomination at all levels to make this a priority. The goal of establishing a minimum of ten new congregations a year was required. In order for this to happen, the committee recommended, first, that "funding for such development be shared by Congregations, Presbyteries and General Assembly Funds and that the Board of World Mission be asked to co-ordinate the achievement of this goal"; second, that the Administrative Council "be invited to study how the church might examine its priorities and fund-raising base to share in the administration of the ten new congregations"; and third, that representatives of the church growth committee, the Board of World Mission, and indeed all other boards and organizations in the church work to find specific ways to reduce the cost of new church development "through new ministry patterns and financial policies."[48] These recommendations were all approved by the Assembly.[49] The Committee on Church Growth to Double in the Eighties was calling on the denomination to invest massively again in church extension projects. The current decline, it argued, was the result of losing sight of this as a priority. Decline could be reversed and the denomination could move back to growth if it put its energy into this project.

Ten congregations a year for the next ten years was an ambitious goal to say the least. Financing this was a significant challenge. The Administrative Council managed the budget of the church, working to see that the church did not return to a situation where it was spending more than it was receiving. This placed that body in the unfortunate position many times of saying "no" to the plans of committees, theological colleges, boards, and even special committees of the denomination, such as the Committee on Church Growth to Double in the Eighties. The financial solution proposed by the committee was more hopeful than detailed. Costs might be reduced, but there were still the significant operational and capital costs. There were also the administrative costs at the national office of administering these new congregations. Planning for ten congregations involved considerable work. Managing the ten congregations established the previous year, while planning for ten new congregations, would require even more work. It was perhaps not surprising that the church growth committee came to the next General Assembly in 1983 with a moderately scaled-back plan and more specifics. Reminding the current Assembly that the previous Assembly had agreed to the goal and funding of ten new congregations a year, the committee restated its belief that this was doable even if challenging: "the costs will be great, but the reward so much greater."[50] The goal was clarified: what the committee was suggesting was the establishment of ten congregations a year over the five-year period from 1985–89. The committee confessed to having come up empty-handed in terms of how this could be financed: "We wish we could report that we have discovered some simple and inexpensive formula by which new congregations can be established! Rather, we must urge the Church to realize that unless church extension becomes a major priority throughout the Church, and unless we significantly increase our commitment to this aspect of gospel ministry at all levels – in our congregations, presbyteries, synods and national structures – the prayer of this goal will be defeated. But we are encouraged by the fact that other denominations have demonstrated that this level of church extension can be sustained in Canada."[51] The committee argued this needed to become an immediate priority. Presbyteries had to take the "primary responsibility" if this were to succeed: "We believe that it would be unfair and unrealistic for the Church to place the burden of our venturesome extension goal upon the shoulders of national structures alone. It is essential that presbyteries take primary responsibility for church extension within their bounds. Needs and opportunities for this ministry are best identified at the local level, and funds for local causes are more easily found. Yet there will always remain an important role for our national Church in aiding our smaller and less-endowed presbyteries to realize their opportunities."[52] The committee then suggested things which the presbyteries might do: create a satellite congregation of an existing congregation; have a group of congregations support a new congregation; or, the entire presbytery could fund this one new congregation. Later in the report the committee proposed motions to clarify the responsibilities of the national church and the responsibilities of the presbytery.[53] None of this was necessarily wrong-headed. What is notable, however, is that in focusing on church growth the committee seemed to propose that the denomination return to how church extension had been done prior to it being centralized in 1963, when the position of a national coordinator was created. It did this without realizing this was what it was doing or taking into account any of the challenges that had led to the creation of the national coordinator, let alone Synod Corporations, in the first place. Some of those challenges had only grown with time. Indeed, any role for the national church in this process seemed unclear, as new congregations were least likely to be needed in "our smaller and less-endowed presbyteries." To be fair, the precise wording of the motions gave more oversight to the national church. They also challenged all of the national boards and committees to see how they "might support the goal of establishing ten new congregations a year," and indeed to report "specific plans to meet this goal" to the next General Assembly.[54]

In addition to these recommendations, the committee also specified how the number of fifty congregations would be reached and how much this would cost. It argued that the presbyteries could establish twenty-five congregations (five per year) using their resources, while the national church could establish fifteen congregations (three per year) using national funds. The remaining ten new congregations would be achieved by "affiliating with our denomination" currently independent "'ethnic churches' (e.g. Korean)" who wished to be connected to a larger denomination.[55] The costs were outlined and noted to be "considerable." It was estimated that the minister would cost (including housing) $30,000, the land for a church would cost $125,000 while the down payment on the manse would account for an additional $25,000. These were the costs for each new congregation established. The committee was clear that this was a significant financial investment: "Some of the financial requirement can be met by redirecting the use of existing budgets. But the acceptance of our church extension goal as a priority of our Church requires additional funds."[56]

The committee laid out its vision as to how this would be implemented. There needed to be "incentive grants" for presbyteries. Presbyteries needed to find ways to finance these projects, such as "releasing established presbytery capital funds" or getting grants from existing congregations, that fell under their authority. The Board of World Mission, it was suggested, needed to be able to "budget for capital expenditures" and it was noted that the church growth committee was requesting the Administrative Council find a way for the mission board to receive $300,000 a year for the next five years in order to provide for "capital costs related to new church development." This was to be reviewed annually, in order to ensure that it was adequate to establish the new congregations (three per year) that the national church had committed to establishing from its own funds.[57] The denomination was in essence being asked to make this not only a priority but the major priority of its work over the next five years.[58]

What was surprising, given the amount of energy the Committee on Church Growth to Double in the Eighties had given to the centrality of church extension, was to see no significant statements on church extension in its report to the 1984 General Assembly. That report focused instead on other important issues, such as evangelism, lay ministry, a task force on ministry in metropolitan areas, and the committee's research findings. The committee continued to do important work in various areas related to helping the denomination deal with its situation (numerical decline) and work to reverse these trends. Yet the focus on church extension as a vital solution seemed to disappear. Why? The Administrative Council and the denomination had worked to provide the funds that would be needed. One possibility would be that, having named the importance of church extension as vital to church growth, the committee now felt its task was done. It was now up to the presbyteries and to the Board of World Mission to implement what it had advocated. Was there enough money? Was the analysis of the church growth committee accurate? In the push to establish new congregations, were wise decisions made as to where those congregations were established? A detailed examination of all of the congregations established at this time would be necessary to answer these questions. What is clear is that the church growth committee and the denomination failed to take seriously how different Canada was religiously in the early 1980s from what it had been in the 1950s. Those reporting "no religion" on the Canadian census in 1981 had risen to 8 per cent of the Canadian population, a dramatic growth in twenty-years.[59] Canadian Presbyterian membership had declined and now stood lower than it had in 1945 (see figure 10.1). Serious consideration was given to none of these factors, just as this crucial reality had not significantly altered how those responsible for church extension had done their work prior to the intervention of the church growth committee. Build it and they will come. This might have worked in the 1950s. It largely did. This was no longer the case by the 1980s, something that all of those involved in establishing new congregations in this period conveniently ignored.

EVALUATIONS AND CRITIQUES

Church extension was centralized in the national offices in 1963, believing that such centralization was necessary. Central planning was good. Costs needed to be more efficiently managed. All these reasons contributed to the decision and one can understand the rationale. Under this new system, Canadian Presbyterians continued to build congregations. The pace may have slowed but costs were increasing. It would be hard to argue that presbyteries left to their own would have been able to do a better job. At the same time, it is also hard to argue that centralizing church extension solved some of the challenges of church extension. Consolidation of congregations and the closing of weak urban and suburban congregations remained a challenge. The denomination continued to offer support. The denomination also continued to build smaller congregations. If sites were more carefully chosen, the preference for neighbourhood churches as opposed to larger churches serving more extensive areas continued. Presbyterians built a lot of churches, many of them smaller, in the 1950s and early 1960s. They continued, even after the appointment of a national coordinator, to build neighbourhood churches. The soaring costs of buildings – and it is important to remind ourselves that it was the congregation that largely paid for the building – tended to encourage smaller, and sometimes less well-constructed, buildings.

There were voices that called for the denomination to do things differently. Critics were always suggesting better ways in which church extension should be done. One of the most damning critiques was provided as part of the report in 1971 of the Board of Evangelism and Social Action on membership decline (discussed in chapter 6). No evidence was provided, but the report provided a stinging critique of how the denomination had gone about new church development:

> It has been stated that our Church Extension policy has not been true to the New Testament pattern of starting in the homes of the people with a group of believers. Instead elders have been suborned from other congregations and we have established charges of twenty or sixty people. New elders and managers were elected who were barely or not Christians; buildings were erected and people were saddled with large debts. The net results were congregations who had to learn what it meant to be a community of faith and as the financial burdens became greater, focus was upon maintenance and not Christian mission. This turning inward meant an inevitable shrinkage in numbers.[60]

The report was circulated to the General Assembly but was not printed in the minutes of the General Assembly. In an unusual move, a motion was passed that removed this section from the report; there is thus a very interesting blank place of the *Acts and Proceedings* in 1971 where this paragraph should be.[61] The paragraph, with commentary, was published in January 1972 as a special edition of *Presbyterian Comment*. But was this how the denomination did church extension in the 1950s and early 1960s? It is not self-evident that it was, nor do most accounts of successful congregations being established in that period (see chapter 2) support this narrative. The centralization of church extension brought change yet it is still not clear that the specific critique offered was valid. Almost a decade later, the Committee on Church Growth to Double in the Eighties also criticized, not how church extension had been done, but that more congregations had not been built.

Criticizing church extension and how it was done is easy. Understanding how it was done is much harder. This is true not only of the Presbyterian Church in Canada but of other denominations in Canada and in the United States. There are local studies that have been conducted, but no serious study of how an individual denomination built new congregations as suburbs grew around major and minor metropolitan areas has been attempted.[62] The overview given here and in a previous chapter is unique. What it demonstrates was the transformation of the Presbyterian Church in Canada as it built these new congregations, moving from a denomination of large downtown churches in the major cities, to one stronger in the suburbs and weaker in the central urban areas. Major urban area churches did not disappear. But the number of them, and the number of large major urban churches, did decrease. Where the denomination gained strength were in new areas of Toronto, Ottawa, Montreal, Vancouver, Hamilton, and many other smaller cities. Church extension successfully followed Presbyterians as they moved out into the suburbs and new housing developments in smaller cities and towns. These congregations became central to the ongoing work of the denomination. Whether these congregations were established under local direction (1945–63) or coordinated by the denomination (1963–85), they largely succeeded. Centralization brought clearer policies and provided different kinds of resources. The success of each venture, however, remained largely with the individuals who attended these congregations and the ministers who led them. Church extension in this period, locally or centrally directed, was largely a success. What the denomination failed to consider adequately as time went on was the changing religious nature of Canada. The denomination did not adjust enough to the decreasing religiosity of Canadians. They continued to imagine, as the Committee on Church Growth to Double in the Eighties exemplified, that if you build it, they will come. By 1985 this was no longer the case. Canadian Presbyterians failed to see this.

8

Contesting the Place of Women

Decision? What Decision?

"Perfume in the pulpit." "Muting the Trumpet." *Time* magazine's 17 June 1966 Canadian edition managed to cover a remarkable number of stereotypes in its brief article reporting the decision of the Presbyterian Church in Canada to ordain women in 1966. The "female crusade" had taken place in a "cheerless St. Andrew's Church." The "feminist cause" began, the article suggested, when "God created Eve as an afterthought." St Paul and John Knox were referenced as oppositions that needed to be overcome, the latter for his pamphlet "The First Blast of the Trumpet Against the Monstrous Regiment of Women." One clergyman, called a "male supremacist," was portrayed as quoting Paul "gleefully." His reading of scripture was why this man opposed the decision. An elder supporting the decision was portrayed as dismissing scripture and arguing instead that it is "what we think that counts." Even when Marion Webster, the recent female graduate profiled in the segment, noted she had not yet decided whether or not she would seek ordination, this was turned into a stereotype: she was "exercising a familiar feminine prerogative."[1] These stereotypes distorted what had happened at so many levels. The church had not "muted" Knox. They had consulted other theological voices instead, notably Calvin, and more recent Reformed voices like Karl Barth. The church had neither dismissed nor ignored St Paul but had attempted to hear what it determined was the entire witness of scripture. Marion Webster was not alone in her year: three other women had graduated from Knox College in 1966.[2] *Time* was accurate on one thing: Canada's third largest Protestant denomination now ordained women. An important decision had been made. The immediate impact of the decision was not a possible female ministerial candidate, but women who quickly became elders in their congregations.

Over the next decade the church continued to consider the changing place of women both within society as a whole and within the church. Large issues such as women moving into the workplace (including a minister's wife) and the women's liberation movement were discussed.[3] Smaller issues included the difficulties of having two different women's organizations at the congregational level, and the challenge to traditional etiquette that more women elders at the General Assembly was presenting.[4] It had been the tradition that the Assembly rose when a woman was present; now that women were present in larger numbers, what was the Assembly to do? The editor of the *Presbyterian Record* noted that there were "seven women commissioners" present that year (1971) and wondered "what will happen when there were seventy of them?"[5] This was not stated as a negative, but more a pondering as to how the General Assembly and all the church courts would need to change. This also reflects the reality that it was the ordination of women as elders, serving in local congregations, and eventually as representatives to presbytery, synod, and General Assembly, where the changes made in 1966 were finding the strongest traction in the early 1970s. Women in church courts were more common and becoming a larger portion of those courts. Women were also becoming ministers, but at a slower rate. The denominational magazine chose to profile two of these women in the middle of the 1970s. Shirley Jeffrey, the first woman to be ordained, was an obvious choice. She had now been ordained for eight years and was serving in her second charge, a two-point ministry at Port Carling and Torrance, Ontario.[6] The Reverend Nan St Louis was not as obvious a choice. While she was also serving a multi-point rural charge in Ontario, she was not only married but expecting a second child.[7] Both profiles were positive; intriguingly, each of the profiles raised the issue of women's liberation with the respective ministers. Jeffrey dismissed the movement, suggesting that was not how she thought of herself. Instead, she saw herself as called by God to ministry: "If God calls you, your womanhood comes through in what you do. I would like to see more women and men in the ministry. There is a real need, and God calls people who are willing to do his work."[8] Nan St Louis also rejected the cultural understanding of women's liberation, insisting instead that her "liberation comes from my submission to God's will and to my husband as the spiritual head of the house."[9] Neither woman was presented as a threat, but rather as a devoted minister.

Yet not all of those in the denomination would have been supportive of these changes or positive to a woman, however devout, being in a position of leadership. As noted in chapter 4, ministers who opposed the ordination of women to the eldership could simply work with their sessions to see that no women were elected as elders in their congregations. Women ministers posed a different challenge. The denomination had made the decision in 1966 to open the eldership and ministry to women; yet advocacy, let alone enforcement, had been lax. Indeed, the denomination had continued to admit into ministry those who disagreed with the 1966 decision. D.A. Codling later noted that the Presbytery of East Toronto licensed and ordained him in 1970 even though it was known "by some members of the court who disagreed with him" that he was opposed to the ordination of women.[10] Such a practice, however common it may have been, was designed to create conflict, particularly as more women moved into ministry. And from the mid-1970s on more women were studying in theological colleges and becoming ministers. What had once been a rarity – an occasional, isolated woman who those opposed to women in ministry could ignore or even bully during her theological training – had grown to become a significant cohort within each of the theological colleges.[11] Conflict was on the horizon.

This chapter will explore in detail the controversy that developed in 1979, and then continued with great intensity over the next few years, related to the place of women in the denomination. Conflict occurred because the denomination had allowed discrimination against women, in particular those wishing to be ministers, despite the decision to allow women to be ordained in 1966. Claims of "liberty of conscience" hijacked the issue and altered the debate completely. Not only did those opposing women in ministry claim the right to disagree with the denomination, they attempted to recast the 1966 decision as voluntary and giving permission rather than a decision that had changed the doctrine and laws of the denomination. To understand what happened it is necessary to begin with the original complaints by students at Presbyterian College, Montreal, against active discrimination in how they were placed upon graduation. We will then turn to consider the novel claim made for "liberty of conscience" when a student for ministry from the Presbytery of East Toronto was turned down because of his stated conviction that he would not participate in the ordination of a woman. This became a major controversy and attempts at two General Assemblies to resolve it failed. A separate task force was created, and its report and the recommendations within it will be considered carefully. The issue was resolved in 1982 with the denomination affirming the 1966 decision, but not without a further deepening of the divisions that already existed within the denomination.

THE MONTREAL MEMORIAL AND 1979 GENERAL ASSEMBLY

In early 1979 a crisis developed, centered at Presbyterian College in Montreal, that exposed the ongoing active discrimination against women. At that time all graduating students were required to take a placement under the Ordained Missionary (OM) appointment system in order to be ordained and thus eligible for employment.[12] While graduating students were allowed to indicate three possible choices from a common list, not all of the choices were available to everyone: female students were restricted in which of these congregations they might be placed (something that did not apply to the male graduating students). In essence there were two lists: a smaller one for everyone, and one that had additional choices exclusively for the men. The students at Presbyterian College objected to this process. A telegram and petition were sent to the Superintendents of Mission of the denomination on 2 March 1979 protesting the "prejudice experienced by women in the appointment process." The petition was signed by thirty-five members of the Presbyterian College community (recent graduates, students) and three professors – twenty-five men and thirteen women in total.[13] A follow-up letter was sent from the Presbyterian College students on 6 March after the appointments to OM placements had been made. They requested another meeting with the mission superintendents who were each responsible for the placement in his (they were all male) region and a "review of possible appointments with reference to sex." In an important follow-up step, this issue was raised at the Presbytery of Montreal at its 13 March meeting.[14] In response to the presentation the presbytery forwarded a memorial to the General Assembly raising issues about the "Place of Women in the Church." This memorial argued that, despite the fact "the ordination of women to the eldership and to the ministry was enacted into the law of the church" at the 1966 General Assembly, women continued to experience "discrimination and prejudice at all levels of church life." The text of the memorial detailed the denomination's decision and goal to uphold equality of men and women. The church had decided this after careful study. The General Assembly in 1965 had sent this down to the presbyteries under the Barrier Act, the majority of the presbyteries had supported it, and it had then passed at the next Assembly and was thus "enacted into the law of the church in 1966."[15] Reality, the memorial noted, had not caught up with what the church had decided. Thirteen years later women in and entering ministry were "experiencing discrimination": "They encounter it in 'jokes' and crude remarks; in examining committees who ask them if they would not be happier at home rather than being ordained; in congregations who object to their appointment only because they are women: from interim moderators who allow that to happen; from presbyters who do not reach out to educate their own congregations; from boards who do not apply the law with equity."[16] As a remedy, the memorial called for education to remind everyone of what the church had decided, a change in attitudes (both related to women as ministers and women as ruling elders), and finally, a "modification of the church's language and terminology, both oral and written, on all church bodies, so as not to be exclusive of women." Particular attention was drawn to church law (the *Book of Forms*), worship (the *Book of Common Order*), and hymnody (the *Book of Praise*).[17] Memorial 1 from the Presbytery of Montreal was received by the General Assembly.[18] A special committee was named by the moderator to study the issues raised in the memorial and report to the next General Assembly. The committee was appointed with Irene Dickson as convenor, a male and a female minister, and a male and a female elder, who would serve alongside representatives of each of the theological colleges, the Board of Ministry, and the Board of World Mission.[19] The Senate of Presbyterian College, in its 1979 report, also raised this issue directly: "There are some congregations applying to Board of World Mission for [OM] appointments which specify that they do not wish to have a woman appointed as their minister. Discrimination exists and steps have not been taken to educate our congregations and to eliminate this discrimination and denial of the opportunity for women to exercise their calling and gifts of ministry."[20]

The issue of the active discrimination faced by women in the church, particularly those moving into ministry, was an issue at the 1979 General Assembly.[21] Despite this the spotlight rapidly shifted to the Presbytery of East Toronto, and away from female candidates for ministry to one specific male candidate. The Board of World Mission had appointed this candidate, Daniel MacDougall, to an OM placement and he was ready to be ordained.[22] Because he had not done his education at one of the two denominational colleges, MacDougall had been required to appear before the Board of Education. That board recommended in its report that he move to the next step and be taken "on trials for license subject to the usual stipulations."[23] It was all seemingly routine. The presbytery now needed to act.

A CASE OF CONSCIENCE

The May meeting of the Presbytery of East Toronto had granted the committee responsible for students permission to take MacDougall on his trials for license. The committee was also given authority to approve them. The General Assembly met the first week of June. The examination for trials for license took place at a special meeting on 12 June.[24] The meeting with the committee did not go well. It was reported at the next presbytery meeting, 26 June, that the committee had not sustained the trials for license; in other words, the candidate had failed and could not move on to be licensed, was not eligible to be ordained, and ultimately could not serve in ministry in the Presbyterian Church in Canada. No reasons were recorded in the minutes. The clerk of presbytery noted that he had received a letter from MacDougall, indicating that he would be "appealing the decision concerning his trial for license." The Rev. Ed McKinlay, the candidate's minister, also made it clear that he would ask the presbytery to reconsider its actions at a later meeting of presbytery.[25]

The issues behind this unexpected turn of events became clearer when the candidate's session, Bridlewood Presbyterian Church, met on 5 September. The session approved a letter to the presbytery arguing why this candidate from their congregation should be approved:

> Daniel MacDougall has stated that he is willing to be bound by the Ordination Vows of our Church which he accepts without any reservation whatsoever. His only wish is to serve Jesus Christ in our Church and be subject to its teaching and standards in accordance with Holy Scripture.
>
> His reticence regarding the Ordination of Women is one which, on the basis of his understanding of Scripture, he shares with many others in our Church, Bridlewood Session submits that since the Ordination of Women is not of the essence of the Gospel, liberty of conscience be granted to those who dissent from this view.[26]

The letter requested that the student be licensed. This was forwarded to the presbytery for the 11 September meeting. The presbytery moved *in camera*. The minutes of presbytery reveal very little; it is from the November 1979 *Presbyterian Record* that we learn that it was a close vote (50/47).[27] The presbytery affirmed the decision of the committee.[28] At the October meeting, it was agreed to forward the student's appeal to the next highest church court, the Synod of Toronto and Kingston.[29]

The issue of "liberty of conscience" was first raised in the session's letter to the presbytery. This phrase, "liberty of conscience," came to frame the debate at the time and has persisted as how the denomination remembers these events. What has been forgotten is how novel this particular understanding of the term was. When Canadian Presbyterians used the phrase "liberty of conscience" or the related phrase "liberty of opinion," they were normally using it in a very specific and limited sense. It related specifically to the way in which one subscribed or agreed to the Westminster Confession of Faith, noting two specific areas where different views were permitted (see chapter 5). What was argued here – and the novelty of this needs to be stressed – was that an individual should be ordained as a minister while disagreeing with a doctrinal decision of the denomination. It was also claimed that the decision to ordain women was unimportant and not of the "essence of the gospel."

When the appeal of the presbytery's decision to deny licensing MacDougall was heard at the Synod of Toronto and Kingston, these claims were restated and additional claims were added. The committee established by the synod to deal with the appeal tried to have it both ways.[30] When the committee's recommendations were presented before the entire synod, the synod agreed with the committee that the presbytery had acted appropriately but rejected the suggestion of the committee that the candidate should nevertheless be licensed. Nine members of synod dissented from the decision. Some offered reasons for their dissent.[31] Liberty of conscience became one common theme. One dissenter, C. MacInnis argued against "the implied restriction and virtual extinction from practice of Sec.II of Chap.XX of the W.C.F. re: Liberty of Conscience which this decision renders."[32] In his dissent, A. Dallison protested that the decision had "in effect placed the matter of the ordination of women in the category of the fundamentals of the faith, on which matter no liberty of opinion may be held by office-bearers" in the denomination. Liberty of conscience was raised as a battle standard. But as one dissenter, D.A. Codling, quickly noted, "of course we cannot allow liberty in those matters which are essential to the life of the church." He proceeded to catalogue what he considered essential. The Codling dissent was very long. It included arguments that this decision "illegally adds to the law and practice of our church" and that as "many loyal and proven" ministers and elders held similar views they were "indict[ed]" by this decision.[33] Many of these reasons would reappear in the debates that followed. And those debates would follow: the synod passed a carefully worded overture to General Assembly asking for direction on these issues given that the "issue has been raised."[34] MacDougall now had the right to appeal the synod's judgement to General Assembly.[35]

It was now clear that two issues were going to be presented to the General Assembly in 1980. One was the report of the Committee on the Place of Women, created to respond to the issues of discrimination faced by women in the church. The second matter was the appeal of the Synod of Toronto and Kingston's decision not to take a candidate for ministry on trials for license. Those attending Assembly were well aware of the issues prior to June 1980, as they had already been raised in the pages of the denominational magazine throughout the year. In the May issue prior to Assembly, the editor James Dickey noted this was one of the two important issues coming before the annual gathering. (The other issue was church growth.) Dickey argued the denomination needed to gain clarity. He observed that one of the underlying issues was the different understandings of how the Bible should be read. He also noted the challenge of allowing too much to individual conscience. These were significant issues, one the editor argued needed be dealt with.[36] Some of the issues had been rehearsed before Assembly met; it is also clear that issues around "liberty of conscience" had already pushed aside a key issue raised at the 1979 General Assembly – the active discrimination against women.

CONTROVERSY: THE 1980 GENERAL ASSEMBLY

The 1980 Assembly dealt with these two distinct issues. The Committee on the Place of Women had done research, including a questionnaire, and reported its findings: it considered attitudes towards women elders to be generally positive, but noted that a minority of responses showed a very negative attitude to women as ministers from some who did not believe that the Bible allowed such a position.[37] The committee suggested more education was one way to respond to the reluctance. It noted the key role played by interim moderators (the ministers in charge when a congregation was looking to call a new minister). One challenge was the fact that some interim moderators would not consider female candidates. The continuing use of language which excluded women in the church was also noted, with suggestions for how this might be addressed. Education was one proposed solution. The committee made a series of recommendations that arose from its findings.[38] Having done its task, the committee asked that it be dissolved (the normal practice). All these recommendations passed when presented to Assembly: indeed, a motion related to interim moderators was strengthened to require them to give "equal," not just "fair" treatment to female candidates. An additional motion on inclusive language also passed that suggested everyone in the church be "sensitive to their own use of exclusive language" in all situations.[39] No dissents were registered on any of these motions. Reading this report in isolation from what else happened at the 1980 General Assembly, one would assume that the denomination was moving forward seeking ways to strengthen the place of women in the church, in particular women in ministry. But in fact, this was not the case at all.

The appeal of Daniel MacDougall was the second matter to appear before the Assembly in 1980. Hearing an appeal related to a decision made by a lower court is a fairly standard matter under presbyterian polity. The General Assembly acts in effect as a supreme court. What was unusual in this case was that multiple overtures had arrived alongside the appeal. In addition to the overture from the Synod of Toronto and Kingston, there were overtures from the candidate's session, from another church and a presbytery, as well as a memorial from an individual, all speaking directly to this case.[40] During the Assembly a special committee was created to deal with these four overtures and the memorial. The appeal also referred to this same special committee that was given permission to meet during Assembly.[41] When it reported on its deliberations, the report on the overtures was brief and to the point. The special committee affirmed the decision taken by the denomination in 1966. It declared that "our theology of ministry has since 1966 included both women and men in the Order of Ministry of the Word and Sacrament," and that this was an essential part of the doctrine of the church that could not be dismissed. Liberty of conscience, the committee argued, did not apply in this case: "the ordination of women clearly belongs to this category of doctrine."[42] The committee thus concluded that participation at ordinations was not an option, but was required of all in the church. They then moved from the principle to the specific practical issue before them. The committee did allow an exception in the case of MacDougall and instructed the presbytery to license him (the necessary action required if he was to be ordained by a different presbytery). No further exceptions were to be made. The special committee finally determined that those within the denomination who struggled with this issue might be "excused from participation" in the ordination of women for a period of ten years as long as they cooperated with all ministers and abstained from "prejudicing their people against the election of women to the ruling or teaching eldership."[43] These motions were printed in the *Presbyterian Record*, which noted that, although there was debate, they passed by standing vote.[44] While the vote was a standing vote – not by secret ballot or a recorded vote – there were dissents to the motion. There were also attempts to have the decision reconsidered.[45] While it seemed a good idea to deal with these overtures during the Assembly, the resulting dissents spoke of deep divisions and came from both sides of the issue. Some dissented without submitting their reasons. Others gave lengthy arguments as to how the church had erred, both at this Assembly, and previously. Some objected to the ten-year provision, seeing it as a compromise. Others argued that the decision in 1966 was, in essence, flawed. The special committee was reconvened in order to answer these dissents.[46] The overtures sent to support the appeal dominated the discussion: the appeal of the synod's decision itself was almost forgotten. A separate report specifically referencing the appeal by D. Codling on behalf of MacDougall was dealt with during a later sitting of Assembly. The sole recommendation was that the action taken in terms of the overtures was the "answer to the complaint." There were no dissents to this particular recommendation.[47] The result of attempting to deal with this while Assembly was meeting pleased neither side. There were clearly two basic disagreements evident in the debates at General Assembly in 1980. First, there were deep disagreements (from those on all sides) with the proposed resolution to the situation that emerged, in particular with the timeline of ten years. But the second, deeper issue, was the fundamental one of whether the church was correct in 1966 in declaring that ordination (elders and ministers) was open to all, regardless of whether they were male or female.

CONTROVERSY: THE 1981 ASSEMBLY

The General Assembly in 1981 repeated the experience of the 1980 Assembly. This time there was no report from the Committee on the Place of Women in the denomination as that committee had, somewhat ironically, been disbanded in 1980; nor was there an appeal of a decision from a lower court. But there had been an explosion of overtures, memorials, and petitions responding in different ways to the decisions made at the 1980 General Assembly. There were twenty-six overtures, sixteen memorials, and three petitions presented related to this issue.[48] Of the overtures that took a clear side, five supported the decision of the 1980 General Assembly while eight were opposed.[49] One overture was particularly strong in its wording. The congregation of St Andrew's, Virden stated that it was "opposed to being deprived after 1990 of a ministry in harmony with our convictions"; it was also opposed "to the present restriction being placed upon ministers which forbids them to speak out before their people against the election of women to the ruling and teaching eldership"; and, after listing a series of other objections, they suggested that the General Assembly reconsider its decision and refer it to the presbyteries "in the hope of producing a more mature and adequate decision." The optimism that presbyteries might do as the congregation wished seemed ill placed, as the Presbytery of Brandon did not support this overture, but simply passed it on without comment.[50] All of these petitions, memorials, and overtures became a major issue before the 1980 General Assembly.

In response, the 1981 General Assembly appointed a committee representative of the various opinions to respond to these overtures. Again, the committee met during Assembly and then reported. It detailed nine themes in the overtures. Many dealt with process and the seeming confusion (the ten-year deadline, uncertainty for candidates for ministry) that the decisions in 1980 had generated. The final two themes outlined the divisions within the denomination; on the one hand there were those concerned that women not be held back from service, while on the other hand there were those concerned about the possibility that "qualified men" might be rejected based on "conscientious scruple on this issue."[51] Based on the reality of these divisions, the committee recommended a task force (which would become the Task Force on Liberty of Conscience) be established to look at this issue and report back to the next General Assembly. The committee also expressed its pastoral concern for three groups: women who had been ordained or were preparing to be ordained as ministers and elders; men "whose interpretation of the biblical and doctrinal literature" has led them to not want to participate in the ordination of women and who were thus appealing for "liberty of conscience"; and, thirdly, for young people seeking a call to ministry amidst the uncertainty. The recommendation to establish a Task Force was clear and acceptable. It was in trying to deal with pressing issues in the meantime that controversy again erupted. The committee tried to go down the middle: it removed the ten year restriction (the period by which everyone had to come in line with the denominational policy on the ordination of women) while at the same time insisting that, until any provisions were made in church law that would allow those with "conscientious reservations" a way "to ease their crisis of conscience" everyone should participate fully in the ordination of women (though this was not expressed as clearly as it might have been).[52] The committee directed candidates for ordination or reception into the denomination to "study the Preamble and Ordination Questions as a directive in their preparation" for service in the denomination. Even within the committee there was dispute about these recommendations, with three members noting they found this went too far in potentially allowing "exemption" which was not permitted under the law of the church, and one member suggesting the committee had not gone far enough in allowing for liberty of conscience, as was permitted in other Protestant denominations.[53] The debate was long and confusing.[54] An unusual step was taken in which a pastoral statement by the Clerks of Assembly (who were responsible for the overall operation of Assembly) was read and then included in the minutes.[55] It was something of an anticlimax when the convenor of the newly appointed Task Force, Margaret Taylor, had a statement read to the Assembly asking the church to pray for the Task Force, affirming that all in the denomination were needed and that "God's Spirit will bring reconciliation to the Body if we will allow it."[56] The creation of the Task Force was the major accomplishment of the 1981 Assembly.

In 1980 and again in 1981, the denomination attempted unsuccessfully to have the issue resolved at the national gathering. In each of these years the normal process was followed with an issue that was deemed urgent: a committee was established which met during the Assembly and then reported back to Assembly with a suggested resolution. Yet each time the proposed solutions failed to resolve the issue and divisions only intensified. It is important to recognize, alongside these official debates, Canadian Presbyterians fought the issue out in the denominational magazine, the *Presbyterian Record*.[57] Individual congregations, presbyteries, and even individuals (or groups of individuals) made their voices heard through the flood of overtures, memorials, and petitions that were directed to the General Assembly. These different forums were interconnected: what was reported or expressed in the *Record* influenced the language of the overtures; the actions taken at one Assembly were reported and led to more overtures and renewed debate. During the 1981 Assembly it became clear that the divisions in the denomination were too deep for this to be resolved by a committee meeting during Assembly. Attempts to deal with the immediate issues only created greater consternation. The deeper issues needed to be confronted. These deeper issues were given to the Task Force.

REPORT OF THE TASK FORCE ON LIBERTY OF CONSCIENCE, 1982

The "Task Force on Liberty of Conscience as it pertains to the Ordination of Women" was appointed at the 1981 Assembly, chaired by Margaret Taylor, and represented the theological diversity of the church. There were twenty members: seven (including the convenor) were women. The Task Force met in person three times (seven days in total) over a six-month period seeking "unanimity." At the third meeting a minority report signed by six members was received related to the issue of active participation in the ordination service. After this issue of "exemption" from participation was raised, the committee met for a further two days to discuss this central issue. The result was a report with recommendations, which was followed by a minority report. The committee also published appendices of supportive material.[58] The committee's report was carefully structured. It considered the context of the denomination's decision to ordain women, the denomination's doctrine of ministry, the concept of liberty of conscience and specifically how this related to the ordination of women, and the issue of ecclesiastical authority, before turning to the issue of whether individuals were permitted to exempt themselves from attending any minister's ordination. This was followed by recommendations.

The Biblical basis on which the church made its decision in 1966 to ordain women as ministers and elders was affirmed – indeed the "entire task force" declared itself in agreement that this "corporate decision" needed to be respected. As there were different Biblical texts

Figure 8.1 Margaret Taylor, Presbyterian Congress, 1971. Taylor was a leading Presbyterian lay-woman. She led the denomination's Task Force on Liberty of Conscience related to the ordination of women that reported to the General Assembly in 1982.

that could be referenced there had been a "need for clarification." The committee noted that "quoting text against text" did not resolve anything, but instead concluded: "while recognizing the diversity of witness in Scripture the Church arrived at a decision concerning the ordination of women, a decision based on the intention of the whole Biblical witness and the revelation of the gospel of Jesus Christ heard in Scripture." The value of this "corporate interpretation" was strongly affirmed.[59] The committee then turned to consider the denomination's doctrine of ministry, with specific references being made to the Westminster Confession of Faith and to the theology of John Calvin and then concluded: "It is into the one ministry of Christ that men and women are called and ordained by the Lord through the Spirit in the Church, and they have no ministry of their own which they individually may define."[60] This theme of the corporate nature of ministry continued as the committee discussed the ordination of ministers and elders. The Task Force was clear: "Since 1966 the Presbyterian Church in Canada has affirmed that the ministry of Christ in all its aspects and offices is exercised by both men and women. Theologically and spiritually speaking, there are not male and female ministers or elders, there are only ministers or elders. The Church spiritually, does not ordain a female or a male, it ordains elders and ministers!"[61] The Task Force noted that this had been reaffirmed by actions of the two previous General Assemblies. The distinction being made by those who argued for the right to not participate at the ordination of anyone based on their sex was thus rejected. To disagree with the ordination of anyone (in this case based on sex) was to challenge the denomination's understanding of "our Church's doctrine of ordination."[62] There was only one ministry. The consequences of this were made clear: "Were the Church to legislate exemptions for elders or ministers from sharing in the ministry of ordaining women it would destroy the oneness of the office of elder and minister and divide them into two orders – one order that ordains women and one order that does not."[63] The committee rejected this as bringing disharmony to the church and as contrary to the denomination's understanding of its doctrine. Having explored the issue of Scripture and doctrine, the Task Force then turned to the specific issue of liberty of conscience.

The Task Force focused its discussion of liberty of conscience on chapter 20 of the Westminster Confession of Faith. As it noted, this "statement on 'liberty of conscience' is unique" in the development of Reformed confessions in the sixteenth and seventeenth centuries. It argued the authors "certainly did not envisage the individual minister being at liberty to exercise ministry as he or she determines in the light of conscience."[64] It then turned to what it considered an analogous situation, the sacrament of baptism, and concluded that as long as the church practiced the baptism of infants, every minister, regardless of personal conscience, was "obligated to participate" in (more accurately, lead) that sacrament. This being noted, the Task Force turned to explore this issue related to the specific issue of the ordination of women. The church had decided in 1966 that women could be ordained: "This equality of status granted to women is now entrenched in the law and doctrine of the Church, and demands a corresponding equality of treatment in the whole life and work of the Church. This precludes all forms of discrimination and any false distinctions based solely on the sex of the candidate."[65] In case this was not clear, the point was hammered home: no provision was made in 1966 for "exemption" from participation, no one in 1966 who dissented from the decision had requested any such exemption, nor had anyone requested this prior to 1980. After stating that any such request would undermine the decision taken in 1966, the committee noted in a parenthetical comment that "suggestions sometimes made that the 1966 legislation was somehow only 'permissive' or 'enabling' have no legal sanction whatsoever."[66] A clear course of action was already possible, it was suggested, for anyone who disagreed and wished to "assuage one's conscience before God" – namely, one could register one's dissent. This could and should be done, but one was then not allowed to "opt out" or seek the right to do so, for they were "seeking the 'freedom to disobey' the doctrine and polity of the church."[67] This point was made in several different ways, but the Task Force argued that any "refusal to participate," given that this was the law of the church, was detrimental to the "authority of the Church and results in a form of ecclesiastical anarchy."[68] Dissent was allowed. One could attempt to reverse decisions made by Church courts. But any such change "must be sought by means of lawful process through petitions and overtures."[69] Chapter 20 of the Westminster Confession of Faith, the Task Force was arguing, was not applicable in this situation.

The Task Force's report suggested that there was consensus on all these matters. Where the committee divided was whether it was possible to give permission to not participate at the ordination of female ministers or female elders. It was here that the minority divided from the majority. As mentioned above, the report of the committee stated that by the third regular meeting of the committee, it was evident that there would be dissents from the report on this issue. These divergent views can be seen respectively in the report itself and in the minority report that followed. The committee (seemingly everyone supported these) laid out seven points it believed were crucial. First, it argued that providing any legislation or agreement which would allow people to not participate at an ordination would be "retreat" from what the church decided in 1966. Here the committee noted that no church it was aware of had retroactively allowed this exemption. It did note two denominations, the Reformed Church in America and the Anglican Church of Canada, which had allowed for exemptions "*at the time they enacted the original legislation* to ordain women," but argued that neither situation provided a positive model. Second, the committee argued that allowing exemptions would "cast doubt on the validity" of the ordinations of women that had already, or would, occur. The committee's third point was that allowing an exemption after sixteen years was contrary to, and dangerous to, the presbyterian approach to church law. The committee argued that not only would such an act "distort our doctrine of ministry" (fourth point), it would not bring peace to the denomination (fifth point). The committee then argued that such an exemption might specifically discriminate against women being elected as elders in congregations where the minister had asked for an exemption (sixth point), before making the concluding argument that such a step was unnecessary as there was already a mechanism to deal with one's conscience: dissent (seventh point). The committee quickly noted, "Dissent never permits non-participation."[70]

It was on this basis that the committee made its statement of affirmation and its recommendations. Four of the six affirmations were accepted by the majority and the minority. It was agreed that individuals had a right to their opinions and judgements, but that liberty of conscience was nonetheless not absolute. It was agreed that elders and ministers were "required to act in such a way that the equality of women with men in Christ and their access to a full and valid ministry" as either elders or ministers needed to be "recognized and upheld and neither denied nor prejudiced." Finally, it was agreed that anyone wishing to change church doctrine or practice needed to work through the courts of the church. There was disagreement, however, on the statement that dissent was the option for ministers and elders who wished to "liberate their conscience before God and all people" and that while there might be "freedom of belief" ministers and elders did not have freedom of action; they must attend all ordinations, regardless of the sex of the candidate. There was also some disagreement whether or not presbyteries had the "authority to grant permission to disobey church law and doctrine on the question of the ordination of women."[71]

The minority report provides rare insight into the position of those six members of the committee who could not agree on the issues related to exemptions.[72] Despite having seemingly signed on to the report, the minority challenged key points. They argued that church courts could be fallible. They reminded the church that there were different verses in scripture, and different ways of interpreting these (some of which might exclude women from "official teaching/ruling functions"), before opining: "This duality of the biblical data explains why divergent positions are held on this subject, and underlines the need to allow liberty of conscience in regard to mandatory participation in the ordination of women." The minority went on to argue that the 1966 decision was "permissive rather than prescriptive or proscriptive in character." In evidence of this, the minority made the rather unusual argument that this was so because the Assembly in 1966 "did not decree the disciplinary expulsion of ministers or elders holding conscientious reservations on the matter" nor did the denomination "preclude the ordination or reception of ministers sharing such reservations."[73] The minority also wondered if this current action was not creating a divisive course. They objected that the decision might preclude called men from serving in the denomination: "If it would be wrong to deny a woman called and endowed of the Lord an opportunity to serve, what makes it right to deny that same privilege to men solely on the grounds of their conscientious reservations on the subject under consideration? To disqualify them on this criterion alone not only deprives the Church of their consecrated skills but does despite [*sic*] to the Spirit who enlists and empowers for Christian ministry."[74] The minority made one final procedural objection before making its proposal: individuals could absent themselves from ordination services, as long as they stated their views when they entered a presbytery; promised to use "no unlawful means" to exclude women from various offices in the church; allowed presbytery to appoint a moderator *pro tem* (a temporary moderator) "to preside at such nominations, elections, ordinations, or inductions"; and finally, agreed "to cooperate with all ministers and elders in the work of the Church." The minority argued that this did not "retreat from the decision of 1966, nor challenge the authority of the Church," and would in the end "reverse the trend to polarization" in the denomination.[75] How this might have worked in practice was not explored, particularly the suggestion regarding a moderator *pro tem*. One assumes this would happen in a situation where an election of elders was taking place within a congregation where the minister disagreed with the ordination of women. It might also occur if that particular minister were moderator of presbytery and thus have a key role at the ordination of a woman into the ministry or the induction of a woman minister into a pastoral charge, but these details were not spelled out. Nor was it clear how a female elder (if elected) would then serve on a session with a minister who did not accept women elders. Finally, there is one small detail in the minority report that merits comment, as the cultural values influencing the attitudes expressed seem on display. Throughout the committee's report the convenor is referred to as "Mrs Margaret Taylor." In the opening of the minority report, while thanking her for her leadership, the minority refers to the convenor as "Mrs K. Denton Taylor."[76] This convention – with a woman not only taking her husband's surname but also being referred to by his given names – is cultural, not biblical. It was a telling choice.

DECISION AND DISSENT

Not surprisingly, the Task Force report was a key issue at the 1982 General Assembly. The divisions within the denomination that year are well remembered; at the same time, the content of the Task Force report itself and the agreement on so many issues is less well remembered. The existence of a minority report appended to the main report was unusual; in the end, the Assembly received only the majority report and defeated a later amendment to replace the majority report with the minority report. The report was debated extensively over two days and approximately three hours, with a full range of opinions being expressed. In the end the recommendations of the report were passed. Seventeen commissioners to the General Assembly registered their dissent. A Declaratory Act which clarified church law was also passed. It is important to pause and note this: what the Assembly believed itself to be doing was clarifying the implications of what had been passed in 1966, not creating any new doctrine or church law. The Declaratory Act stated that while all "already ordained and inducted" ministers and elders in the denomination had "freedom of belief on the question of the ordination of women" they did not have "freedom of action" and thus must participate in the ordination of women.[77]

Not everyone accepted this decision. Several overtures appeared after the 1982 General Assembly that continued to challenge the decisions of the denomination. Overture 7 to the 1983 General Assembly from Knox Church, Toronto, challenged whether the denomination had ruled correctly, citing the Westminster Confession of Faith's understanding of liberty of conscience as one of its arguments, a point echoed by overture 8 that same year from the Session of Cote de Neiges Church, Montreal.[78] Disagreement continued. At the same time, a novel development had occurred already during the course of the debate from 1979 to 1982. As Donald MacLeod has suggested, it was this debate over liberty of conscience which led to the formation of the Renewal Fellowship within the Presbyterian Church in Canada. Even as that organization moved, in MacLeod's words, "from reaction to renewal," an organization now existed outside of the courts and the committees of the church which represented one theological voice (evangelicals).[79] This was new within the post-union Canadian Presbyterian church. While there had been disagreements and different wings of the church, the creation of an organization inside the denomination which organized its constituency in this way had not been common. (The Caledon Contemporaries might be the only other example.) The denomination now had a permanent organized body reflecting one theological position.

WHY DID THIS HAPPEN THIRTEEN YEARS AFTER THE DECISION?

Why 1979? Why in this year did the Presbyterian Church in Canada, which had seemingly decided to accept the ordination of women thirteen years earlier, find itself embroiled in a major controversy? Was the request reasonable? Donald MacLeod, in his article on the origins of the Renewal Fellowship, suggests several reasons for the delay, including the reality that in 1966 many of the conservative orthodox were more concerned about the proposed new confession of faith than the issue of women's ordination, which they nonetheless opposed.[80] Jo-Ann Dickson drew attention to the increasing number of women moving into ministry in the late 1970s, and in particular the challenge that this created at the Mission Board given that all moving into congregational ministry needed to be placed under the Ordained Missionary appointment system. She documents the tensions between the Mission Board and the students of Presbyterian College (as discussed above) which led to a memorial coming to the 1979 General Assembly raising the issue of the discrimination women moving into ministry were facing.[81]

There were clearly factors within the denomination which led to the issue of the ordination of women – specifically to the ministry – becoming an issue in 1979. At the same time, it is worth noting that it was a pivotal year within the broader political context, not only in Canada but throughout Western nations. This was the historical moment when the cultural changes which began in the 1960s were being contested, sometimes very strongly.[82] New political figures were emerging who strongly disagreed with the values and attitudes that had emerged as a result of the 1960s and the direction in which their nation seemed to be heading. In Canada, Brian Mulroney represented a mild version of this: Margaret Thatcher in Great Britain and Ronald Reagan in the United States provide clearer evidence of this reaction. Thatcher was elected Prime Minister in 1979. Reagan was emerging in this year as one of the strongest contenders for the Republican nomination for President. Even more tellingly, it was in 1979 that the United States failed to ratify the Equal Rights Amendment (ERA) to the American Constitution. The ERA would have made men and women equal in terms of law. This seemed an innocuous idea and an important step forward when it was first proposed in 1972. Many individual States quickly ratified this amendment; however, as the decade progressed, opposition and backlash increased. Some States that had already ratified the ERA rescinded their previous decisions. By 1979 it was clear it would not pass. The ERA failed to receive the necessary approvals to be added to the constitution and thus died.[83]

This is important context for the debates within the Presbyterian Church in Canada. These debates were in society, in newspapers, and on television. Organizations were being formed challenging ideals of female equality. There was thus a conflict within culture: we should not be surprised to see debates of the broader culture reflected in the debates within the Presbyterian Church in Canada. Indeed, these broader cultural clashes are evident in Jim Dickey's reporting on the 1979 General Assembly, specifically as it relates to the issues of the place of women in society and the church. One minister who "had reservations of conscience about the ordination of women" spoke of feeling "singled out for pressure" and being "forced to affirm" more than he felt he could. The issue of inclusive language was also briefly noted.[84] These issues simmered beneath the surface. In 1982, the Board of Ministry noted in its report that priority should be given by the colleges "to the appointment of women (to the faculty) where candidates of equal qualifications are being considered." One critic was quoted as wondering what values were behind this: "Is it

Christ or women's lib'?"[85] Canadian Presbyterians were clearly aware of and influenced by the broader cultural debates on the place of women within society as a whole, not simply their place in the church.[86]

The controversy about "liberty of conscience" succeeded in obscuring the issue which began the debate. It is not clear that the issues of discrimination, first noted in the Montreal Memorial, were ever dealt with. It did become church policy that all interim moderators were not allowed to discriminate against female candidates. What is not clear is how many cases emerged where interim moderators were challenged or disciplined on this issue. Presbyteries did not intrude into congregations and demand that there be female elders elected. Congregations continued to have all male sessions. Some presbyteries remained exclusively male in their composition when it came to ministers. While clear decisions were made, the denomination did not go after those who objected (or even continued to defy the decision), and certainly not in the manner the minority report suggested might have or should have occurred after the 1966 decision.

The issue of discrimination being faced by women wishing to be ministers emerged in 1979. This would have been before the General Assembly in 1980, regardless of any other events. It is also clear that those opposed to the decision of the denomination in 1966 to ordain women as ministers and elders continued to act as if that decision had never been made. This was easy to do. The main impact of the decision in the years immediately following 1966 was on the local congregation. Women could now serve as elders on session; however, it was easy for sessions and ministers who did not accept the ordination of women to simply not allow for the election of women elders. This was self-evident. There had thus been no reason to request exemption or liberty of conscience in 1966. It might be challenging to have women elders at General Assembly or at presbytery meetings, but one might simply continue to address the court in the time-honoured way, "Fathers and brethren," thus ignoring those women present.[87] Active discrimination was tolerated – the obvious example being the Mission Board having one "list" of possible OM placements for male and female candidates, and one (larger) list for only male candidates. It was only as the number of female candidates for ministry grew, as it did in the later 1970s, that these practices came under greater and greater stress. With more women studying to be ministers and then entering the ministry, a crisis was seemingly inevitable. Those opposed could no longer pretend that the decision, at least as it applied to women as ministers, had never been made. There would be ordinations or inductions they might need to attend. Ignoring the decision made in 1966 and pretending it had never been made was becoming more and more difficult, if not impossible. This is one reason why in 1979 a crisis developed: liberty of conscience seems an inappropriate term to describe what occurred.

Did the Presbyterian Church in Canada remember the significance of its decision, in terms of doctrine and church law, of the 1966 decision to ordain women as both ministers and elders? The amnesia of some in the Presbyterian Church in Canada is something that needs to be recognized. Some clearly did forget. The 1980 General Assembly had to remind everyone that since 1966 the denomination's "theology of ministry" had included both women and men as those eligible to serve as ordained ministers.[88] The Task Force on Liberty of Conscience similarly made it clear that this was a doctrinal issue.[89] This was clearly stated and even restated: yet what is notable is how frequently those who disagreed either ignored it, claimed it was not the case, or otherwise dismissed what the denomination had decided. The clear statement made by Louis Fowler in 1955 that the reason the ordination of women needed to go down under the Barrier Act was that this was a change to the Westminster Standards, both in terms of doctrine and polity, seemed largely forgotten. The reality that this careful process had been followed was also not clearly remembered. The 1975 first edition of John Moir's recent history of the denomination, *Enduring Witness*, noted the decision in 1966 which passed the "desired legislation," but missed key details. Moir mentioned the recommendations of the Committee on the Place of Women in 1964 and that the proposals were sent down to the presbyteries. Moir recorded the results related to the ordination of women as elders in the informal poll the committee reported in 1965, but did not report the results on women as ministers (see table 4.2). Absent as well was any discussion of the decision in 1965 to send this matter down officially to the presbytery under the Barrier Act, or the positive results that were reported in 1966. Instead, Moir suggested Assembly had "delayed for one year" before the decision was made that "finally allowed women to enter into complete 'partnership' with men" in the life of the denomination.[90] In fact, the church had followed exactly the process that was required to change doctrine and polity. The history of the denomination's handling of the issue was incomplete and thus not helpful during these debates.

The Presbyterian Church in Canada was also not always good at updating what it believed in terms of doctrine. As was discussed in chapter 5, the denomination prided itself on its connections to the Westminster Confession of Faith. At the same time (see chapter 9) it had commented on, and fundamentally changed, aspects of its doctrinal understanding: notably, the church rejected the statements in its own doctrine that suggested the pope was the anti-Christ. But, this was not the case here. While the section in the 1977 *Book of Forms* on "Standards and Subscription" (chapter 8) did not make note of the fact that the church had decided women could be ordained as elders and ministers,[91] this was explicitly noted earlier in chapter 1, which laid out the denomination's doctrinal standards. Here, alongside references to the denomination's "Declaration of Faith Concerning Church and Nation" and the decision around Parallel Secondary Standards, it was stated unequivocally that the denomination had determined that "women are eligible" to be both elders and ministers (see figure 8.2). This was clearly expressed, as it had been in the 1970 edition.[92] Claims that the 1966 decisions were somehow only permissive strain credibility, given the reality that the denomination was clear in noting this change to its doctrine and polity.

Does everyone get to establish on what terms they wish to take their ordination vows? Those arguing for liberty of conscience on the issue of women ministers were in essence saying yes to this question. Those supporting the request continually asserted that this was all reasonable and not remarkably audacious. For example, in supporting Daniel MacDougall's request to be licensed and ordained, his home session stated the following: first, he was "willing to be bound by the Ordination vows of our Church which he accepts without any reservations whatsoever"; second, he was willing to "be subject to its [the denomination's] teaching and standards in accordance with the Holy Scripture"; but, third, he disagreed with the denomination on its stance on the "Ordination of Women." Since he believed this based on his personal understanding of scripture, and since others agreed with him, he should be allowed "liberty of conscience" on this issue.[93] It was all presented as a reasonable request, with some seeming confusion as to why it was not immediately conceded.

But this was not a reasonable request. Indeed, the combination of statements made in support of this by the session are nonsensical. The ordination vows taken from the 1977 *Book of Forms* which the

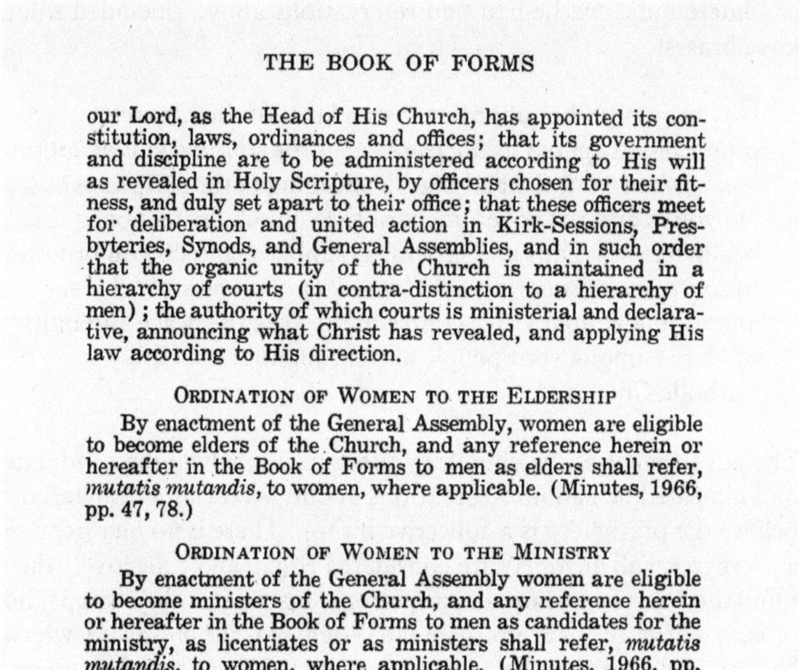

THE BOOK OF FORMS

our Lord, as the Head of His Church, has appointed its constitution, laws, ordinances and offices; that its government and discipline are to be administered according to His will as revealed in Holy Scripture, by officers chosen for their fitness, and duly set apart to their office; that these officers meet for deliberation and united action in Kirk-Sessions, Presbyteries, Synods, and General Assemblies, and in such order that the organic unity of the Church is maintained in a hierarchy of courts (in contra-distinction to a hierarchy of men); the authority of which courts is ministerial and declarative, announcing what Christ has revealed, and applying His law according to His direction.

ORDINATION OF WOMEN TO THE ELDERSHIP

By enactment of the General Assembly, women are eligible to become elders of the Church, and any reference herein or hereafter in the Book of Forms to men as elders shall refer, *mutatis mutandis*, to women, where applicable. (Minutes, 1966, pp. 47, 78.)

ORDINATION OF WOMEN TO THE MINISTRY

By enactment of the General Assembly women are eligible to become ministers of the Church, and any reference herein or hereafter in the Book of Forms to men as candidates for the ministry, as licentiates or as ministers shall refer, *mutatis mutandis*, to women, where applicable. (Minutes, 1966, pp. 47, 78.)

DECLARATION OF FAITH CONCERNING CHURCH AND NATION

For full text see Minutes, 1954, pp. 243-245.

PARALLEL SECONDARY STANDARDS

For full text see Minutes, 1962, pp. 288, 289.

2

Figure 8.2 At the beginning of the 1970 *Book of Forms* and the 1977 *Book of Forms* (pictured here), the section outlining the doctrine of the church included the decisions related to the ordination of women as elders and ministers. Pictured is the version in place when debate on women's ordination began in 1979 and continued through 1982. For reasons that remain unclear, these sections were removed from the 1981 edition.

candidate indicated he had "no reservations above" included some key phrases:

2 Do you accept the subordinate standards of this Church, promising to uphold its *doctrine under the continual illumination and correction* of the Holy Spirit speaking in the Scriptures?
3 Do you accept the government of the Church, by sessions, presbyteries, synods and general assemblies, and do you promise to *share in and submit yourself to all lawful oversight* therein, and to follow no divisive course but to seek the peace and unity of Christ among your people and throughout the Holy Catholic Church.[94]

The government of the church by presbyteries, which the candidate had indicated he had no reservations about, is crucial. Presbyterians believe the presbytery is a collective bishop. There is no hierarchy in a presbytery; all members are considered equal, and collectively they fulfill the role of a bishop. In an episcopal system it is the bishop who ordains all clergy. In the presbyterian system, it is the presbytery which has the exclusive right to ordain Ministers of Word and Sacrament. They in turn ordain ruling elders in congregations. This is the system which one promises to uphold in the ordination vows.

Stating ahead of time that one objects to, and thus will not participate in, the ordination of women creates immediate problems. At the congregational level, is it likely that the session, chaired by the minister who objects to the ordination of women, would approve a female elder? Let us imagine they actually did: what happens next? If the minister will not ordain this duly elected elder, who will? How can one claim a person is accepting the system of church courts (as set out in the vow) if one is not doing what the General Assembly has stated one should do? Even the inaccurate claim that what was decided in 1966 was "only permissive not proscriptive" collapses when one considers the practical issues of the stance being advocated here. By choosing not to participate, one is essentially vetoing any woman elder being ordained in a congregation. There seems to have been some evidence that those supporting MacDougall understood this. Ed McKinley refers several times in his article in the *Presbyterian Record* to the fact that the young man would work with all women who had been "lawfully ordained."[95] But, the issue of how women could be ordained in a session of which he was a minister was avoided.

In the case of a woman in a presbytery of which MacDougall was a member – and thus a crucial part of the collective bishop – what this would look like was again unexplored. What if a female graduate were to be ordained in the presbytery? The act of ordination in the presbyterian system is by the laying on of hands: that is, all of the clergy present place their hands on the candidate's head. What is being asserted theologically is by doing this collectively the power of the Holy Spirit is given and sets the candidate aside for their ministry. Based on the limited information that was provided by those arguing for exemption, what seems to have been proposed was that this individual (if a minister) would not, because of his conscience, participate. What does it mean if one part of the bishop chooses not to ordain? Does that invalidate the ordination? What was being requested was not a casual absence. One promises in the ordination vows to "share in and submit yourself to all lawful oversight." How can one take this vow, knowing that one does not intend to "share in" this responsibility in all cases? In absenting oneself from the service, how can this not be considered following a "divisive course"?

The answer may be that one has decided that the church erred and therefore the oversight was not "lawful." But the church made this decision at the level of a General Assembly. All of the rules of church law were followed. How is one following the hierarchy of church courts in rejecting this as a lawful decision? How can one claim they are upholding the denomination's *"doctrine under the continual illumination and correction* of the Holy Spirit speaking in the Scriptures"? The church modified its doctrine and polity when it moved to open ordination to all, men and women, in 1966. This was decided, as we have seen in chapter 4, after careful debate and on the basis of a study of scripture. Not all agreed. But this was what the denomination – collectively – stated was permissible according to scripture. Here the banner of "liberty of conscience" was unfurled. Several voices at the time noted that this was an unusual, new, and not necessarily fair use of this concept of liberty of conscience.[96] These arguments were ignored and calls for liberty of conscience simply became louder. It was boldly and persistently argued that the church had not changed its doctrine but only "permitted" women to be ordained, that the ordination of women was not of the essence of the gospel and, that because many members of the church understood the Bible differently, not participating in the ordination of women was reasonable. This flood of related arguments created chaos and diverted attention away from a blunt reality. The church had decided this matter. Ordination was open to all, men and women. This was the doctrine and polity of the church that had been decided. Being part of a presbyterian system meant that one participated – as the ordination vows clearly stated – in the shared responsibilities of the system. This was clear.

But what if you believed the church had strayed? What if you believed the denomination had made the wrong decision in 1966? What if you believed that the church's approach to scripture was wrong; even more, what if you believed the church had listened to culture, not scripture? What if you believed these changes were "unlawful"? Variations on all of these themes were heard in the arguments made at the time. The persistence and assurance with which these arguments were being made is what stands out. Canadian Presbyterians had been divided – in the nineteenth century, at the time of the debates about church union, and certainly after the 1925 union. Was this a simple continuation of those divisions, or was the divergence in this period symptomatic of something new? This is an important, though difficult, question to answer. Certainly the reality that the denomination was no longer growing fed the sense that the church had taken the wrong path. Was there a need for more change as the church was not changing fast enough? Or, had the church changed too much and strayed too far from the Bible? Did the church need a new revised statement of faith or did it need to go back to the firm foundation of the Westminster Confession of Faith? The state of the church and the sense of decline and loss of membership and influence certainly intensified these debates. So too did the state of the culture. The emerging reaction against the changes – usually seen as extremely negative – of the 1960s can be seen broadly in the culture. This cultural reaction strengthened those who believed the church had also gone too far. The place of women was one of those contested elements in culture. Perhaps it should not surprise us that it also came to be a point of conflict in the church.

9

A Late Consensus?

The cover had one word on it: "Worship." Above the word was a silver chalice and flanking it on each side were two books: the 1972 *Book of Praise* and the even more recently published abridged edition of the *Book of Common Order* (1978).[1] The February 1984 cover of the *Presbyterian Record* highlighted the denomination's achievement in producing its own contemporary resources for worship. A few months later, a third publication could have been added – the denomination's long desired contemporary statement of faith called *Living Faith*, which was expressly designed for use in worship. The message in 1984 seemed clear. Canadian Presbyterians were not stuck in the past but were modernizing, current, and producing resources for the times. This may have been true but the journey to these achievements had been more complex and at times torturous. What remains striking is not that Canadian Presbyterians had produced these resources but how long it had taken them to get to this point. The denomination had been relying since church union on the hymnbook that was first published in 1918. Why did it take until 1972 for Canadian Presbyterians to publish a new *Book of Praise*? A contemporary statement of faith was proposed in 1943 and finally adopted forty-one years later. Was this a result of a new consensus that had emerged, or were there other factors at play? This chapter will explore these questions looking at various decisions made in terms of doctrine and worship. Times were changing. Presbyterians wanted to, and frequently did, move forward. Presbyterians were surprisingly willing to change their relations with Roman Catholics, even declare that the Westminster Confession was wrong, as the impact of the Second Vatican Council became evident. They were not, however, willing to change the text of that historic creed. Nor were they, as will be seen in the next topic to be considered, able in the mid-1960s or early 1970s to agree on a contemporary statement of faith. They were able to revise their hymnbook, but concerns about respectability led them to relegate any song that might be played on guitar to a separate songbook. The charismatic movement, on the other hand, was met with surprising openness when it became a major topic for discussion at the Church Doctrine Committee (the successor to the Committee on Articles of Faith). Overall, change was slow. Presbyterians struggled to alter what were understood as key parts of their heritage.[2] When they succeeded, was this a sign of consensus? Or does it provide evidence that those in the denomination were no longer as engaged in fighting each other for the soul of the denomination?

THE SUBORDINATE STANDARDS: ORDINATION VOWS AND THE POPE

As was discussed in chapter 5, Canadian Presbyterians had not succeeded in creating a contemporary statement of faith. The Westminster Confession of Faith and the surrounding documents remained central to their understanding of themselves as Reformed Protestant Christians. An additional statement clarifying the obligations of the state to the church and the church to the state known as the "Declaration of Faith Concerning Church and Nation" had been approved in 1954 and confirmed in 1955. The status of this declaration, however, was not clear. It did not replace the relevant chapter in the Westminster Confession nor did the denomination abandon its long-held practice of allowing liberty of conscience on this particular section of the confession when ministers or elders took their ordination vows. The ordination vows themselves and how one subscribed to or agreed to the Westminster Confession became the focus of considerable work on the part of the Committee on Articles of Faith. The committee worked on this for over fourteen years.[3] It began by proposing some new questions and asking for feedback. Eventually in 1970 a preamble and revised questions for use at an ordination were accepted by the General Assembly. The preamble detailed the confessional history of the denomination and noted: "Our subordinate standards are the Westminster Confession of Faith as adopted in 1875 and 1889, the Declaration of Faith concerning Church and Nation of 1954 and such doctrine as the Church, in obedience to Scripture and under the promised guidance of the Holy Spirit, may yet confess in her continuing function of reformulating the faith."[4] One accepted these standards in the ordination questions "under the continual illumination and correction of the Holy Spirit speaking in the Scriptures."[5] It had taken a long time to get here, but Canadian Presbyterians had agreed upon these questions that spoke to how they accepted and understood their doctrinal statements.[6] At the same time, there were unresolved issues. How could one affirm the "Declaration of Faith Concerning Church and Nation" while still asserting "liberty of conscience" on this issue as the church had agreed in 1875? The denomination had also recognized in 1962 other Reformed confessions (the Second Helvetic Confession, the Belgic Confession, the Gallican Confession, and the Heidelberg Catechism) "as standards parallel to our own."[7] What did this mean? These documents, though produced by Reformed Christians in the sixteenth century, did not all agree with each other. While certainly indicating the denomination's desire to be a home for all Reformed Christians, not just those from the British Isles and Ireland, how these various confessional standards stood in relation to each other was unclear.[8]

In this period Canadian Presbyterians also admitted the Westminster Confession was imperfect. As relationships with Roman Catholics notably thawed due to the openness displayed by the Second Vatican Council, some in the denomination raised the issue of the language used in their subordinate standard.[9] In April 1964 the Presbytery of Temiskaming sent an overture to the General Assembly. As respectful as they were of the Reformation heritage, the presbytery noted that article 6 of section 25 of the Westminster Confession identified "the Pope as antichrist." This, the presbytery argued, could no longer be said of recent popes. Even more to the point, it conveyed its conviction that "the present wording of the said article, besides failing to reflect the love of Jesus Christ, proposes an attitude of hatred, judgement and suspicion."[10] Noting that another Presbyterian church, the United Presbyterian Church USA, had already reworded this section, the presbytery asked the General Assembly to change that wording to the one used by the United Presbyterian Church.[11] The Committee on Articles of Faith reported to the next General Assembly that although it was "sympathetic to the prayer of the overture in its concern over the harsh language" used for the pope, the challenge was that the Westminster Confession of Faith was a historic document and "its actual text ought not to be tampered with."[12] The committee proposed a different solution. It would prepare an "explanatory note" explaining the theology within the confession and the concern regarding individual abuses of power that might happen but "nevertheless would make a serious attempt to assess the positive role of the papacy in recent decades."[13] This approach was met with support from the church.[14] At the next Assembly, the full text of the explanatory note was presented. The use of the term "anti-Christ" in reference to the pope was placed in historical context. Recent popes were applauded for "a changed attitude from that of their predecessors in office." Given these changes, "we must be willing to revise our attitudes concerning the papacy."[15]

This solution did not please everyone. A second – and much more strongly worded – overture appeared in 1967. The Presbytery of Sarnia asked the General Assembly to "take action to amend for subscription purposes the Westminster Confession of Faith" by omitting four statements. In addition to chapter 25 section 6 (which called the pope "that antichrist, that man of sin, and son of perdition") the presbytery objected to chapter 22 section 7 (against celibacy and monastic vows), chapter 24 section 3 (prohibiting marriage with "infidels, Papists, or other idolaters"), and chapter 29 section 2 (against "the Popish sacrifice of the mass").[16] The presbytery used strong language to challenge its own confessional standards, speaking of them as "derogatory references to other theological positions," "not essential," and "calculated to give offence to our Roman Catholic brethren."[17] The Committee on Articles of Faith again cited the Canadian Presbyterian practice of not altering historic creeds and advised against deletion. No explanatory note was proposed, but the committee added this comment: "Regarding our present-day attitude to the issues raised in the overture, we draw attention to the fact that the Church of Rome is herself currently re-thinking these matters, and we are watching with great interest the changes taking place in that Church (e.g. Hans Küng, 'The Council, Reform and Reunion'). While we recognize the offensive nature of these statements and do not regard them as true, we nevertheless advise against making any definite judgment on these matters at this time."[18] Unwilling to change a historic document, the Committee on Articles of Faith was willing to state plainly that the Westminster Confession contained errors. But how was this conveyed to the denomination? And for those taking the ordination vows, what were they accepting (or modifying)? And who got to make that determination? These were all important and unresolved issues, even as the denomination tried, again, to create a contemporary statement of faith.

1966 "DRAFT STATEMENT OF FAITH" AND *CONFESSING THE FAITH TODAY*

The General Assembly had approved the creation of a contemporary statement of faith in 1943. That project had stalled in 1949 when the General Assembly directed the Committee on Articles of Faith to focus on the issues related to church and nation. After the completion of the "Declaration of Faith Concerning Church and Nation" in 1954, the committee focused on other issues. The work on a contemporary statement of faith remained stalled. An overture in 1965 asking the church to clarify its confessional position led to the creation of a joint committee made up of members of the Committee on Articles of Faith and the Inter-Church Relations Committee, which created a "Draft Statement of Faith" in 1966.[19] The statement was divided into four parts: a preface followed by three main sections – "Where Is Man?" "Good News: Jesus of Nazareth," and "Life in the Spirit." The preface sought to explore why Christians created confessions of faith and what these meant and how different historical circumstances led to the need to restate the faith in appropriate terms. The simple structure, beginning with humanity before moving to talk about Jesus, did not reflect the way confessions had been traditionally organized. It did accurately reflect the spirit of the 1960s. While the structure was simple, the text of the statement of faith itself was not. The prose was dense. The logic underlying the organization was not readily apparent. In one section under the heading "Where Is Man?" the statement attempted to discuss God's presence in history, including the motivation underlying the incarnation:

> God makes himself known to men in various ways, but in a decisive and unique way in the events of Israel and Jesus Christ. This is the content of the apostolic witness, and the distinctive message of the Christian Gospel. The human situation is understood not as tragedy, in which the dark side of existence wins out, but as a victory over the darkness wrought out within our history by God's own activity. Man is the good creature

> of God intended for fellowship with him and life in his presence. As a creature, he is able to know God only through means, through mediation. But this mediated knowledge is darkened and complicated by the sinister presence of an alien power in God's creation, the power called sin.[20]

This was not a simple point. It is difficult to imagine how the average Canadian Presbyterian in 1966 might relate to or use this document. To state "the demonic perversion of human authority, creativity and mastery over nature pose the gravest threat to authentic human existence, to the very meaning of life together on this planet earth," and then pledge oneself to the healing power of Jesus did not clearly convey the idea that it would be good if Christians were active in fighting against pollution or other threats to human existence.[21] The theological obscurity of the Westminster documents and seventeenth-century language had been replaced by the theological obscurity of the mid-twentieth century. This document was sent to the presbyteries, and the result was a variety of different responses. Little progress was made.

In an attempt to jump-start the process, the Church Doctrine Committee produced a volume edited by William Klempa entitled *What It Means to Confess the Christian Faith Today* in 1972.[22] As the convenor of the committee, Klempa noted: "It is still our conviction that a brief contemporary statement of faith is very much needed by our Church and it must be attempted." Klempa noted the other denominations, the United Presbyterian Church in the United States of America, the United Church of Christ, and the Presbyterian Church in the Southern States, who had all managed to produce a contemporary statement of faith. The book, which featured the 1966 Draft Statement, was intended to "stimulate the Church in its thinking" and galvanize support for the project: "It is our sincere hope that it will give impetus to a renewed interest in and a serious effort to write a new statement of faith."[23] The "Draft Statement of Faith" produced in 1966 began the collection. The other essays provided a wide variety of perspectives, with most addressing the question posed in the title of the book. Diverse voices were heard, including the voices of two women. Essays were provided by, among others, William Stanford Reid, Stuart Coles, Joseph McLelland, Mariano Di Gangi, Max Putnam, Enid Pottinger, Brian Fraser, and Valerie Dunn. The divergent opinions of Canadian Presbyterians in 1972 was clearly evident. What was not clear was how this expression of viewpoints might lead to a contemporary statement of faith. In 1972 Presbyterians could at least look forward to a new hymnbook.

REVISING THE *BOOK OF PRAISE*

The need for a new collection of hymns had been apparent since the end of World War II. Canadian Presbyterians called their hymnbook the *Book of Praise*, perhaps as a way to stress the importance of metrical psalms as well as hymns. Overtures in 1950, 1952, and 1958 all raised different issues related to the adequacy of the current *Book of Praise* and the need for a new one.[24] It seems odd that no action was taken. Canadian Presbyterians had revised their music book frequently before, producing editions in 1880, 1898, and 1918.[25] The desire for a new *Book of Praise* was certainly one of the major concerns of the committee responsible for worship in this period. Acting on the instructions of the General Assembly in 1952, the committee met with delegates from various American Presbyterian denominations to consider a joint hymnal. Canadian Presbyterians went to the first meeting with their position clear: any book would need to have "a metrical psalter as a distinct and separate section."[26] This position was not acceptable to the other denominations involved in the discussion, and so the Canadians withdrew from the discussions. They also noted that, whereas the *Book of Praise* was the one book that had "official standing" in the denomination, the proposed book was only one of several from which American Presbyterian congregations in their denominations might choose.[27] These were clearly different projects. But the committee continued to insist that it needed to produce a new book in cooperation with others: "It is obvious that great advantage would accrue from the use of a book by us in common with other Presbyterians of the English speaking world. It is for that reason, apart from other reasons, that we cannot recommend the revisions of our own book."[28] Committee members suggested they go back to what they had suggested in 1951 when the issue had been raised. Their original plan had been to wait for a revision of the *Church Hymnary* (a British hymnbook used by many Presbyterian denominations) and to become one of the denominations working on that revision. They were confident that a revision of this hymnbook used by Presbyterians throughout the Commonwealth was the correct approach.[29] Year after year they kept telling the denomination that this was the path to take, even when they had received no assurances that such a project was imminent. The advantages of a common book of worship music shared with other denominations are clear. So too are the disadvantages. As Canadian Presbyterians had quickly discovered in their brief work with American Presbyterians, they would be but one of many at the table and not able to get their way on issues such as a distinct psalter. What were the "other reasons" for cooperation that the committee had alluded to in 1953? The issue of cost seems to have been in the background of this and many other decisions. To produce a denominational hymnbook would require a considerable investment of time and money. The committee continued to wait for a suitable partner with whom a hymnbook could be produced.

While the committee continued to wait for a partner, many in the denomination continued to raise concerns that the present hymnbook was inadequate. The committee replied in somewhat scolding terms, suggesting it was adequate if used properly. In 1963 an overture sent to General Assembly again raised the need for a new *Book of Praise*.[30] The committee responded the next year suggesting three options. The first was for the denomination to produce its own hymnbook. It dismissed this as too costly. The second option would be to wait for a revision of the *Church Hymnary*. This was the current strategy. The third option was to work with the United Church of Canada on a joint hymnbook. This was what it proposed.[31] This was soundly rejected by the denomination, and instead a committee was established to begin the process of revising the *Book of Praise* (the first option).[32] The committee – chaired by William Fitch, the minister of Knox Presbyterian Church, Toronto – met over the following years and worked to revise the *Book of Praise*. Members of the committee brought a variety of skills, including musical expertise, and represented the theological breadth of the church.

The revised *Book of Praise* published in 1972 was a striking contrast to the 1918 *Book of Praise*. The cover was not black but a vibrant shade of blue. The font choices were modern. The music notation was in quarter notes, not half notes, with the words between the treble and bass clefs whenever possible for easier congregational singing. There was a psalter at the beginning, though it consisted of only 68 selections in contrast to the 134 in the 1918 *Book of Praise*. What it did contain was a selection of responsive psalms at the back of the book. These were designed for easy congregational use with the ministers' lines in bolded type, the responses in regular font, and a selection and presentation which made use in worship easy. The translations used in the Psalms were also modern, most coming from the Grail translation, a sharp contrast to the King James Version in use in so many congregations in 1972.[33] The revised *Book of Praise* felt contemporary. It was widely embraced and used in the denomination.

Many in the denomination were grateful for any revision that allowed them to abandon the 1918 *Book of Praise* that was still in their pews. But as congregations bought and used the new book, there came an awareness of some challenges and quirks. The one that drew perhaps the greatest criticism was the choice of the hymn tune "Glasgow" for the song "Amazing Grace." Thanks to the rendition by the Royal Scots Dragoon Guards, this hymn somewhat surprisingly featured on the popular music charts in 1972, after which the rather odd and difficult to sing tune in the new hymnbook became even more jarring. British hymn tunes (as in the case of "Amazing Grace") seem to have been chosen over more common American tunes. The new book had a strong selection of Canadian tunes and hymns.[34] There were some wonderful choices. But there were also some odd inclusions. What congregation could possibly have sung "I Bind unto Myself Today," a difficult version of the words of St Patrick that took eight pages and had two different tunes? The omissions were even more glaring. Alongside the feeling of being modern, the 1972 *Book of Praise* also had (one discovered over time) a feeling of being correct. This was the right kind of music the Presbyterians should sing. It was respectable. This excluded many of the contemporary folk hymns and songs (there are no examples of folk hymns or choruses in the 1972 *Book of Praise*). Indeed, the committee was clear in their intent: "It would be very easy for us to yield to pressures from many sources and produce a song book to vie with the spirit of the age. But this is not our commission. We are persuaded that only the best is good enough for God; and that we must offer to Him as pure a sacrifice as we can. Our praise must be from the heart, tuneful, strong, melodious and inspiring. It need not, however, be poor music. The Committee on Revisions has tried to maintain the highest standards of musical excellence. This is not easy for dedicated musicians when some hymns of dubious quality are already favourites in many congregations." Thankfully, the committee noted, the "gifted group of musicians" who had worked on the committee had prevented this from happening, an increasing challenge in a time when they noted "beat [*sic*] music" was being played around the clock on popular radio stations.[35]

The process of creating a songbook began even before the 1972 *Book of Praise* had been completed. An overture in 1968 requested that there be a supplement to the proposed new hymnbook.[36] In the preface to the *Book of Praise* itself it noted that a "supplementary hymn-book suitable for open-air services, camp fires, youth groups, informal get-togethers and the like" was in preparation. A separate committee – there was no overlap of membership between the committees – met and produced this under the title *Praiseways* which was published in 1975 (the denomination's centennial year). *Praiseways* used the familiar traditional American tune for "Amazing Grace." It had choruses, folk hymns such as "Kum ba yah!" and "Let Us Break Bread Together," and contemporary favourites such as "We Are One in the Spirit" and "In the Stars His Handiwork I See." It also included gospel hymns such as "Just a Closer Walk" and "I Know Not Why God's Wondrous Grace" that did not, for whatever reason, make it into the *Book of Praise*.[37] Indeed, what is most remarkable about *Praiseways* is how many hymns (as opposed to songs and choruses) there were and the inclusion of hymns by Canadian Presbyterians. The role of those involved in the Presbyterian Music Camp in the creation and selections for this book has recently been noted.[38]

Praiseways added helpfully to the possible repertoire of songs that Canadian Presbyterians could use during worship, but also at church camps and less formal gatherings. *Praiseways* sought to fill what was perceived to be a need in the church for more contemporary songs and songs not all played on piano or organ. Alongside the 1972 *Book of Praise* it exemplified the desire of Canadian Presbyterians to make their worship more contemporary and relevant. It also demonstrated some of the challenges of attempts to do this. Some of the newer selections were challenging if no one was there in person to teach them. The choice of guitar chords for some songs was unnecessarily complicated. It also stood in sharp contrast to the vision of musical propriety and respectability that underlay the choices in the 1972 *Book of Praise*.

THE NEO-PENTECOSTAL (CHARISMATIC) MOVEMENT

As they had done with their calls for a new hymnbook, Canadian Presbyterians called their denomination to look at various theological issues during the 1970s and early 1980s. Some of these issues created little controversy, even as they envisaged major changes to current practices. One such issue was the issue of allowing baptized children to participate in the communion service. Traditionally, a separate confirmation needed to take place before anyone who had been baptized as a child was allowed to take communion or, as it was referred to during these discussions, be admitted to the Lord's Table. The Church Doctrine Committee studied this issue and proposed children who had been baptized could participate without yet going through the confirmation process and becoming full church members. No change is ever unopposed, but this seemed to be widely accepted in the denomination.[39] On the issue of abortion, Presbyterians maintained their existing position of being opposed to abortion in most circumstances. Attempts were made to make this a key issue for the denomination in the 1970s and early 1980s when the evangelical movement in North America was positioning itself to make the anti-abortion/pro-life position central to Christian faith.[40] Canadian Presbyterian voices urged the denomination to take a stronger position in opposition to abortion. The denomination maintained its traditional opposition but did not make this a central theological issue.[41] The Church Doctrine Committee kept busy on a variety of theological and ethical issues; indeed, the trend seemed to be to send every and all theological or potential theological issues to this one committee. This stands in contrast to earlier decades when theological and ethical issues had been the responsibility of all committees in the church, with some of the most significant work being done by joint committees.[42] One clearly theological issue which came before the Church Doctrine Committee was the issue of how to respond to Christians who had charismatic experiences.

The most successful Christian movement globally in the twentieth century was the charismatic, or Pentecostal, movement. Armed with a conviction that the Holy Spirit was active and continued to provide the gifts described in the New Testament, including speaking in tongues, charismatics formed their own congregations and denominations. The Pentecostal Assemblies of Canada, the largest Pentecostal denomination in the country, grew exponentially in the post-war period and became one of Canada's largest denominations.[43] Pentecostal ideas were shared in popular Christian paperbacks such as David Wilkerson's *The Cross and the Switchblade*.[44] Charismatic experiences moved beyond Pentecostal churches to seemingly unlikely places including Roman Catholic communities and Anglican, United Church, Baptist, and Presbyterian congregations. Emotional religious experiences were welcomed by many as a sign of revival. The "Jesus People" movements that seemed to be attracting younger people into the church were strongly evangelical in theology and often charismatic.[45] Other Presbyterians were cautious, even negative, not only about what they might characterize (rightly or wrongly) as the over-emotional aspects of the worship services, but about many of the theological ideas being expressed. The potential for divisiveness in congregations, between those who had experienced a charismatic experience and those who had not, was always a possibility. Attention was brought to these issues quite concretely in 1971 when it was reported that there had been a conflict in First Church, New Westminster, British Columbia. Hints could be gleaned from the report that the Church Doctrine Committee had been asked to study the "doctrine of the working of the Holy Spirit with specific reference to glossolalia (speaking in tongues) and other charismatic gifts."[46] A special committee, the Committee to Study the Charismatic Movement, was also established in 1973. Its report to the 1974 General Assembly set out to explain the charismatic movement, suggesting that while all Christians "should have the experience of the presence of Holy Spirit," it was not necessary to speak in tongues in order to be a Christian. This distinction was clearly made. At the same time, the report showed great sympathy for the charismatic movement. The experiences that those in the charismatic movement were having were affirmed as valid. To the question: "Did these things only happen in the Bible or do they still happen today?" the report gave the direct answer: "They still happen today."[47] In discussing faith healing, the report argued this was "also manifested today, as are the other gifts of the Spirit."[48] In terms of emotion in church, the report simply noted that people express themselves in different ways, but did "not rule out emotional expression, because people are emotional creatures." Instead, people should worship as seemed natural, "remembering that their purpose is to glorify God, not to make a show of their religion."[49] The committee suggested it continue for an additional year to do more work, but nonetheless proposed that the General Assembly agree with the statement, "The 'Charismatic' experience is the experience of the presence of Jesus Christ through the Holy Spirit in a gathering of Christians or in an individual's personal life and of an enthusiastic or ecstatic response thereto. This is documented in Holy Scriptures and, therefore, has a legitimate place in the life of the Body of Christ, the Church."[50] The General Assembly passed an amended positive statement.[51] That same year the Church Doctrine Committee noted that a subcommittee was continuing to study this important topic and were working with the special committee.[52]

At the next General Assembly, the special committee continued to express sympathy for the charismatic movement. For the committee, the charismatic movement was a revival movement, offering signs of life when too often "we hear of the deadness of the church."[53] There were a few cautions along the way. The committee suggested that "no one gift can, therefore, be singled out as a touchstone of the Spirit-filled life," but still offered a very positive assessment of the movement. In its advice to the denomination, it encouraged "ministers and sessions to make provision for charismatic fellowship within the church, under their oversight, in order that those who long for spiritual fellowship of a charismatic nature, may not feel rejection by their church."[54] Again, it urged the church to support the position it had taken the previous year; again, the matter was referred, this time to the Church Doctrine Committee which would be continuing to study this issue, with members of the special committee assisting. Given this reluctance, one might anticipate great hostility from the Church Doctrine Committee in its report in 1975. Caution, yes. Hostility, no. As one would anticipate, this was a much more learned report, drawing on the Westminster Standards and Scripture to discuss the Holy Spirit in the Christian life. The committee directed attention to the differences it had with the movement but did not reject it. Indeed, the committee noted, "some phenomena of the charismatic movement are alien to our tradition, but at this point our tradition is seriously lacking."[55] The committee then disputed a specific section of the Westminster Confession (21:3) that argued that prayer must be, "if vocal, in a known tongue." The report noted the challenge for Presbyterians of accepting what was not part of their experience, but did note that this was "clearly part of the New Testament experience of the Holy Spirit." Speaking in tongues as a "test of life in the Spirit" was rejected but the reality of speaking in tongues was not questioned.[56]

Presbyterians received what the Church Doctrine Committee drafted as the final report on the charismatic movement in 1976. The report was extensive and thorough to a fault. The report explored history and theology. It defined its terms, differentiating between the Pentecostal movement and denominations, and the charismatic movement, which it saw as taking place "largely within the established historic churches," then divided this further between Roman Catholic and Protestant traditions. The committee used the term "Neo-Pentecostalism" to refer to the charismatic movement within Protestant churches.[57] The report was detailed in its explorations and not an easy document to read. This might explain why its generally favourable position towards the Neo-Pentecostal movement has been forgotten.[58] Clear distinctions between Presbyterian and Pentecostal theology – particularly around speaking in tongues – were made; however, the report never denied the reality of these experiences. It complexly argued (rather than simply suggested) that speaking in tongues was acceptable but not necessary (from a Presbyterian perspective) for Christian faith. Near the end of its report, the Church Doctrine Committee provided an appraisal of the Neo-Pentecostal movement using five points. These items were expressed in a complex way: "Neo-Pentecostalism is not in itself a threat to the life of the Church unless and until it is used as a pretext for division or a weapon to gain power."[59] This is a positive statement, despite the caution. In its comment the committee was also positive, suggesting that Neo-Pentecostalism was "an evidence that God is at work in His Church" and not necessarily a threat. In the section on pastoral relations, the report advocated that ministers and sessions consider allowing gatherings of Neo-Pentecostals within the church. This was expressed in cautious language, with these being "under their supervision," but there was support for these meetings. The committee also stated that "Disciplinary measures should not be taken against those who participate in the charismatic movement but follow no divisive course."[60] The Church Doctrine Committee did not reject the charismatic movement and even attempted to make a place for it within its structures. What it failed to do, however, was convey this clearly.

Such a lack of clarity might have been why the Church Doctrine Committee a few years later published a popular report entitled "The Neo-Pentecostal Movement and the Presbyterian Church in Canada."[61] One of the writers of the 1976 report objected in the *Presbyterian Record*: "In this booklet, generally speaking, the treatment of Neo-Pentecostals is wholly negative and breathes a spirit of rejection. By contrast, the 1976 Report, though critical of certain aspects of Neo-Pentecostalism is positive, conciliatory, and breathes a spirit of acceptance. It speaks, for instance, with sympathy and understanding of the characteristics of Neo-Pentecostalism."[62] That was the intent of the report; the need for a popular edition suggests it failed to convey its message clearly.

The Church Doctrine Committee was also not clear where and how it was departing from the traditional Reformed theology in its reports. The Church Doctrine Committee in 1976 brushed aside one concern it had received: "One Presbytery wished that we provide arguments for our rejection of a view long held in the Reformed tradition, viz. that extraordinary gifts of the Spirit have ceased. As we found no Scriptural support for that view, we consider that the burden of proof lies on the other side."[63] The report argued that "we must question some results of the Reformation" and spoke directly to two specific gifts that were part of the modern charismatic movement: "As far as healing and glossolalia [speaking in tongues] are concerned, we dare not maintain that miracles are confined to special periods of revelation in the past."[64] These were bold statements. There was a tradition within Protestantism as a whole, as well as the Reformed tradition itself, that argued that certain of the gifts of the Holy Spirit had been limited to the apostolic age.[65] This tradition was not described but simply, as the above quote illustrates, dismissed. Who gets to determine which parts of Reformed tradition should be rejected and which should be supported? And when a position is being rejected was there not a greater responsibility to say more than simply that it is up to the other side to prove the case?

LIVING FAITH

In 1981 the Church Doctrine Committee turned its attention to the creation of a contemporary statement of faith. Three years later the confession, known as *Living Faith*, was presented and approved by the General Assembly by a nearly unanimous vote.[66] *Living Faith* begins with the bold assertion that "in every generation the church needs to confess its faith anew."[67] While arguably true, this had not been the experience of the denomination, which had struggled since the idea was first agreed upon in 1943 to produce a contemporary statement. There are two obvious questions: First, why did it take so long? Second, why did it succeed at this point in time? The first question has been explored in various ways throughout this book, particularly in chapter 5, as well as earlier in this chapter. The simplistic answer might be that they could not overcome their differences. This does not make answering the second question any easier.

It should also be noted that, while the committee produced this document in a remarkably short time, it did not cut any corners. The committee had consulted widely, as was noted by the Rev. Stephen Hayes, the convenor of the subcommittee of the Church Doctrine Committee responsible for producing *Living Faith*, in the May 1984 *Presbyterian Record*.[68] After being formed in 1981, the committee worked until, at the end of 1982, it had a draft which was then sent out for study and comment. Changes were made in response to the criticisms; however, it was noteworthy how the committee members working on the new statement of faith responded to these criticisms. They treated them with respect. At the same time, they were conscious that they would never achieve unanimity: "The fact that not everyone will like it, and that a few may loudly proclaim against it, does not alter the fact that we have every reason to believe that it will be enthusiastically received by the vast majority of our people and that it will find its way into both the worship and the study of our church."[69] That confidence and the ability to listen to, but not be hindered by, the 10 per cent who it was reported asked for rejection of the document might be one key reason for the committee's success.

The clarity of the product might be another reason. Hayes noted that in the statement "each line normally expresses but one thought" and in language that was "simple and direct."[70] The introduction to *Living Faith* attributed "the inspiration for the style and general outline" of the statement to *A Declaration of Faith*, the 1977 document by the Presbyterian Church in the United States.[71] This attribution overstates the debt.[72] The authors of *Living Faith* did follow the general framework of *A Declaration of Faith* but they did not do so slavishly. Each document has ten chapters but the chapters are similar, not identical. The most significant change in terms of structure was the addition of a chapter on faith, which included not only a section on faith but one dealing with doubt: "Here, perhaps for the first time, a confessional statement recognizes doubt, and in the midst of its ringing affirmation of Christian truth acknowledges the difficulties of belief and the ambiguities of the life of faith."[73] The differences in style were also more significant than suggested in *Living Faith*. In discussing how Christians should study scripture, *A Declaration of Faith* affirms: "Therefore we use the best available methods/to understand them [the scriptures] in their historical and cultural settings/and the literary forms in which they are cast."[74] *Living Faith* expresses the same idea in these words: "The writing of the Bible was conditioned/by the language, thought,/and setting of its time./The Bible must be read in its historical context."[75] Each line expressed one thought, as Hayes had stated. The document had an intentional poetry and clarity. Here it stood in stark contrast to the previous attempts at contemporary confessions, notably the 1966 "Draft Statement of Faith." The 1966 statement declared: "Jesus Christ is the fulfilment of Israel's calling and hope, God in person active among them to found his church in their midst. Thus the 'new' Testament takes precedence, providing a new way of interpreting the Hebrew scripture. Indeed, in the Gospel, the proclamation of the Christ event, we are given a criterion for judging all scripture and all human wisdom; we are bound to subject everything to the criticism of the divine act in Jesus the Christ."[76] Section 5.4 of *Living Faith* simply stated: "The Bible is to be understood in the light/of the revelation of God's work in Christ."

The accessibility and clarity of writing was one factor, alongside the determination to not let a minority of voices derail the project, that led to the success of *Living Faith*. Another reason may have been the willingness of the committee to reflect the theological consensus of the denomination and not push the boundaries with the latest theological ideas (at the time these would have been process theology and liberation theology). This was a document that most Canadian Presbyterians could understand and which reflected how they had come to understand the faith. One place where this was evident was in the discussion of that most thorny of issues – as we have already noted – predestination. *Living Faith* placed predestination within the chapter on God in Christ, in the section "Salvation in Christ." It began "Salvation comes from God's grace alone/received through faith in Christ./From all eternity, and through no merit on our part,/God calls us to life in Christ./ Here is the good news of the Gospel!" This was something that the average Canadian Presbyterian could understand and accept, as they would the positive statement that "we have been predestined to be like Christ and to serve God." The text states its conviction: "God chooses us."[77] It does not focus the discussion on those who were not chosen by God. This concern for both the chosen and the condemned (double predestination) was a feature of the Westminster Confession of Faith. The Church Doctrine Committee was aware of this but did not let this prevent them from creating a contemporary statement of faith. Intriguingly, William Stanford Reid, who had been so critical of earlier work, did not criticize the position taken on predestination and was generally positive about *Living Faith*.[78] The wise leadership of Hayes needs to be recognized as one reason for its success. The Church Doctrine Committee had also made a strategic decision that made the success of the contemporary statement more likely. The committee did not suggest that this should become a subordinate standard, either replacing or being on the same level as the Westminster Confession of Faith. By making the decision that this would be a statement for use in worship and study, it sidestepped the potential controversies, debates, and delays of attempting to create something that would be a subordinate standard. By not trying to achieve too much, the drafters undercut the arguments of those who might have been doctrinal purists. This is not to say there was no opposition. There was, from both those who wanted the statement to go further and those who believed it departed too much from the tradition.[79] The committee responsible argued back vigorously, confident that this was something the denomination needed. Its reward was the remarkable fact that *Living Faith* passed in 1984 with little opposition, would sell thousands of copies, and would be widely used as intended, in worship and study.

CONSENSUS?

Living Faith sold over 6,000 copies and went into several printings. Meanwhile, the denomination continued to look to the Westminster Confession of Faith as its subordinate standard, central to denominational life and theology. The challenge was that Canadian Presbyterians did not publish their own version of the Westminster Confession, complete with references to where the "Declaration of Faith Concerning Church and Nation" intersected with the confession. Nor did they include any of the explanatory statements regarding issues such as how they now believed the pope was not the anti-Christ. This remains one of the strangest things about Canadian Presbyterians in the period after 1945. They were proud that they, unlike American Presbyterians, did not change the historic text of the document.[80] The Westminster Confession was still their subordinate standard but they could not be bothered to print it. What place did it have in the denomination? Was anyone even reading it anymore, or did it emerge only to be cherry-picked for a particular theological point to be made? Not surprisingly, the reality that the church had already dealt with the issue of the language used to describe the pope was forgotten. Beginning in 1998, the issue appeared again before several General Assemblies.[81] One can criticize those who were unaware that this had been dealt with already, but was there not some responsibility for the denomination generally, and the Church Doctrine Committee specifically, to publish a Canadian version of the Westminster Confession?

The production of an abridged version of the *Book of Common Order* was problematic in a different way. An updated version was needed, the worship committee noted, for two specific reasons: first, the questions at the ordination service had been changed in 1970 and were thus different from those asked in 1964; second, the prayers were in more traditional formal language and there was a need to provide more contemporary prayers. A revision was needed. This would be costly, both in terms of time and money. The solution, shared with the church, was an abridgement that focused on only certain services. The result was that the evening services were not included in the abridgement. This made sense as very few congregations still had an evening service. What made less sense was that all of the regular orders for morning service (those without communion) were also not included. The only service of worship included was the service of Word and Sacrament.[82] Given the amount of controversy that this service had created fourteen years earlier, the fact that it was the only morning worship service in the abridged edition is astounding.

What are we to make of these transitions? One argument would be that the denomination had gradually developed a consensus and was willing to make changes. This is certainly a possibility. It could also be pointed out how *Living Faith* represented not the latest theological ideas but a theology that reflected the neo-orthodox consensus that had been a central feature of the denomination for at least three decades. This is true, to be sure. Yet at the same time, it is apparent when we look more broadly that we see many in the Presbyterian Church in Canada were increasingly looking outside the denomination for inspiration and support. The Presbyterian Church in Canada was shrinking. One could legitimately argue that something was wrong. Presbyterians also conveyed the belief that they were the only denomination shrinking; or if others were declining, not nearly as fast as they were. In this situation, solutions outside of the denomination were a natural attraction. Ecumenically minded Presbyterians looked to the World Council of Churches as well as partners in other denominations. Evangelical Presbyterians looked to the vibrant and growing neo-evangelical movement. These movements seemed to offer more than could be gained by engaging in yet another bitter internal debate. A late consensus may have been achieved, as much by indifference, as common views.

Conclusion

The Presbyterian Church in Canada finds itself in a very different place as it celebrates its 150th Anniversary in 2025 than it did when it celebrated its centennial in 1975. The church has changed a great deal. Canadian culture has changed even more. And this change in the place of Christianity within the broader society is the more significant change, one that Canadian Presbyterians have struggled – alongside almost all other Christian denominations in Canada – to accept and respond to effectively. In 1961, the population of Canada was 90 per cent Christian according to the census.[1] Less than 1 per cent of the Canadian population in 1961 identified as having "no religion." By the time of the centennial, the 1971 census had reported a sharp increase – now 4 per cent – in those claiming no religious identity.[2] But the dominance of Christians in the Canadian population was still the overwhelming reality. Fifty years later things could not be more different. Those claiming "no religion" are now 35 per cent of the Canadian population; those identifying with any form of Christian faith are 53 per cent.[3]

We have explored the history of the Presbyterian Church in Canada in the crucial years from 1945–85. This book has argued that this was the tipping point in the denomination's fortunes. Continuing Canadian Presbyterians experienced the church union in 1925 as a disruption. Those in the continuing denomination found themselves, despite their careful planning, with a massive task of rebuilding. The denomination was also different, focused more in central Canada than it had been previously. Despite the enormous challenges, the denomination rebuilt and was moving forward only to have the twin crises of the Great Depression and World War II derail those plans. The end of World

War II in 1945 saw improved finances and a determination to move forward and grow. This is what the Presbyterian Church in Canada did in the years following the war. New congregations were built in frontier areas, in the suburbs around major cities, and in smaller cities. Membership and Church school membership increased. The church grew and expanded. Presbyterians were confident and proud. They continued to focus on mission, both in Canada and overseas. They continued to raise moral concerns in the broader society and participate in various forms of evangelism. They began the process of considering the place of women in the denomination, including the possibility of ordination of women both as elders and as ministers. The denomination agreed to that in 1966. It did this based upon its own convictions that this was a biblical decision. It also did it aware that the place of women in the broader Canadian culture was being reconsidered. It saw itself as a church speaking to the culture, not as separate and distinct from that culture.

All of this occurred at a time when Christianity was dominant in Canada. The cultural shift that began in the 1960s affected the denomination. Membership declined. Fewer children came to Church school. Building new congregations continued but these were more costly to build and grew at a slower pace. Amidst these changing circumstances, the denomination began to ask questions. Various reforms were proposed and some attempted. Radical change did not happen. What became evident, however, was that the differences within the denomination were becoming clearer. Should we listen to society and change? Should we get back to basics and ignore what the culture was saying? These positions only grew more entrenched over the decade of the 1970s. Those holding these positions looked outside the denomination to groups who shared their convictions. The fight over the World Council of Churches Program to Combat Racism in 1979 was one indication of these divisions. The arguments over what to do with those who could not accept the denomination's decision to ordain women in the late 1970s and early 1980s only deepened these divisions. Remarkably, it was at this moment that the denomination created its long-awaited contemporary statement of faith, *Living Faith*.

This book has argued that church extension, whether done locally or centralized by the denomination, was necessary and largely successful. Various committees and their attempts to make the work of the denomination more efficient have been discussed. The long, careful process leading to the ordination of women in 1966 has been outlined, as has the challenge to this decision almost a decade and a half later. The twisted path to changes in doctrine, as well as in how worship was conducted, has also been outlined. These internal decisions are all important. What can be seen is a denomination attempting to adapt and meet the needs of the time. Whether it did this successfully or not, and where it succeeded and failed, is all worthy of discussion. At the same time, the external changes in Canadian culture need to be recognized. What we see is a denomination trying to adjust, creating a committee to double membership, planning an ambitious campaign of building new churches, and otherwise seeking to maintain its position as a significant church on the Canadian landscape. This is a story of having a model that worked effectively in one era, then attempting to adjust that model when it no longer worked. Whether Canadian Presbyterians understood that at the time, or understand that today, is an interesting question. If one were to carry this story past 1985 down to the present, one would see the divisions only grow wider, with each position blaming the other side for all that had gone wrong. Instead of recognizing the changed context, the two sides seem content to pay lip service to these broader cultural changes, and then suggest if only they had been listened to, all would be well, or could be well again.

This is not the story that Canadian Presbyterians have generally told themselves. For many in the Presbyterian Church in Canada – in particular ministers – the arguments made in this book may be a challenge. Over the years I have listened to countless conversations expressing various points of view about what went wrong with the denomination, why the Presbyterian tradition is in decline, and what should be done to correct it. For example, some have argued we built too many new congregations, and we built them in the wrong places. Others have argued the denomination moved into decline, numerically and spiritually, because it stopped building congregations. What these differing opinions share in common is that they are only opinions. Often they are strongly held, yet infrequently has there been a willingness to test one's opinions by actually doing research or take seriously the research that has been done. I have been surprised that the dramatic changes in context that Brian Clarke and I demonstrated in *Leaving Christianity* have not, with some notable exceptions, been taken more seriously in these conversations. My hope is that this book will challenge those in leadership, as well as those in congregations, to be willing to reconsider the stories they have told so fervently for so many years.

What I would ask all readers to do is simply listen to the story. If there are other facts that have not been considered, these can become part of an ongoing conversation. Argue with the interpretations – but take the facts seriously. There are certain places where those facts are clear and well documented. The church recovered after 1925. The new congregations built in the first period of church extension exploded and became vital to the denomination. Canadian Presbyterians reformed and attempted to adapt to changes. The decision to ordain women in 1966 constituted a change in doctrine and polity that was properly approved by the denomination. These are facts that need to be accepted. On this basis, one can then suggest how the denomination might have acted more effectively. Those suggestions of what the denomination did wrong, or should have done, need to be placed within the larger context of the changing place of religion in Canadian society in this period. They should also be tested against other denominations who made similar decisions. The United Church of Canada listened to culture and made a series of changes, including an openness to more liberal theological positions. It did not grow. Other denominations held firmly to their traditions and embraced more conservative ethical and theological positions. These traditions did better between 1965 and 1985; they have not all done as well in more recent years.[4]

On balance, the Presbyterian Church in Canada struggled to adapt to the changes brought about by the 1960s. In particular, the denomination failed to modernize its structures, including its financial and administrative structures. The denomination had a national office and national staff. But could it effectively raise the money it believed it needed in order to achieve what it saw as its mission? Could it work together to meet the challenge – agreed to by everyone by the late 1970s – of declining church membership? Could the denomination work together? By the early 1980s the divisions were growing deeper. The arguments about the place of women in the church in this period did not create those divisions, but only brought them to the surface and deepened them. Presbyterians no longer had common enemies like the Roman Catholics and the United Church of Canada to unite them. What they failed to discover was a common vision or a common direction. Canadian Presbyterians had always been a diverse group that fought amongst themselves but worked together. Now they argued amongst themselves – but were they willing to work together? Or did they even see this as important?

These are the questions facing the denomination in 1985 when the story told in this book concludes. These remained the questions Canadian Presbyterians continued to face as new issues emerged and as numerical decline continued. As noted earlier, the denomination did not double its membership in the 1980s, despite some determined work by the Committee on Church Growth to Double in the Eighties. Instead, membership continued to decline. That decline continues, with no indication of when or how it will be reversed (see figure 10.1 and figure 10.2). What has become clearer – though again those within the denomination frequently fail to take this into account – is that allegiance to Christianity as a whole has declined dramatically in Canada. Numerical decline has been the white noise in the background of all the denomination has done in the four decades since 1985. While it has been constant, new realities and new issues have emerged that have become central to the life of the Presbyterian Church in Canada. Korean Canadians, an emerging and important community by the early 1980s, have become a significant linguistic and ethnic component of the denomination. In 1997 the decision was made to allow for Korean language presbyteries.[5] Korean Canadians have been joined by Presbyterians from other parts of the world, notably Africa. In 1994 the denomination offered a confession related to the attitudes it displayed towards Indigenous people during its mission work in Canada.[6] This came as a surprise to many in the denomination. The damage done by residential schools had not been widely discussed. (This is one reason why residential schools are not a major theme in this book.) As Lorenzo Veracini has noted, "Where it is most triumphant, settler colonialism effectively covers its tracks."[7] In later years, Canadian Presbyterians would come to know far more about their role in residential schools and their responsibility for participating with the Canadian government in what the Truth and Reconciliation Committee determined was a "cultural genocide." Relations with Indigenous people in Canada were always framed within the overall home mission work of the denomination, with little sense that anything had gone wrong. This changed with the denomination's 1994 Confession (a confession of sin), which was followed in 2024 with a detailed apology for the denomination's "complicity in colonization and the Residential School System."[8]

The same year, 1994, was also the year the denomination's Church Doctrine Committee released its long-awaited report on human sexuality. The origins of the report go back to 1984 and an overture from

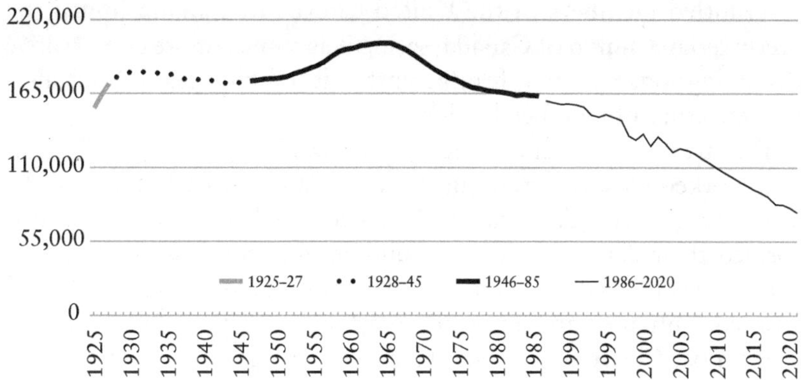

Figure 10.1 Membership in the Presbyterian Church in Canada, 1925–2020

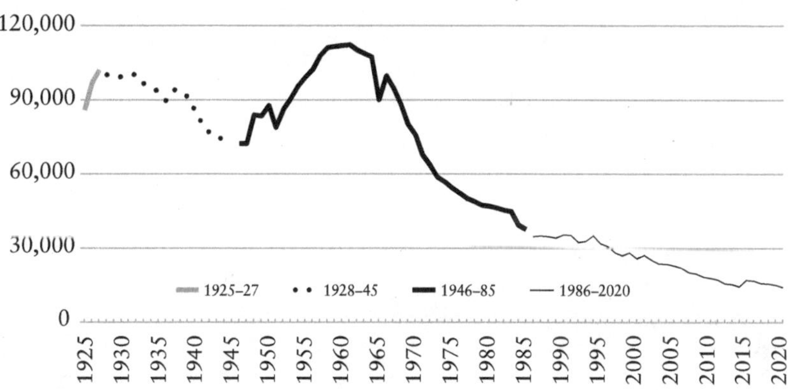

Figure 10.2 Church school membership, 1925–2020

the Presbytery of Cape Breton asking the denomination to state clearly its belief that homosexuality was a sin.[9] The Church Doctrine Committee wrestled with this for years and provided a series of reports along the way. In 1994, the denomination adopted the report of the committee in a way that suggested that the discussion was now closed. The report concluded that gays and lesbians were not allowed to be ordained as clergy in the denomination, and reaffirmed the traditional view that marriage could only be between a man and a woman.[10] This affirmation was done at a time when no province in Canada legally accepted same sex marriages (these would become legal across Canada in 2005). The denomination stood firmly by its tradition. A few disgruntled members of the United Church of Canada joined the Presbyterian Church of Canada, seeing it as a much more conservative denomination. Standing firm against cultural changes did not alter the trajectory of membership loss.

That trajectory began in the crucial decades of the 1960s – what had worked so successfully in the 1950s and the early parts of the 1960s no longer did. Canadian Presbyterians had grown and transformed their denomination by building new congregations. Those suburban congregations were crucial in the years that followed. Things worked. Until they no longer did. Adapting to a different Canada, one that is post-Christian and post-Christendom, remains a challenge.

Notes

INTRODUCTION

1 Finlay G. Stewart, "Here it is – 1975!," *Presbyterian Record*, January 1975, 2.
2 Ross, *The Holy Spirit and the Eagle Feather*, 39–40; Bush, *Western Challenge*, 86–118. Grant, *Moon of Wintertime*, 161, 163, makes notes of the first significant engagements with Indigenous peoples. The lack of Presbyterian missions in the mid-nineteenth century, 71–95, is notable.
3 Presbyterian Church in Canada, "List of Residential Schools Operated by the Presbyterian Church in Canada," in *Brief Administrative History of the Residential Schools & the Presbyterian Church in Canada's Healing and Reconciliation Efforts*, 8–9, https://presbyterian.ca/wp-content/uploads/Administrative%20History%20of%20Residential%20Schools.pdf.
4 Allit, *Religion in America*; Clarke, "English-Speaking Canada."
5 Clarke and Macdonald, *Leaving Christianity*.
6 Wilkinson and Ambrose, *After the Revival*; Wilkinson, *Canadian Pentecostalism*; Flatt, *After Evangelicalism*; Stewart, *New Canadian Pentecostals*; Fay, *Canadian Catholics*.
7 The second edition of *Enduring Witness* was published in 1987 and the third in 2004. References to the book in the notes are to the third edition unless otherwise noted.
8 Hayes, *Anglicans in Canada*.
9 Schweitzer, *United Church*; Airhart, *Church with the Soul of a Nation*.

CHAPTER ONE

1 Moir, *Enduring Witness*, 224.
2 Ibid., 128–45; Johnston, "No Slippery Undertaking."
3 Clarke and Macdonald, "No Need to Turn Out the Lights," 200–1.
4 Laverdure, *Sunday in Canada: The Rise and Fall of the Lord's Day*.
5 Methodists, Presbyterians, and Congregationalists were the denominations that united with independent union congregations, which had been established after the Basis of Union had been drafted, in 1925 to form the United Church of Canada.
6 Fraser, *Social Uplifters*; Farris, "Fathers of 1925," 95–124.
7 Given its importance, it is not surprising that there is extensive literature reflecting various perspectives on church union. Some key works include: Moir, *Enduring Witness*, 197–223; Airhart, *Church with the Soul of a Nation*, 30–64; Clifford, *Resistance to Church Union*; Grant, *Church Union*.
8 Moir, *Enduring Witness*, 209–11.
9 Scott, "*Church Union*," 81.
10 Ibid.
11 Moir, *Enduring Witness*, 212; *Acts and Proceedings of the Presbyterian General Assembly* (hereafter *A&P*), 1917, 52–3.
12 Moir, *Enduring Witness*, 217.
13 Ibid., 218.
14 Clifford, *Resistance to Church Union*, 142–206; Corbett, "Legal Problems," 53–65; Knight, "Voices United?" 39–64.
15 This is evident in the Presbyterian Church Association (PCA) fonds in the denominational archives, particularly in these files: 1982-1003-17; 1982-1003-4-1; and 1982-1003-4-2, which includes a list of votes by province as well as the printed report prepared for the Ontario Legislature. Presbyterian Church in Canada Archives (hereafter PCC Archives).
16 Pre-Assembly Congress file, 1982-1003-3-18, PCC Archives.
17 There are two different versions of the *A&P* of the 1925 Presbyterian General Assembly, one ending on 9 June 1925 and one continuing through to 16 June 1925. Both versions are available (as two separate volumes) at the PCC Archives, or in the References section of the Caven Library at Knox College in Toronto, Ontario (where they appear in the same bound volume).
18 The meeting of this body on 11 June and 12 June 1926 at Knox Church in Toronto is noted in WMS-WD General Records, opening page, 1988-7004-63-6, PCC Archives.

19 For church membership, see table 1.1; for church school enrolment, see *A&P* 1925 (3 June–9 June), Summary by Synods to December 31, 1924.
20 Clifford, *Resistance to Church Union*, 173.
21 PCA fonds, 1982-1003-4-2, results for Saskatchewan, PCC Archives.
22 Ibid.
23 Ibid.
24 Ephraim Scott, *Presbyterian Record*, July 1926, 199.
25 Moir, *Enduring Witness*, 225–6, cites an article by Scott in the April 1926 *Record* where he makes the same misleading claim, which Moir disputes. For a discussion of the UCC in this period, see Airhart, *Church with the Soul of a Nation*; McIntyre, "Unity among Many;" and Stebner, "The 1930s."
26 *Presbyterian Record*, July 1928, 197–8.
27 *Presbyterian Record*, vol. 50, nos 6–7, published in Toronto in June 1925, was produced by pro-union Presbyterians. Scott published, from Montreal, *Presbyterian Record*, vol. 50, 6, June 1925.
28 *Presbyterian Record*, vol. 50, no. 7, July 1925, cover.
29 Dunn, "Great Divorce," 58–96.
30 Ibid., 80. Mission fields were later opened in Manchuria and among Koreans in Japan, 88–9.
31 Anderson, *Kimchi and Maple Leaves*, 171–95.
32 Jess, "Young People," 27–36.
33 Clifford, *Resistance to Church Union*, 194–206, 219–22.
34 *Presbyterian Record*, July 1927, 199–200.
35 *Presbyterian Record*, August 1928, 231.
36 *Presbyterian Record*, August 1929, 253.
37 Ibid., 256.
38 *Presbyterian Record*, August 1928, 236.
39 Ibid.
40 Ibid.
41 *Presbyterian Record*, July 1930, 195.
42 *Presbyterian Record*, August 1930, 229.
43 *Presbyterian Record*, July 1930, 198.
44 Ibid., 201.
45 Ibid., 197–8.
46 *Presbyterian Record*, August 1930, 227.
47 Farris, "Fathers of 1925," 95–124.
48 Vissers, "Recovering the Reformation Conception," 240. Vissers, *W.W. Bryden*.
49 *Presbyterian Record*, July 1931, 198.
50 *Presbyterian Record*, August 1932, 235.

51 *A&P*, 1932, 44–5, 133–5, 137.
52 *Presbyterian Record*, August 1933, 237.
53 *Presbyterian Record*, August 1935, 240–3.
54 Ibid., 243.
55 Ibid., 245.
56 *Presbyterian Record*, August 1936, 231.
57 *Presbyterian Record*, August 1939, 229.
58 *Presbyterian Record*, August 1943, 227.
59 *Presbyterian Record*, August 1944, 230.
60 *Presbyterian Record*, July 1935, 202–5.
61 *Presbyterian Record*, August 1935, 236.
62 *Presbyterian Record*, July 1935, 209–10.
63 Moir, *Enduring Witness*, stresses the UCC challenge in 1932, 232; see also Clifford, *Resistance to Church Union*, 207–18.
64 *Presbyterian Record*, August 1938, 235.
65 *Presbyterian Record*, July 1939, 199.
66 Ibid., 202.
67 *Presbyterian Record*, August 1939, 230.
68 Clifford, *Resistance to Church Union*, 234–5.
69 Moir, *Enduring Witness*, 245. This quote has been present in all editions of the book.

CHAPTER TWO

1 Minutes, Presbytery of Toronto, September 1944–June 1945, 1977-3011, PCC Archives. This topic was discussed in an earlier publication, Macdonald, "Taking God into the Suburbs."
2 *A&P*, 1946, 8.
3 Ibid., 10.
4 The Presbytery of Toronto divided into West Toronto and East Toronto in 1949 but continued to work together on church extension.
5 *A&P*, 1948, Appendices, 7.
6 *A&P*, 1952, Appendices, 9.
7 Ibid.
8 Ibid. See also the discussion later in this chapter on extension work in Montreal.
9 Rev. J.J. Edmiston, Historical sketch, dedication of the building, Synod of the Maritime Provinces, Historical Committee, 1973-2005-1-6, PCC Archives.

10 Jackson, *Crabgrass Frontiers*, is the classic study of suburbanization. The Canadian experience shared some similarities, but was also different. Harris, *Creeping Conformity*; Solomon, *Toronto Sprawls*. For a contemporary Canadian Presbyterian view of the suburbs, see Welch, "Ministry of the Church in Suburbia."
11 The *A&P* gave data from which the computer-generated maps of congregations were produced. This information was confirmed using Adamson, "The Presbytery of West Toronto."
12 John McNab, "Evangelizing the Growing Suburbs," *Presbyterian Record*, December 1954, 10–12.
13 John McNab, "Presbytery Tackles New Frontiers," *Presbyterian Record*, January 1955, 10–12.
14 Allister E. Morrison, "Prospecting on the Eastern Seaboard," *Presbyterian Record*, March 1955, 4–5.
15 John McNab, "Church Extension Beckons in the West!" *Presbyterian Record*, September 1955, 18–20.
16 John McNab, "Lengthen the Cords and Strengthen the Stakes," *Presbyterian Record*, October 1955, 12–14.
17 Ibid., 13. Calgary seems to have been unique in their willingness to relocate congregations. Synod of Alberta History Committee, "Growth," 118–19.
18 McNab, "Lengthen the Cords," 14. It was not clear if this was an Indigenous or European-Canadian congregation.
19 "Kenora's new Fellowship Centre," *Presbyterian Record*, July–August 1971, 19.
20 McNab, "Lengthen the Cords," 15.
21 John McNab, "The Challenge of the Prairies?" *Presbyterian Record*, November 1955, 4.
22 Ibid., 5.
23 Ibid.
24 Ibid.
25 McNab, "Church Extension Beckons," 20.
26 John McNab, "Montreal Suburbs Welcome the Church," *Presbyterian Record*, March 1957, 12–14.
27 "Montreal's Outreach," *Presbyterian Record*, June 1959, 8–9, 28. The article has no byline, but notes that it was "based on material" provided by the convenor of the extension committee, the Rev. Dr W. Stanford Reid.
28 Ibid.
29 Moir, *Enduring Witness*, 77–95.

30 Bush, *Western Challenge*, 55–61, 66–71.
31 *A&P*, 1955, overture 25, 336–7.
32 Synod of Alberta, "Growth," 26–7.
33 Corporation files, Corporation of the Synod of Toronto and Kingston, Annual Report, 1982-2002-1-1, PCC Archives.
34 Corporation files, Corporation of the Synod of Toronto and Kingston, Third Annual Report, 2, 1982-2002-1-1, PCC Archives.
35 Corporation files, Corporation of the Synod of Toronto and Kingston, Letter from D. McCullough, October 27, 1959, 1982-2002-1-1, PCC Archives.
36 Corporation files, Corporation of the Synod of Toronto and Kingston, First Annual Report, 4–5, 1982-2002-1-1, PCC Archives.
37 Corporation files, "The Corporation of the Synod of Toronto and Kingston of the Presbyterian Church in Canada," n.d. but c. 1962, 1982-2002-1-1, PCC Archives. There are individual profiles of congregations. No information was given about St Paul's. The new congregation was anticipating a membership of 500 and a church school membership of 350.
38 Ibid.
39 Corporation files, Synod of Hamilton London, 1987-2002-1-11, PCC Archives.
40 Presbytery of West Toronto Minutes, 1977-3012-1-4, December 11, 1956, April 2, 1957.
41 Ibid., May 7, 1957, June 25, 1957, May 6, 1958.
42 This analysis is based upon the denominational statistics in the *A&P*, 1961.
43 *A&P*, statistics, 1966.
44 Order of service for the dedication of the Christian education building, Presbytery of West Toronto, 1977-3012-35-36, PCC Archives.
45 Chadwick, *The Scots Kirk*, 60, 135.
46 *A&P*, statistics, 1946, 1966.

CHAPTER THREE

1 "Westmount Churchgoers See Banned Film," *Presbyterian Record*, July–August 1955, 3; "The Film That Quebec Banned!," *Presbyterian Record*, February 1954, 3; Macdonald, "Vatican II," 83–5.
2 "The Film," 3.
3 "Westmount Churchgoers," 3.
4 *A&P*, 1945, overture 29, 151–2.
5 *A&P*, 1946, overture 2, 128–9.

6 Moir, *Enduring Witness*, 252.
7 *A&P*, 1947, overture 28, 1947, 156–7.
8 Ibid., overture 37, 162, and overture 42, 165–6.
9 Moir, *Enduring Witness*, 252–3.
10 *A&P*, 1961, 361.
11 There is a stark contrast between the Committee on Inter-Church Relations, "Presbyterians and the Church Catholic" and Stanford Reid, "In the Unity of Faith."
12 *A&P*, 1964, 437.
13 *A&P*, 1967, 53; *A&P*, committee report, 1969, 375.
14 Macdonald, "Presbyterian and Reformed," 182–8.
15 *Presbyterian Record*, July–August 1945, 199.
16 One example was pictures of Chinese and Ukrainian dress at the 1963 General Assembly. *Presbyterian Record*, July–August 1963, 9.
17 *Presbyterian Record*, July–August 1947, 199.
18 *Presbyterian Record*, July–August 1956, 7.
19 *A&P*, 1962, 98, 288–9.
20 General Board of Missions, "Looking Ahead," 9.
21 Ibid.
22 Mark, "Synod Address," 2–7.
23 Ibid., 8–9.
24 Ibid., 9–10.
25 Reith, "Our Commission … in Canada … and Overseas," 18–19.
26 Ibid., 19.
27 Ibid., 56–64, 70–1.
28 Ransom, *No Time To Falter*, 43–77.
29 *A&P*, 1947, Appendices, 19–21.
30 Ibid, 54.
31 James A. Munro, "Home Missions in Review," *Presbyterian Record*, January 1958, 24–5.
32 *Presbyterian Record*, September 1965, 30.
33 *A&P*, 1947, 214–15.
34 *A&P*, 1957, 358–67.
35 A&P, 1965, 526–7, 529.
36 Airhart, *Church with the Soul of a Nation*, 228–30.
37 Angus, "Political Values," 57.
38 William Fitch, "Scotland Welcomes Billy Graham," *Presbyterian Record*, May 1955, 18–20; Fitch, "Billy Graham Tells Scotland," *Presbyterian Record*, June 1955, 6–7, 29; John McNab, "The Editor Reports," *Presbyterian Record*, September 1955, 7.

39 John McNab, "The Secret of Billy Graham's Crusade," *Presbyterian Record*, November 1955, 18–19, 32; "Graham Follow-Up Rally Held in Toronto," *Presbyterian Record*, December 1955, 26.
40 Report on Assembly, *Presbyterian Record*, July–August 1959, 11.
41 *A&P*, 1947, Appendices, 85; *A&P*, 1948, 351–6; *A&P*, 1949, 155.
42 *A&P*, 1948, 342–350.
43 Report on Assembly, *Presbyterian Record*, July–August 1962, 8.
44 In using this comparison in 1971, the report on Declining Church Membership was following a common pattern. *A&P*, 1971, 290.
45 A building committee was created in 1958.
46 Staff moved into the building in August 1966. The official dedication was held 30 November 1967 with the Governor General in attendance.
47 Report on Assembly, *Presbyterian Record*, July–August 1945, 199.
48 Ibid. See also, Moir, *Enduring Witness*, 248–9; *A&P*, 1946, Reports, 96.
49 *A&P*, 1947, 355.
50 Ibid., 356. Italics in the original.
51 Report on Assembly, *Presbyterian Record*, July–August 1955, 10.
52 *A&P*, 1957, overture 2, 346; overture 6, 348–9; overture 16, 355–6.
53 Ibid., 75.
54 *A&P*, 1958, overture 31, 369.
55 Ibid., overture 32, 370.
56 Ibid., overture 8, 357. This overture from the Presbytery of Westminster is the one generally cited. Among the other overtures raising concerns about finances that year were overture 17, 362, overture 18, 362–3, and overture 28, 368, each with quite a different diagnosis of the issues.
57 *A&P*, 1958, 354–72; *A&P*, 1959, 567–604; *A&P*, 1960, 416–18. The financial crisis in this period is not a major topic within Moir, *Enduring Witness*. MacLeod, *Evangelical Calvinist*, discusses this with a focus on the role played by Stanford Reid, 147–51.
58 *A&P*, 1959, 567–70.
59 Ibid., 568–9.
60 Ibid., 571–4.
61 Ibid., 575.
62 Ibid., 576.
63 Ibid.
64 Ibid., 577.
65 Ibid., 581.
66 Ibid., 580.
67 *A&P*, 1960, 416–18.
68 Editorial, *Presbyterian Record*, November 1967, 4.

69 Malvina Reynolds, "Little Boxes," track 3 on *Malvina Reynolds Sings the Truth*, Columbia Records, 1967.
70 Macdonald, "Vatican II," 78–105; O'Malley, *Vatican II*.
71 Berton, *The Comfortable Pew*, 110.
72 Ibid., 129.
73 Byfield, *Just Think*.
74 Kilbourn, *The Restless Church*.
75 Board of Evangelism (UCC), *Why the Sea*.
76 McLelland, "Why Our Pond," 5.
77 Ibid., 6.

CHAPTER FOUR

1 The picture and caption appeared in the July–August edition of the *Presbyterian Record*, 1967, 12. For a biography of Mary Whale see Nutt, "Mary E. Whale," 110–7.
2 Airhart, "Women in the United Church," 361–8; Boyd, "Presbyterian Women," 352–61; Brown Zikmund, "Protestant Women's Ordination," 940–50. For discussion on women in the Presbyterian Church in Canada see Moir, *Enduring Witness*, 255–6; Bush, "Women's Ordination Debate," 1–6; Macdonald, "What were they thinking," 16–30.
3 Korinek, "No Women Need Apply," 473–509.
4 Wilson, *Turning the World*, 20–35.
5 Airhart, "Women in the United Church," offers a parallel example, esp. 365–6; see also Klempa and Doran, *Certain Women*.
6 Klempa and Doran, *Certain Women*.
7 *A&P*, 1953, overture 2, 393.
8 Ibid., 33–4, 89, 96.
9 *A&P*, 1954, 33–4. While the committee reported to the General Assembly in 1954, their report was not included in the appendices in 1954. The text of the 1954 report was published as part of a document, "Report of The Committee Re: The Place of Women in the Church," General Assembly 1955, and went from page 9 to 11. Again, this was not printed in the appendices of the *A&P* in 1955, but seems to have been distributed to the Assembly. "Report of the Committee Re: The Place of Women in the Church," General Assembly, 1955, 1973-1023-1-3, PCC Archives. A copy of this report is included in a file folder containing minutes from the Committee on the Place of Women in the Church in the Caven Library at Knox College in Toronto, Ontario (hereafter cited as CPWC file folder).

10 The committee was sometimes referred to as the "Special Committee," while other times it was referred to as simply the "Committee."

11 "Report of the Committee Re: The Place of Women in the Church," General Assembly, 1955, 9, 1973-1023-1-3, PCC Archives.

12 Ibid., 10.

13 Ibid., 10–11.

14 Ibid., 11.

15 Ibid., 3.

16 Ibid., 3.

17 Ibid., 4; *A&P*, 1955, 58–9. The report itself was again not published (see above).

18 Louis H. Fowler, "The Place of Women in the Church," *Presbyterian Record*, September 1955, 10–11.

19 "Report of the Committee Re: The Place of Women in the Church," General Assembly, 1955, 6–9, 1973-1023-1-3, PCC Archives.

20 Fowler, "Place of Women," 10.

21 Ibid, 11.

22 L. Jean Black, "The Place of Women in the Church," *Presbyterian Record*, May 1956, 5.

23 John A. Johnson, "Reasons for Opposing the Ordination of Women," *Presbyterian Record*, May 1956, 6–7.

24 Frank S. Morley, "Women Should be Ordained," *Presbyterian Record*, May 1956, 18–19.

25 Helen Scott Sinclair, "An Order of Women," *Presbyterian Record*, March 1958, 4–5, 30.

26 Ibid., 5.

27 Ibid., 30.

28 Editor, "Presbyterian Alliance Examines the Status of Churchwomen," *Presbyterian Record*, April 1953, 11; Madeleine Barot, "Men, Women, and the Church," *Presbyterian Record*, January 1959, 26.

29 Other articles include: Mary MacNicol, "A student tells the story of Our Deaconess School," *Presbyterian Record*, February 1959, 16–17; James D. Smart, "The Ministry of Women," *Presbyterian Record*, February 1959, 10–11, 32; Helen Scott Sinclair, "Is Woman-Power Wasted in Our Church," *Presbyterian Record*, October 1959, 6–7.

30 This was reported in the *A&P*, 1956, as part of the report of the committee, 312–13. The results from presbyteries have been noted in the literature and are fairly widely known.

31 For the report see *A&P*, 1956, 312–14. The Assembly's actions are in the minutes, 74–5, 85.

32 *A&P*, 1957, 77.
33 Ibid., 259–60.
34 Ibid., 260.
35 Ibid.
36 *A&P*, 1957, 260–1.
37 *A&P*, 1958, 284; *A&P*, 1959; *A&P*, 1960. This concern is also demonstrated in the minutes of the committee, CPWC file folder.
38 "Memoranda from Convenor to Committee Members: Dec., 1959," CPWC file folder.
39 *A&P*, 1960. The text of the overture is printed on page 456.
40 Ibid., 39, 54, 71, 103.
41 For these results see *A&P*, 1961, 350.
42 Ibid., 415.
43 Minutes of the Committee on the Place of Women in the Church, Minutes of the Committee, November 16, 1960, CPWC file folder.
44 *A&P*, 1961, 290. The minutes record this using slightly different words.
45 Ibid.
46 Ibid.
47 Minutes, November 16, 1960, 2, CPWC file folder.
48 *A&P*, 1961, 290.
49 Ibid.
50 Minutes, January 24, 1962, CPWC file folder.
51 Minutes, May 10, 1962, CPWC file folder.
52 *A&P*, 1962, 288.
53 *A&P*, 1963, The Articles of Faith report, 301.
54 Committee on the Place of Women in the Church, "Putting Woman in Her Place," c. 1963, inside cover. MacLeod, "Reaction to Renewal," 179, suggests Eoin Mackay was the primary author of this document. Eoin Mackay was clearly a key figure on the committee, but there is no evidence in the document itself to support this contention.
55 "Putting Woman in Her Place," 1.
56 Ibid., 2–4.
57 Ibid., 5.
58 Ibid., 6–7.
59 Ibid., 8.
60 Ibid., 10.
61 Ibid., 11.
62 Ibid., 13.
63 Ibid.
64 Ibid., 14–16.

65 Flatt, *After Evangelicalism*, 12, includes neo-orthodoxy with liberalism under the term "modernism." The argument being made in this chapter is that neo-orthodoxy is distinct from, and should not be understood as a form of, liberal theology.
66 Everett Bean, "Regarding the Ordination of Women," *Presbyterian Comment* (June 1961): 3–4.
67 DeCourcy Rayner, "Editorial," *Presbyterian Record*, June 1964, 4.
68 *A&P*, 1964, 386. This suggests it was well used: committees were often clear in noting their disappointment when their work was not used.
69 *A&P*, 1964, 386.
70 Ibid., 387.
71 Ibid.
72 Ibid., 387.
73 Ibid.
74 The differences in wording between these motions is interesting, with motion 4 (ordination of women as elders) being much briefer, clearer, and more direct. Ibid., 388.
75 Ibid., 386–8; for the actions of Assembly in regard to these motions, see 48, 103.
76 Note the underlined numbers are the only ones mentioned in the denomination's history. Moir, *Enduring Witness*, 255–6.
77 *A&P*, 1965, 384. The committee reported the number of presbyteries who had responded and the number who had voted in favour of each motion.
78 Ibid., 52.
79 Ibid., 108.
80 Ibid., 52, 108; Report of the committee, 384–5.
81 The vote under the Barrier Act was reported in *A&P*, 1966, 456.
82 Text of Remits, *A&P*, 1966, 47.
83 Ibid., 52, 57–8.
84 Ibid., 75–8, 98–9, 99–100.
85 Ibid., 116. While the reasons for dissents for women as ministers were similar, no special committee was established to respond.
86 *Time* magazine (Canadian edition), June 17, 1966, 14.
87 Tippins, "Celebrating the 50th Anniversary."
88 *Presbyterian Record*, June–July 1967, 16. This was reported under "Other matters" which details some seemingly humorous moments at Assembly alongside other minor, but important, matters.
89 *A&P*, 1967, 357–9.
90 Knox College *Bulletin*, Autumn 1968, 1; *Presbyterian Record*, June 1968, 5.

91 Tippins, "Celebrating the 50th Anniversary."
92 Chaves, *Ordaining Women*, 32–6, 49.
93 *A&P*, 2021, overture 1, Presbytery of Western Han Ca, 740; Overture 20, Presbytery of Eastern Han Can, 750.
94 MacLeod, "From Reaction to Renewal," 179.
95 A. Donald MacLeod, "'Good-bye' is Never Easy," *Channels* (Summer 1987): 2.
96 *Presbyterian Comment* 6, no. 4 (September 1966): 1. This is the first issue in 1966 that exists in the PCC Archives. Whether commentary was made in previous numbers that year is unclear.

CHAPTER FIVE

1 Moir, "Who Pays the Piper," 67–81.
2 Scott, "*Church Union,*" 132.
3 "A Deliverance of the Presbytery of Paris," *The Presbyterian Student* 4, 4 May 1939, 5–9. The origins and distribution of the Deliverance are included in the preface, 5, with the text of the Deliverance following.
4 Moir, *Enduring Witness*, 254; Klempa, "Declaration Revisited," 86–96; Klempa, "Canadian Presbyterians and Westminster Standards," 132–3. The very different character of the two memorials from the Presbytery of Paris is not clear in these discussions. Macdonald, "Protest or Loyalty," discusses this but confuses the two memorials from the Presbytery of Paris.
5 Paris Deliverance, 5–6.
6 *A&P*, 1939, 29. The custom at the time seems to have been to only print the text of overtures, not petitions or memorials.
7 *A&P*, 1939, 66.
8 Peddie, "*The King of Kings.*" There is no pagination, but this document appears on the first page.
9 Ibid.
10 Ibid., section 6.
11 Ibid., end of section 6.
12 *A&P*, 1942, overture 18, 112–13.
13 Ibid. Not everyone in the synod agreed: the overture was not approved by the synod, but simply passed on to the General Assembly without comment, approval, or disapproval. One dissent was noted.
14 *A&P*, 1942, overture 24, 117.
15 Ibid., 117.
16 *A&P*, 1942, 19, 22.

17 Ibid., 26, 42–4.
18 Ibid., 44–5.
19 *A&P*, 1943, 130. Mackenzie King, the Prime Minister, was a Presbyterian.
20 Ibid., 131.
21 Ibid.
22 Ibid., 52.
23 *A&P*, 1944, 57.
24 *A&P*, 1945, 301–8.
25 Ibid., 304.
26 Ibid., 304–5.
27 WCF, chapter 23, 3.
28 *A&P*, 1945, 306.
29 Ibid., 307.
30 Ibid., 307–8.
31 *A&P*, 1947, 183. The committee's name was changed to the Committee on Articles of Faith in 1946, *A&P*, 1946, 77.
32 *A&P*, 1947, 182.
33 *A&P*, 1948, 129.
34 Ibid., 131.
35 Ibid.
36 Ibid., 131, 133.
37 Ibid., 137.
38 *A&P*, 1949, 313–17. Each of these descriptions, called "Articles" now, was approximately two pages. Two members of the committee, William Stanford Reid and Scott Mackenzie, resigned before the 1949 report, 310.
39 *A&P*, 1949, overture 18, 110.
40 Ibid.
41 Ibid.
42 *A&P*, 1951, 87.
43 Ibid., the Preamble, 88–91, the Articles of Faith, 91–98. The Declaration itself was not printed in the *A&P*, perhaps because it had been distributed at Assembly and was being actively discussed.
44 Ibid., 88.
45 Ibid.
46 This is the only time the Preamble appears. The Articles were reprinted in the 1952 report.
47 *A&P*, 1954. The debate extended over serval sederunts. The motion is on 65; the dissent is recorded on 66.

48 *A&P*, 1955, 46–7, 288; Dissent, 90–91.
49 Ibid., overture 14, 330–1, overture 37, 343–4.
50 *A&P*, 1955, 288. The report on Remittances notes East Toronto passing this with dissents. Overture 30, 340.
51 Ibid., overture 30, 340.
52 Ibid.
53 Ibid.
54 McNab, "What Do Presbyterians Believe?," ii.
55 Mariano Di Gangi, "The Task of Evangelism," in McNab, "What Do Presbyterians Believe?," 44.
56 F. Scott Mackenzie, "Predestination," in McNab, "What Do Presbyterians Believe?," 53–4.
57 Ibid., 55.
58 Reference to the 1939 edition, *Presbyterian Record*, 1940, 203; Presbyterian Church in Canada, *Book of Common Order* (BCO), 2nd revised edition, 1948.
59 Ibid., preface to the first edition, v.
60 Ibid., preface to the second edition, iii.
61 *A&P*, 1953, overture 22, 403.
62 Ibid.
63 *A&P*, 1956, 74–5, 373; *A&P*, 1957, 250–2; *A&P*, 1958, 268–270; *A&P*, 1959, 298 300.
64 *A&P*, 1957, 343. The survey went from 341–5.
65 *A&P*, 1956, 321.
66 *A&P*, 1960, 311.
67 *A&P*, 1965, 383.
68 Presbyterian Church in Canada, BCO, 1964, Preface, v–vi.
69 Ibid., vi.
70 Ibid.
71 Farris, "Fathers of 1925," 95–124.
72 Moir, *Enduring Witness*, 261.
73 *A&P*, 1961, 302–3.
74 *A&P*, 1958, 42.
75 *A&P*, 1960, 83.
76 *A&P*, 1962, 49.
77 *A&P*, 1964, 61–2.
78 MacLeod, *Evangelical Calvinist*, 157–9.
79 Ibid.
80 *A&P*, 1963, 50.

CHAPTER SIX

1 For an exploration of the 1960s, see Marwick, *The Sixties*; Petigny, *The Permissive Society*; McLeod, *Religious Crisis*; Brown, *Death of Christian Britain*. For Canada in this period, Owram, *Born at the Right time*; Christie and Gavreau, *Sixties and Beyond*; Miedema, *For Canada's Sake*.

2 Joseph McLelland, "Blueprint for a new model," *Presbyterian Record*, September 1967, 8–17.

3 William Stanford Reid, letter to the editor, *Presbyterian Record*, November 1967, 9.

4 Administrative Council, *A&P*, 1965, 479.

5 Ibid., 482.

6 Committee on Recruitment, *A&P*, 1965, 375.

7 Committee on Synod Corporation, *A&P*, 1968, 299–300.

8 Stuart B. Coles, "Crisis = Danger + Opportunity," *Presbyterian Record*, May 1968, 11. Italics in the original.

9 Ibid., 10. Italics in the original.

10 Ibid., 10–11.

11 These documents can be found in Congress of Concern file, 1988-1005-2-15, PCC Archives.

12 Valerie M. Dunn, "A Congress of Concern: were they rebels or reformers?" *Presbyterian Record*, July–August 1968, 16–17.

13 Congress of Concern file, 1988-1005-2-15.

14 Dunn, "A congress of concern," 17.

15 Congress of Concern file, 1988-1005-2-15.

16 Ibid.

17 *A&P*, 1968, 94.

18 Charles Cochrane, "The Nature of Renewal," *Presbyterian Record*, April 1969, 12.

19 Ibid., 13.

20 "Can we face these explosive issues," *Presbyterian Record*, May 1969, 15. The article noted that material was contributed by R.P. Carter and Wayne Smith.

21 Cover, *Presbyterian Record*, July–August 1969. Quotation is taken from the description of the cover, 5.

22 *A&P*, 1969, 377–99.

23 News item, *Presbyterian Record*, December 1969, 18.

24 Committee on Life and Mission, *Into the 70's* (LAMP report).

25 Ibid., 11.

26 Ibid., 12.
27 Ibid., 25–6.
28 Ibid., 32.
29 Ibid., 54.
30 Ibid., 55, 63.
31 Final Ross Report, October 1969, xi, 1973-1025-1-5, PCC Archives.
32 Valerie Dunn, "Whatever Happened to the Ross Report?" *Presbyterian Record*, February 1971, 2.
33 *A&P*, 1970, 33, 60–1, 104–5, 374–83.
34 Final Ross Report, October 1969, 61–5.
35 Ibid., 68–71. The data provided on the reformers in this section of the report came from sources largely outside of the process undertaken by the Ross Report. Comments made during the Congress of Concern were reported in such a way that it gave them similar validity to those discovered during the process of research conducted for the report.
36 Ibid., 68.
37 Ibid., 71.
38 Interim Ross Report, 13, 1973-1025-1-4, PCC Archives; Final Ross Report, 89.
39 "Declining Church Membership," Board of Evangelism and Social Action, *A&P*, 1971, 290–3.
40 Ibid., 290. Italics in the original.
41 Ibid., 292.
42 Ibid., 295.
43 Ibid., 296.
44 Ibid., 298.
45 Ibid., 299.
46 Ibid., 300–1. There is a space on 301. Thc paragraph was deleted from the report. This is discussed in chapter 7.
47 McGillivray, "Educating Baby Boomers."
48 William Fitch, "Revising the Book of Praise," *Presbyterian Record*, February 1968, 18–20.
49 Zander Dunn, "The Crux of the Matter: the 1971 Presbyterian Congress," *Presbyterian Record*, September 1971, 20–3; "Over 800 Presbyterians Came to Congress '75," *Presbyterian Record*, September 1975, xx; James Dickey, "Congress '79: Guelph, Ontario," *Presbyterian Record*, September 1979, 12–14.
50 Dunn, "The Crux of the Matter," 20–3.
51 "Knox College students tour Nova Scotia," *Presbyterian Record*, July–August 1972, 21.

52 Wayne Smith, "A Youth Ministry on Wheels," *Presbyterian Record*, November 1974, 18–19.
53 Zander Dunn, "A New Kind of Camp," *Presbyterian Record*, November 1972, 11.
54 On the Christian Pavilion at Expo '67, see Sheldon MacKenzie, "The Christian Pavilion," *Presbyterian Record*, January 1966, 17; and the editorial "Is the Christian Pavilion Effective," *Presbyterian Record*, July 1967, 4. On the importance of evangelism, see *Presbyterian Record*, January 1961, back cover; Wayne Smith, "More than just another Church Meeting," *Presbyterian Record*, October 1970, 16–17; and the exploration of evangelism in the United Church of Canada in Plaxton, "Evangelize with the Whole Gospel."
55 Advertisement, "Presbyterian Youth Hostel Expo '67," *Presbyterian Record*, February 1967. 25. "The Carpenter Shop," *Presbyterian Record*, November 1970, 26; DeCourcy Rayner, "Nuts 'n Bolts 'n Things," *Presbyterian Record*, June 1973, 18–19; Douglas Lowry, "The Unity of the Spirit," *Presbyterian Record*, October 1977, 18–19.
56 Fonds level description, PWS&D fonds, 1972–1998, 2, PCC Archives.
57 Willoughby Belch, "The Gift of Life," *Presbyterian Record*, March 1985, 8; Editorial, *Presbyterian Record*, April 1985, 4. The moderator in office at the time, Alex Calder, was opposed to abortion.
58 Various pamphlets on current ethical issues were published by the denomination in this period. One example, Tattrie, *Euthanasia*.
59 This controversy can be followed in the *Presbyterian Record*. Glen Davis, then an Associate Secretary for Board of World Mission, wrote an article on Nicaragua, March 1985, 14–17, and then one on El Salvador, April 1985, 22–5. His views were challenged in Rudolph Placek, "A Reply to Glen Davis," June 1985, 8–9, and in various letters to the editor. Canadian Presbyterians were clearly divided on one of the major political issues of the day – American foreign policy in this region.
60 Gabe Rienks, "Presbyterian identity," *Presbyterian Record*, November 1974, 2–3.
61 DeCourcy H. Rayner, "Our new Church history: Enduring witness. A Centennial gift from the author John S. Moir," *Presbyterian Record*, November 1974, 13. Another centennial project was a photo album of the denomination: Bailey, *Covenant in Canada*.
62 Ibid.
63 Ibid.

64 Brian Fraser, "Into the twentieth century," *Presbyterian Record*, April 1974, 16–17. The description of Fraser's role is given on 17. Three other articles appeared by Fraser exploring these themes.
65 Stewart, "Here it is," 3.
66 Ibid., 3.
67 Advertisement, "Presbyterian Centennial Tours," *Presbyterian Record*, February 1974, 21. It was noted that this project was authorized by both the Centennial Committee and the History Committee of the denomination.
68 "Celebrate with Music," *Presbyterian Record*, July–August 1975, 18–19.
69 Sheila Kirkland, "Every banner a winner!" *Presbyterian Record*, July–August 1975, 2–3. This list of the tour of the Centennial banners and where they would be was published as a news item April 1975, 20.
70 Judy Melanson, "The Centennial in Song," *Presbyterian Record*, June 1975, 16.
71 Clarke and Macdonald, *Leaving Christianity*, 27–71.
72 Ibid., 28–32.
73 *A&P*, 1979, 42.
74 Assembly report, *Presbyterian Record*, July–August 1979, 10.
75 *A&P*, 1979, 68–9.
76 *A&P*, 1978, 384.
77 Ibid., 385. This is a quotation with a quotation inside it.
78 Ibid., 390–1.
79 *A&P*, 1979, 477–9.
80 Assembly issue, *Presbyterian Record*, July–August 1979, 11.
81 Dennis Oliver, "Renewal and Growth in an Old-Line Church: The Presbyterian Example," Canadian Church Growth Leadership Letter, Easter, 1981, 2, 1982-1012-1-3, PCC Archives.
82 Ibid., 4.
83 *A&P*, 1980. This report is 272–9. Quote is from 277.
84 Ibid., 391.
85 Ibid.
86 Ibid., 392.
87 *A&P*, 1981, 238.
88 *A&P*, 1984, 278.
89 "Presbyterians in Canada," *Christian Century*, July 25, 1984, V101, 706.
90 *A&P*, 1985, 253.
91 *A&P*, 1981, 238–240.
92 *A&P*, 1983, 231–47.

93 *A&P*, 1984, 278–87.
94 Macdonald, "Vatican II," 104.
95 *A&P*, 1978, 76, 330, 335. The Inter-Church relations committee shows an openness to the UCC, including the passage of a motion for the mutual recognition of ministers of the UCC.
96 File related to W5 program, GS 83-2, box 2, file 4. Anglican Church of Canada, General Synod Archives.
97 James Dickey, *Presbyterian Record*, July–August 1979, 8. Capitalization as in the original.
98 *A&P*, 1979, overture 24, 452.

CHAPTER SEVEN

1 *A&P*, 1962, 201.
2 Report on Assembly, *Presbyterian Record*, July–August 1965, 13.
3 *A&P*, 1965, 203. This is stated in the opening paragraph of the report on Church Extension.
4 Jack Cooper, "Theology of Church Extension," presented at a workshop on church extension held at Knox College, December 28–9, 1966, 2; National Church extension committee, 1988-1003-71-6, PCC Archives.
5 Ibid., 4.
6 Ibid., 6.
7 Ibid.
8 G.D. Johnston, "Address by the Very Rev. G.D. Johnston to the National Church Extension Committee," September 1967, 1, 6, 1988-1003-74-14, PCC Archives. While Johnston was a former moderator, the title given to Johnston – "Very Rev." – was not used by the PCC in this period.
9 Ibid., 7. Note that this was after women could be ordained.
10 "Preliminary Study of Our Methods of Financing Church Buildings," 1–2, 1988-1003-74-14, PCC Archives.
11 Ibid., 2.
12 *A&P*, 1966, Church extension report, 245.
13 PCC Extension, "Report on London," 2, 1988-1003-74-10, PCC Archives.
14 Cooper, "Report to the Presbytery of Westminster," 6, 1988-1003-74-13, PCC Archives.
15 Ibid.
16 Ibid.
17 PCC Extension, "Report to the Presbytery of Assiniboia," 5, 1988-1003-74-11, PCC Archives.

18 Ibid., 6.
19 Ibid., 10.
20 Ibid., 18, 19. The report on Calvin Presbyterian church is, 13–17.
21 *A&P*, 1967, 255.
22 *A&P*, 1968, 202.
23 J.C. Cooper, "Church extension today," May 22, 1968, 8–9, 1988-1003-71-6, PCC Archives.
24 *A&P*, 1968, 47.
25 *A&P*, 1970, 259.
26 Ibid., 259–60.
27 Moir, *Enduring Witness*, 3rd edition, 265. The latter quote in Moir suggests that this failure was caused by the "unexpected decline" in church membership, and led, alongside the escalating costs, to the freeze in 1962. The freeze was clearly related to the financial challenges of the church; it is not clear that declining membership played a role in this. What is important for the discussion is that, based on the evidence provided in the report in the *Acts and Proceedings*, Moir concluded church extension in the denomination had failed. This has been a common, if not *the* common, assumption since.
28 General Board of Mission minutes, March 11, 1970, 15, 19881003-12-10, PCC Archives.
29 Ibid.
30 Ibid.
31 "Church Campus Concept." April 1970, 1988-1003-74-14, PCC Archives.
32 *A&P*, 1978, 433–4.
33 *A&P*, 1979, 431–2.
34 Ibid., 431–2.
35 *A&P*, 1980, 424. They noted "full support of the minister" was to be for only three years.
36 Ibid., 424–5.
37 *A&P*, 1981, 446.
38 *A&P*, 1981, 54.
39 *A&P*, 1982, 236.
40 Ibid.
41 Ibid., 237.
42 Ibid.
43 Ibid.
44 Ibid., 239.
45 Ibid.

46 Ibid.
47 Ibid, 240. Italics in the original.
48 Ibid.
49 Ibid., 48–9, 58. There were the normal amendments or attempts at amendments, but these did not change the substance of the motion.
50 *A&P*, 1983, 241.
51 Ibid.
52 Ibid., 241–2.
53 Ibid., 242. This is recommendation 23.
54 Ibid., 243. This is recommendation 24.
55 Ibid., 242.
56 Ibid., 243.
57 Ibid., 244–5. Recommendations 32 and 33 related to financing and working with the Administrative Council to ensure financing.
58 Ibid., 76–7.
59 Clarke and Macdonald, *Leaving Christianity*, 163.
60 A. Donald MacLeod, "Church Extension in the '70's," *Presbyterian Comment*, January 1972.
61 *A&P*, 1971, 301. This was not a normal practice. This is the only incident of this I have encountered in this period.
62 Given the importance of the topic of how denominations built new congregations after World War II, this is surprising. Allitt, *Religion in America*, 33–45, discusses this briefly with a focus primarily on architecture. Harrison, "Post-War Trauma," discusses this for Toronto. Roberto Perin, *Many Rooms*, provides an excellent study of places of worship in one area of Toronto.

CHAPTER EIGHT

1 *Time* magazine (Canadian edition), 17 June 1966, 14.
2 There are four women in the Knox College graduation photo, 1966.
3 Alexandra S. Johnston, "The Unrepresented Half," *Presbyterian Record*, November 1969, 2–3; Rosemary Singleton, "This minister's wife has a career of her own," *Presbyterian Record*, February 1974, 2–3; William Klempa, "The Liberation of Men and Women," *Presbyterian Record*, May 1973, 14–15; Flora McKinlay, "Women's Lib or Women's Freedom," *Presbyterian Record*, December 1973, 6–7.
4 Isabel McLaren, "Let's look at women's work," *Presbyterian Record*, September 1971, 7; Editorial, "Are women equal in in church courts," *Presbyterian Record*, July/August 1971, 4.

5 "Are women equal," 4.
6 Lawrence Brice, "She ministers to Port Carling and Torrance," *Presbyterian Record*, November 1976, 10–11.
7 Hugh Thomson, "Reverend Nan," *Presbyterian Record*, March 1977, 18–19.
8 Brice, "She ministers," 11.
9 Thomson, "Reverend Nan," 19.
10 Minutes, Synod of Toronto and Kingston, 1979, 48, 1987-2003-1-3, PCC Archives.
11 Tippins, "Celebrating the 50th Anniversary."
12 Dickson, "Testing 1966," 43–55.
13 Ibid., 44–5.
14 Ibid., 43–50. Quote at 46.
15 *A&P*, 1979, 466. The text of Memorial 1 is printed on pages 466–7.
16 Ibid., 466.
17 Ibid., 466–7.
18 *A&P*, 1979, 26. There is a note that the memorial was not deemed to be in proper form (with no explanation of what was incorrect), but it was nonetheless accepted.
19 *A&P*, 1979, 26, 33. Overture 31, dealing with Graduating Student appointments, also appeared at this General Assembly. It is not clear that this was related other than indicating the issue of graduating students and their appointment was a matter of concern in the denomination at the time.
20 Senate of Presbyterian College Report, *A&P*, 1979, 272–3. Recommendation 5 called on the Board of Ministry to establish a task force to deal with this issue.
21 *Presbyterian Record*, July–August 1979, 12–13.
22 *A&P*, 1979, 19.
23 Ibid. The Board of Education made this recommendation, which then passed the matter on to the Presbytery of East Toronto for their decision.
24 Minutes, Presbytery of East Toronto, May 1979, 81; 12 June, 95. 1988-3026-1-3, PCC Archives.
25 Ibid., 26 June, 105.
26 Minutes, Bridlewood Session, 5 September 1979, 2007-4029, PCC Archives.
27 *Presbyterian Record*, November 1979, 34.
28 Minutes, Presbytery of East Toronto, 11 September 1979, 13.
29 Ibid., 2 October 1979, 18. At this same meeting Ed McKinley's attempt to have his reasons for dissent included in the minutes were ruled out of order; see 16.

30 Minutes, Synod of Toronto and Kingston, October 1979, 41–5, 1987-2003-1-3, PCC Archives.
31 Ibid., 45. Eight names are listed; but one of the written dissents was from someone (A. Dallison) not listed, hence there seem to have been nine dissents.
32 Ibid.
33 Ibid.; for the dissent see 47–9; for the summary see 49.
34 Ibid., 53.
35 Ibid., 50. D. Codling became the person who was named in the appeal.
36 James Dickey, "Editorial: Let us be perfectly clear…," *Presbyterian Record*, May 1980, 4–5. This issue was also discussed in *Presbyterian Comment*, May 1980.
37 *A&P*, 1980, 395. The entire report can be found on pages 393–8.
38 Ibid., 398.
39 Ibid., 63–6.
40 Ibid., overture 3, 452; overture 5, 453; overture 10, 453–4; overture 30, 463; memorial 1, 466–7.
41 Ibid., 25–6.
42 Ibid., 62.
43 Ibid. Officially this report was responding to the overtures.
44 *Presbyterian Record*, July–August 1980, 12–14.
45 *A&P*, 1980, dissents, 61–3, 92–95, 104. Motion to reconsider, 80, 83.
46 Ibid., 104, 112, 116–17.
47 Ibid., 80–1.
48 *A&P*, 1981, 85, lists a total of 45 overtures, petitions, and memorials. It also specifies which overtures were referred to the committee, as well as the memorials and petitions.
49 Ibid. All of the overtures on all topics that year can be found 456–83.
50 Ibid., overture 18, St. Andrew's, Virden (MB), 468–9.
51 Ibid., 85.
52 Ibid., 52–87. A Declaratory Act 407-3 was passed at the 1981 General Assembly. This was thus already the law of the church and it was merely being clarified.
53 Ibid.
54 Ibid., 31, 38, 84–90, 95–6, 112–15.
55 Ibid., 113–14.
56 Ibid., 114.
57 The debate related to the ordination of women was a major issue in this period. There were columns, opinion pieces, and many letters to the editor. The April 1981 issue was focused on "Liberty of

Conscience and the Ordination of Women." These sources were researched but there was not space to engage in a thorough rehearsal of all of the arguments.

58 Task Force, "Report on Liberty of Conscience," *A&P*, 1982, 501–15. The report was also published as two booklets, one was the report and the second was entitled "Supportive Materials: Pertaining to the Task Force on Liberty of Conscience as it pertains to the Ordination of Women." The copy of the Task Force "Report on Liberty of Conscience" in the Caven Library includes both the report and the supportive materials. Unfortunately, the supportive materials were not published in the *A&P*. The references that follow are all to the booklet, "Report on Liberty of Conscience."

59 Ibid., 2–3.

60 Ibid., 4.

61 Ibid., 5.

62 Ibid.

63 Ibid., 6.

64 Ibid., 7.

65 Ibid., 8.

66 Ibid.

67 Ibid., 9.

68 Ibid.

69 Ibid.

70 Ibid.,10–12. Italics in the original.

71 Ibid., 12, 16.

72 Ibid. The document also included the Minority Report, 15–16.

73 Ibid., 15.

74 Ibid.

75 Ibid., 16.

76 Ibid., 15. Contrast this with what the entire committee reported, 2.

77 *Presbyterian Record*, July–August 1982, 13. Reports on this are in the editorial, 6, and then scattered throughout the report on the General Assembly, 10–14. The Report and debate are also in the *A&P*, 1982.

78 *A&P*, 1983, overture 13, 502. See also overture 20, 504–5; overture 21, 505–6.

79 The formation of the Renewal Fellowship is explored MacLeod, "Reaction to Renewal," 187 and elsewhere.

80 Ibid., 179.

81 Dickson, "Testing 1966," 43–55; Macdonald, "What Were They Thinking?," 27–8.

82 The changes in the 1960s have been explored in several books, notably Marwick, *The Sixties* and Petigny, *The Permissive Society*. For the reaction see Jenkins, *Decade of Nightmares*.
83 On the ERA, Jenkins, *Decade of Nightmares*, 85–7, 109–11, 160.
84 Jim Dickey, *Presbyterian Record*, July–August 1979, 12–13.
85 Jim Dickey, *Presbyterian Record*, July–August 1982, 20. The quotation is attributed to Peter Szabo of the Presbytery of Montreal.
86 Dickson, "Testing 1966," notes the cultural influences of Rene Levesque's Quebec and other issues, 43. MacLeod, "Reaction to Renewal," notes the growth among evangelicals in the 1980s, 176, and other contextual factors. Kobes de Mez, *Jesus and John Wayne*, explores the issue of gender and North American Christianity.
87 This seemingly continued even after 1982. At one of my first presbytery meetings while a student in 1984, a retired minister addressed the court in this manner.
88 *A&P*, 1980, 62.
89 Task Force, "Report," 5.
90 Moir, *Enduring Witness*, 264. The same paragraph appears in the 1st edition, 264.
91 Presbyterian Church in Canada, *Book of Forms*, 1977, 111–16.
92 Ibid., 2. This also appears in the 1970 edition of the *Book of Forms*, 2, which would have been the first edition after the decision in 1966. A revision to the *Book of Forms* was agreed to in 1979; for reasons that are unclear, as well as inexplicable, the revision, which appeared in removed the references to the ordination of women from this page. *Book of Forms*, 1981, 2. That this was done at the height of this debate is – to say the least – puzzling.
93 Minutes, Bridlewood Session, 5 September 1979, PCC Archives.
94 *Book of Forms*, 1977, 113. Emphasis added.
95 Ed McKinley, "Divisiveness or Dissent?" *Presbyterian Record*, March 1980, 6–7.
96 Art Van Seters, "How does an appeal to liberty of conscience relate to the ordination of women," January 1980, Committee on Memorial #1, 20007-106-1-1, PCC Archives.

CHAPTER NINE

1 Cover, *Presbyterian Record*, February 1984.
2 This stands in sharp contrast to the United Church of Canada. Schweitzer, *Theology of the United Church*; Bourgeois, "Awash in Theology."
3 Bush, "The Church, Its Subordinate Standards."

4 *A&P*, 1970, 282.
5 Ibid.
6 Bush, "The Church, Its Subordinate Standards."
7 *A&P*, 1962, 98, 288–9.
8 Church Doctrine Committee, "Confessing the Faith Today," *A&P*, 2003, 256.
9 Bush, "Presbyterian Church and the Pope," 111. Macdonald, "Vatican II," 78–105.
10 *A&P*, 1964, overture 25, 500–1.
11 Ibid., 501.
12 *A&P*, 1965, 333.
13 Ibid.
14 The *Record* did receive one letter to the editor protesting the response to the overture. *Presbyterian Record*, October 1965, 34.
15 *A&P*, 1966, 268.
16 *A&P*, 1967, overture 17, 421.
17 Ibid., 421–2.
18 Ibid., 241.
19 *A&P*, 1965, overture 18, 511; Klempa, *What It Means to Confess*, iii.
20 "Draft statement of Faith," 1.
21 Ibid., 2.
22 Klempa, *What It Means to Confess*, iii.
23 Ibid.,
24 *A&P*, 1950, overtures 6, 110, and overture 34, 123; *A&P*, 1952, overture 5, 184; *A&P*, 1956, overture 4, 327–8, and overture 18, 334–5.
25 Redmond, "John Somerville," 1–5; McKellar, "Presbyterian Hymnody," 1–13.
26 *A&P*, 1953, 303.
27 Ibid.
28 Ibid.
29 *A&P*, 1955, 293; *A&P*, 1956, 273; *A&P*, 1957, 250–2; *A&P*, 1958, 268–70.
30 *A&P*, 1963, 113, overture 32, 463–4.
31 *A&P*, 1964, 370.
32 Ibid., 65–6.
33 PCC, *Book of Praise*, 1972, introductory materials. This preface was published as well as an article "The new Book of Praise" in the *Presbyterian Record*, September 1972, 12–14.

34 Ibid. The preface notes two hymns from the United States, but then did not include the United States among the nine countries they cited when noting that the hymns came from "everywhere."
35 Ibid.
36 *A&P*, 1968, overture 19, 401–2. See also Brian Fraser, "A Young Man Looks at the Assembly," *Presbyterian Record*, July–August 1971, 13.
37 Presbyterian Church in Canada, *Praiseways.*
38 Sutherland, "Presbyterian Music Camp," 1–12.
39 Moir, *Enduring Witness*, 279–80; Hans Zegerius, "The Admission of Children to the Lord's Table," *Presbyterian Record*, December 1984, 2–3.
40 Moir, *Enduring Witness*, 278; Fitzgerald, *Evangelicals*, 254–6, 291.
41 The denomination's position did not change. There are various articles on this issue in this period in the *Presbyterian Record*, including Willoughby Belch, "The Gift of life," April 1985, 8, and the editorial, April 1985, 4, 41. There were also two overtures in 1985, *A&P*, 1985, overture 19, 460, and overture 24, 463.
42 Klempa, *An Historical Digest*. See also, Klempa, "History of Presbyterian Theology," and Rennie, "Conservatism."
43 Clarke and Macdonald, *Leaving Christianity*, 107–10.
44 Wilkerson, *Cross and the Switchblade.*
45 Douville, *Uncomfortable Pew*, 206–7.
46 Report on Assembly, *Presbyterian Record*, July–August 1971, 17.
47 *A&P*, 1974, 386.
48 Ibid., 387.
49 Ibid., 388.
50 Ibid.
51 Ibid., 49–50.
52 Ibid., 392.
53 *A&P*, 1975, 323.
54 Ibid., 325–7.
55 Ibid., 395.
56 Ibid.
57 *A&P*, 1976, 375–393.
58 Moir, *Enduring Witness*, 278.
59 *A&P*, 1976, 388.
60 Ibid., 392–3.
61 CDC, *The Neo-Pentecostal Movement.*
62 Hans W. Zegerius, "A tale of two reports," *Presbyterian Record*, January 1980, 6. This was rebutted by Stephen Hayes, "Neo-Pentecostalism: Point-Counterpoint," *Presbyterian Record*, February 1980, 6–7.

63 *A&P*, 1976, 375.
64 Ibid., 387.
65 Eire, *Reformations*, 750–1.
66 *A&P*, 1984, 24; *Presbyterian Record*, July–August 1984, 4, 15, 23.
67 Introduction, *Living Faith*, 3.
68 Stephen Hayes, "A Living Faith: A report on the New Statement of Faith," *Presbyterian Record*, May 1984, 22.
69 Ibid.
70 Ibid.
71 *Living Faith*, 3.
72 Hayes, "Personal recollection," unpublished manuscript in author's possession.
73 *Living Faith*, 3.
74 Presbyterian Church in the United States, *A Declaration of Faith*, 1977, chapter 6, section 3, lines 62–4.
75 *Living Faith*, section 5.4.
76 "Draft Statement of Faith," 1–2.
77 *Living Faith*, section 3.6.
78 William Stanford Reid, "A Consumer's Guide to new statements of faith: how does Living Faith compare?" *Presbyterian Record*, April 1985, 18–21.
79 Robert Gartshore, "Objections to Living Faith," *Presbyterian Record*, March 1984, 8. The committee offered a rebuttal in the same issue, 9.
80 Church Doctrine Committee, "Confessing the Faith today" *A&P*, 2003, 256–7, 264.
81 *A&P*, 1998, overture 38, 539; *A&P*, 1999, overture 4, 461. The Church Doctrine Committee reported on this in *A&P*, 2001, 37–8, 41, 236–8.
82 Presbyterian Church in Canada, *Book of Common Order* (Abridged), 1977.

CONCLUSION

1 Clarke and Macdonald, *Leaving Christianity*, 4. For the changing proportion of Protestants and Roman Catholics, 29.
2 Ibid., 163.
3 Statistics Canada, "Canadian census: A rich portrait," October 26, 2022.
4 Clarke and Macdonald, *Leaving Christianity*, 72–121.
5 *A&P*, 1997, 55, 470–3. This began as an experiment but became permanent several years later. For the Korean experience in the UCC, see Kim-Cragg, *Water from Dragon's Well*.
6 *A&P*, 1994, 29, 40–2, 365–7.
7 Veracini, "'Settler Colonialism,'" 325.

8 The 1994 Confession can be downloaded from the Presbyterian Church in Canada's website, https://presbyterian.ca . The 2024 apology and the report that preceded it: https://presbyterian.ca/wp-content/uploads/RGA2024_Special-Committee-re-Renewed-Apology-re-Role-in-Colonialism-and-Residential-Schools-2024.pdf.

9 *A&P*, 1984, overture 14, 520.

10 *A&P*, 1994, 30, 48, 56, 63, 251–74.

Bibliography

ARCHIVAL SOURCES

Anglican Church of Canada, General Synod Archives, Toronto, Ontario
  File related to W5 program, GS 83-2, box 2, file 4
Caven Library, Knox College, Toronto, Ontario
  File folder containing minutes from the Committee on the Place of Women in the Church [CPWC file folder]
  Knox College Bulletin
  Presbyterian Record
  Time magazine (Canadian edition), 17 June 1966
Presbyterian Church in Canada Archives [PCC Archives]
  Denominational Minutes and Historic Doctrine
  Acts and Proceedings of the General Assembly, 1925–85, 2021, https://presbyterianarchives.ca/finding-aids/acts-and-proceedings *[A&P]*
  Channels
  Presbyterian Comment
  Tippins, Emily. "Celebrating the 50th Anniversary of the Ordination of Women 1966–2016." Online exhibit. Presbyterian Church in Canada Archives. 20 July 2016. Accessed 15 February 2023. https://presbyterianarchives.ca/2016/07/20/celebrating-the-50th-anniversary-of-the-ordination-of-women-1966-2016/.
  Westminster Confession of Faith. 1647. https://presbyterian.ca/resources/resources-od/.

OTHER SOURCES

Adamson, William. *The Presbytery of West Toronto: Historical Sketches.* Toronto: Presbyterian Church in Canada, 1999.

"A Deliverance of the Presbytery of Paris." *Presbyterian Student* 4 (4 May 1939): 5–9.

Airhart, Phyllis D. *Church with the Soul of a Nation: Making and Remaking the United Church of Canada.* Montreal & Kingston: McGill-Queen's University Press, 2014.

– "Women in the United Church of Canada." In Skinner Keller, Radford Ruether, and Cantlon, *Encyclopedia of Women and Religion in North America*, 361–68.

Allitt, Patrick. *Religion in America since 1945: A History*. New York: Columbia University Press, 2003.

Anderson, Robert K. *Kimchi and Maple Leaves under the Rising Sun: The Story of the Involvement of the Presbyterian Church in Canada with the Korean Christian Church in Japan.* Belleville, ON: Guardian Books, 2001.

Angus, James Murray. "The Political Values Present in the Presbyterian Church in Canada's Response to Social Problems, 1925–1975." MA thesis, Department of Religious Studies, Carleton, 1978.

Bailey, T.M. *The Covenant in Canada: Four Hundred Years History of the Presbyterian Church in Canada.* Toronto: Presbyterian Church in Canada, 1975.

Berton, Pierre. *The Comfortable Pew: A Critical Look at Christianity and the Religious Establishment in a New Age.* Toronto: McClelland and Stewart, 1965.

Board of Evangelism and Social Service, United Church of Canada. *Why the Sea Is Boiling Hot: A Symposium on the Church and the World.* Toronto: United Church Publishing House, 1969.

Bourgeois, Michael. "Awash in Theology: Issues in Theology in the United Church of Canada." In *The United Church of Canada: A History,* edited by Don Schweitzer, 259–77. Waterloo: Wilfrid Laurier University Press, 2012.

Boyd, Lois A. "Presbyterian Women in America." In Skinner Keller, Radford Ruether, and Cantlon, *Encyclopedia of Women and Religion in North America*, 352–61.

Brown, Callum G. *The Death of Christian Britain: Understanding Secularisation 1800–2000*. London: Routledge, 2001.

Brown Zikmund, Barbara. "The Protestant Women's Ordination Movement." In Skinner Keller, Radford Ruether, and Cantlon, *Encyclopedia of Women and Religion in North America*, 940–50.

Bush, Peter. "The Church, Its Subordinate Standards, and the Ordination Questions." *Presbyterian History* 64, nos 1–2 (Spring and Fall 2020): 1–5.

– "The Opening of the Women's Ordination Debate in the Presbyterian Church in Canada, 1952–1957." *Presbyterian History* 60, no. 2 (Fall 2016): 1–6.

– "The Presbyterian Church and the Pope: One Denomination's Struggle with Its Confessional History." *Studies in Religion/Sciences Religieuses* 33, no. 1 (2004): 105–15.

– *Western Challenge: The Presbyterian Church in Canada's Mission on the Prairies and North, 1885–1925*. Winnipeg: Watson and Dwyer, 2000.

Byfield, Ted. *Just Think, Mr Berton (A Little Harder)*. Winnipeg: The Company of the Cross, 1965.

Chadwick, Andrew, Bruce McCowan, and Nancy McCowan. *The Scots Kirk: An Oral History of St Andrew's Presbyterian Church, Scarborough*. Toronto: Natural Heritage/Natural History, 1997.

Chaves, Mark. *Ordaining Women: Culture and Conflict in Religious Organizations*. Cambridge, MA: Harvard University Press, 1997.

Christie, Nancy, and Michael Gauvreau, eds. *The Sixties and Beyond: Dechristianization in North America and Western Europe, 1945–2000*. Toronto: University of Toronto Press, 2013.

Church Doctrine Committee (CDC). "Confessing the Faith Today: The Nature and Function of Subordinate Standards." *A&P*, 2003, 247–72.

– *The Neo-Pentecostal Movement and the Presbyterian Church of Canada: A Popular Report*. Don Mills: Presbyterian Church in Canada, c. 1982.

Clarke, Brian. "English-Speaking Canada from 1854." In *A Concise History of Christianity in Canada*, edited by Terence Murphy and Roberto Perin, 261–359. Toronto: Oxford University Press, 1996.

Clarke, Brian, and Stuart Macdonald. *Leaving Christianity: Changing Allegiances in Canada since 1945*. Montreal and Kingston: McGill-Queen's University Press, 2017.

– "No Need to Turn Out the Lights: Anglicans in Canada in the Twentieth and Twenty-First Centuries." In *Reformation Worlds: Antecedents and Legacies in the Anglican Tradition*, edited by Sean A. Otto and Thomas Power, 199–212. New York: Peter Lang, 2016.

Clifford, N. Keith. *The Resistance to Church Union in Canada 1904–1939*. Vancouver: University of British Columbia Press, 1985.

Committee on Inter-Church Relations. "Presbyterians and the Church Catholic." Toronto: Presbyterian Church in Canada, 1962.

Committee on Life and Mission. *Into the '70s in Life and Mission: Report of the Committee on Life and Mission*. Toronto: Presbyterian Church in Canada, 1969.

Committee on the Place of Women in the Church (PCC). "Putting Woman in Her Place." Toronto: Presbyterian Church in Canada, c. 1963.

Corbett, D.J.M. "The Legal Problems of the Canadian Church Union of 1925." *Canadian Society of Presbyterian History Papers* (1979): 53–67.

Dickson, Jo-Ann. "Testing 1966: Unrest in Montreal." *Canadian Society of Presbyterian History Papers* (2012): 43–55.

Douville, Bruce. *The Uncomfortable Pew: Christianity and the New Left in Toronto*. Montreal and Kingston: McGill-Queen's University Press, 2021.

Dunn, Zander. "The Great Divorce and What Happened to the Children." *Canadian Society of Presbyterian History Papers* (1977): 58–96.

Eire, Carlos M.N. *Reformations: The Early Modern World, 1450–1650*. New Haven: Yale University Press, 2016.

Farris, Alan L. "The Fathers of 1925." In *In the Tide of Time: Historical Essays by the Late Allan L. Farris*, edited by John S. Moir, 95–124. Toronto: Knox College, 1978.

Fay, Terrence J. *A History of Canadian Catholics: Gallicanism, Romanism, and Canadianism*. Montreal and Kingston: McGill-Queen's University Press, 2002.

Fitzgerald, Frances. *The Evangelicals: The Struggle to Shape America*. New York: Simon & Schuster, 2017.

Flatt, Kevin J. *After Evangelicalism: The Sixties and the United Church of Canada*. Montreal and Kingston: McGill-Queen's University Press, 2013.

Fraser, Brian J. *The Social Uplifters: Presbyterian Progressives and the Social Gospel in Canada, 1875–1915*. Waterloo: Wilfrid Laurier University Press, 1988.

General Board of Missions. "Looking Ahead in World Mission." Toronto: Presbyterian Church in Canada, 1964.

Grant, John Webster. *The Canadian Experience of Church Union*. London: Lutterworth Press, 1967.

– *The Church in the Canadian Era: Updated and Expanded*. Burlington: Welch, 1988.

– *Moon of Wintertime: Missionaries and the Indians of Canada in Encounter since 1534*. Toronto: University of Toronto Press, 1984.

Harris, Richard. *Creeping Conformity: How Canada Became Suburban, 1900–1960*. Toronto: University of Toronto Press, 2004.

Harrison, David. "Post-War Trauma: Church Growth and Construction in Toronto." In *Trauma and Survival in the Contemporary Church: Historical Responses in the Anglican Tradition*, edited by Jonathan S. Lofft and Thomas P. Power, 103–15. Newcastle upon Tyne: Cambridge Scholars, 2021.

Hayes, Alan. *Anglicans in Canada: Controversies and Identity in Historical Perspective*. Urbana and Chicago: University of Illinois Press, 2004.

Hudnut-Beumler, James. *Looking for God in the Suburbs: The Religion of the American Dream and Its Critics, 1945–1965*. New Brunswick, NJ: Rutgers University Press, c. 1994.

Jenkins, Philip. *Decade of Nightmares: The End of the Sixties and the Making of Eighties America*. New York: Oxford University Press, 2006.

Jess, Rebecca. "Young People and the Future of the Presbyterian Church: Rebuilding Post-Union." *Canadian Society of Presbyterian History Papers* (2020): 27–36.

Johnston, John A. "'No Slippery Undertaking': The Presbyterian Union of 1875." *Canadian Society of Presbyterian History Papers* (1975): 61–106.

Kim-Cragg, David. *Water from Dragon's Well: The History of Korean-Canadian Church Relationship*. Montreal and Kingston: McGill-Queen's University Press, 2022.

Kilbourn, William, ed. *The Restless Church: A Response to the Comfortable Pew*. Toronto: McClelland and Stewart, c. 1966.

Klempa, Lois, and Rosemary Doran. *Certain Women Amazed Us: The Women's Missionary Society, Their Story, 1864–2002*. Don Mills: Women's Missionary Society (Western Division), 2002.

Klempa, William, ed. *The Burning Bush and a Few Acres of Snow: The Presbyterian Contribution to Canadian Life and Culture*. Ottawa: Carleton University Press, 1994.

– "Canadian Presbyterians and the Westminster Standards." In *Exploring the Faith: Essays in the History and Theology of the Reformed Tradition,* edited by William J. Klempa, 115–35. Toronto: Clements Academic, 2009.

– "The Declaration of Faith Concerning Church and Nation Revisited." In *Exploring the Faith: Essays in the History and Theology of the Reformed Tradition*, edited by William J. Klempa, 85–114. Toronto: Clements Academic, 2009.

– *An Historical Digest of the Work in Articles of Faith, 1942–1967.* Don Mills: Presbyterian Church in Canada, 1968.

– "History of Presbyterian Theology in Canada to 1875." In Klempa, *The Burning Bush*, 193–218.

– , ed. *What It Means to Confess the Christian Faith Today.* Don Mills: Church Doctrine Committee of the PCC, 1971.

Knight, Sara J. "Voices United? The House of Commons' Role in the Creation of the United Church of Canada." *Canadian Society of Church History Papers* (2003): 39–64.

Kobes du Mez, Kristin. *Jesus and John Wayne: How White Evangelicals Corrupted a Faith and Fractured a Nation.* New York: W.W. Norton, 2020.

Korinek, Valerie J. "No Women Need Apply: The Ordination of Women in the United Church, 1918–65." *Canadian Historical Review* 74, no. 4 (1993): 473–509.

Laverdure, Paul. *Sunday in Canada: The Rise and Fall of the Lord's Day.* Yorkton: Gravelbooks, 2004.

Macdonald, Stuart. "'1966 and All That:' The Liberty of Conscience Debate (1979–1982) in Context." *Canadian Society of Presbyterian History Papers* (2021): 20–34.

– "Canadian Presbyterians and Vatican II: A Silent Revolution." In *Vatican II: Expériences canadiennes/Canadian Experiences*, edited by Michael Attridge, Catherine E. Clifford, and Gilles Routhier, 78–105. Ottawa: University of Ottawa Press, 2011.

– "Divining the Entrails: One Challenge in Studying How the Presbyterian Church in Canada Looked at Itself and Its Future, 1945–2000." *Canadian Society of Presbyterian History Papers* (2006): 10–28.

– "Presbyterian and Reformed Christians and Ethnicity." In *Christianity and Ethnicity in Canada,* edited by Paul Bramadat and David Seljak, 168–203. Toronto: University of Toronto Press, 2008.

– "The Presbyterian Church in Canada and Extension Work, 1945–1985: Initial Findings." *Canadian Society of Presbyterian History Papers* (2003): 34–48.

– "Protest or Loyalty? The Background to the Declaration of Faith and Nation (1954)." *Canadian Society of Presbyterian History Papers* (2020): 1–14.

– "Taking God into the Suburbs: Canadian Presbyterians and New Church Development in the Toronto Area, 1945–1965." *Canadian Society of Church History Papers* (2019): 37–50.

– "What Were They Thinking? The Place of Women and the 1966 Decisions on Ordination." *Canadian Society of Presbyterian History Papers* (2016): 16–30.

Mark, Malcolm A. "Canadian Presbyterianism in Action, 1761–1961." Toronto: Presbyterian Church in Canada, Address to the Synod of Toronto and Kingston, 1961.

MacLeod, A. Donald. "From Reaction to Renewal: Presbyterian Renewal Fellowship, 1979–1987." In *Studies in Canadian Evangelical Renewal: Essays in Honour of Ian S. Rennie*, edited by Kevin Quast and John Vissers, 175–94. Markham: F.T. Publications, 1996.

– *W. Stanford Reid: An Evangelical Calvinist in the Academy*. Montreal and Kingston: McGill-Queen's University Press, 2004.

Marwick, Arthur. *The Sixties: Cultural Revolution in Britain, France, Italy and the United States, c. 1958–c. 1974*. Oxford: Oxford University Press, 1998.

McKellar, Hugh D. "150 Years of Presbyterian Hymnody in Canada." *Canadian Society of Presbyterian History Papers* (1986): 1–13.

McGillivray, Anne. "Educating Baby Boomers: Sunday School Curriculum Recommendations in the Presbyterian Church in Canada, 1940 to 1970." *Canadian Society of Presbyterian History Papers* (2019): 30–42.

McIntyre, C.T. "Unity among Many: The Formation of the United Church of Canada, 1899–1930." In *The United Church of Canada: A History*, edited by Don Schweitzer, 3–37. Waterloo: Wilfrid Laurier University Press, 2012.

McLelland, Joseph. *Why Our Pond Is Lukewarm, or Forty Years in the Wilderness: Two Addresses to the Toronto-Kingston Synod at Sudbury, Ontario in October, 1965*. n.p.: S.I., 1965.

McLeod, Hugh. *The Religious Crisis of the 1960s*. Oxford: Oxford University Press, 2007.

McNab, John, ed. "What Do Presbyterians Believe?" Toronto: *Presbyterian Record*, 1957.

Miedema, Gary. *For Canada's Sake: Public Religion, Centennial Celebrations and the Re-making of Canada in the 1960s*. Montreal and Kingston: McGill-Queen's University Press, 2005.

Moir, John S. *Enduring Witness: A History of the Presbyterian Church in Canada*. 1st ed., Toronto: Bryant Press, 1974. 3rd ed., Toronto: Presbyterian Church in Canada, 2004.

– "'Who Pays the Piper…': Canadian Presbyterianism and Church-State Relations." In Klempa, *The Burning Bush*, 67–81.

Nutt, Mary. "Mary E. Whale." In *Gifts and Graces: Profiles of Canadian Presbyterian Women.* Vol. 1, edited by John S. Moir, 110–17. Burlington: Eagle Press, 1990.

O'Malley, John W. *What Happened at Vatican II.* Cambridge, MA: Harvard University Press, 2008.

Owram, Doug. *Born at the Right Time: A History of the Baby Boom Generation.* Toronto: University of Toronto Press, 1996.

Peddie, Gordon A. "'The King of Kings': The Basis of Union of the Presbyterian Church in Canada, and Its Relationship to the Present Need of the Church for a Confession of Faith in Jesus Christ as Lord of Church and State." Toronto: Age Publications, 1942.

Perin, Roberto. *The Many Rooms of This House: Diversity in Toronto's Places of Worship since 1840.* Toronto: University of Toronto Press, 2017.

Petigny, Alan. *The Permissive Society: America, 1941–1965.* New York: Cambridge University Press, 2009.

Plaxton, David. "'We Will Evangelize with a Whole Gospel or None': Evangelism and the United Church of Canada." In *Aspects of the Canadian Evangelical Experience*, edited by Rawlyk, 106–22. Montreal: McGill-Queen's University Press, 1997.

Presbyterian Church in Canada (PCC). *Book of Common Order* (1948). Toronto: Presbyterian Publications, 1948.

– *Book of Common Order* (1964). Toronto: Presbyterian Publications, 1964.

– *Book of Common Order: Abridged Edition* (1978). Don Mills: Presbyterian Publications, 1978.

– *Book of Forms* (1933). Toronto: Presbyterian Publications, 1933.

– *Book of Forms* (1970). Don Mills: Presbyterian Publications, 1970.

– *Book of Forms* (1977). Don Mills: Presbyterian Publications, 1977.

– *Book of Forms* (1981). Don Mills: Presbyterian Publications, 1981.

– *The Book of Praise – Revised 1972.* Don Mills: Presbyterian Church in Canada, 1972.

– *Living Faith.* Winfield, BC: Wood Lake Books, 1984.

– *Praiseways.* Don Mills: Presbyterian Church in Canada, 1975.

Presbyterian Church in the United States. "A Declaration of Faith." 1977.

"Presbyterians in Canada." *Christian Century* 101 (July 25, 1984): 706.

Ransom, R.M., ed. *No Time to Falter.* Toronto: Presbyterian Church in Canada, 1962.

Redmond, Chris. "John Somerville and the Presbyterian Book of Praise." *Presbyterian History* 60, no. 1 (Spring 2016): 1–5.

Stanford Reid, William, ed. "In the Unity of Faith: Some Comments on the Position of the Presbyterian Church in Canada in the Modern Ecumenical Movement." Montreal: n.p., 1962.

Reith, Louise A. "Our Commission – in Canada and Overseas." Toronto: Women's Missionary Society, 1947.

Rennie, Ian S. "Conservatism in the Presbyterian Church in Canada in 1925 and Beyond: An Introductory Exploration." *Canadian Society of Presbyterian History Papers* (1982): 29–60.

Ross, Aaron A.M. *The Holy Spirit and the Eagle Feather: The Struggle for Indigenous Pentecostalism in Canada.* Montreal and Kingston: McGill-Queen's University Press, 2023.

Schweitzer, Don, Robert C. Fennell, and Michael Bourgeois, eds. *The Theology of the United Church.* Waterloo: Wilfrid Laurier University Press, 2019.

Scott, Ephraim. *"Church Union" and the Presbyterian Church in Canada.* Montreal: John Lovell and Sons, 1928.

Skinner Keller, Rosemary, Rosemary Radford Ruether, and Marie Cantlon, eds. *Encyclopedia of Women and Religion in North America.* Bloomington: Indiana University Press, 2006.

Solomon, Lawrence. *Toronto Sprawls: A History.* Toronto: University of Toronto Press, 2007.

Statistics Canada. "The Canadian Census: A Rich Portrait of the Country's Religious and Ethnocultural Diversity." *The Daily*, October 26, 2022.

Stebner, Eleanor J. "The 1930s." In *The United Church of Canada: A History,* edited by Don Schweitzer, 39–56. Waterloo: Wilfrid Laurier University Press, 2012.

Stewart, Adam. *The New Canadian Pentecostals.* Waterloo: Wilfrid Laurier University Press, 2015.

Sutherland, Angus. "Presbyterian Music Camp: 50 Years of Harmony." *Canadian Society of Presbyterian History Papers* (2022): 1–12.

Synod of Alberta History Committee. "Growth: A History and Anthology of the Synod of Alberta of the Presbyterian Church in Canada." n.p.: Synod of Alberta, 1968.

Task Force on Liberty of Conscience. "Report of the Task Force on Liberty of Conscience as It Pertains to the Ordination of Women." Toronto: Presbyterian Church in Canada, 1982.

Tattrie, George. "Euthanasia: A Christian Perspective." Don Mills: PCC, Board of Congregational Life, Studies and Statements Committee, 1982.

Vissers, John A. *The Neo-Orthodox Theology of W.W. Bryden*. Eugene, OR: Pickwick Publications, 2006.

– "Recovering the Reformation Conception of Revelation: The Theological Contribution of Walter Williamson Bryden and Post-Union Canadian Presbyterianism." In Klempa, *The Burning Bush,* 239–58.

Veracini, Lorenzo. "'Settler Colonialism': Career of a Concept." *Journal of Imperial and Commonwealth History* 41, no. 2 (2013): 313–33.

Welch, Walter. "The Ministry of the Church in Suburbia." Charles H. MacDonald Lecture, Knox College, 1961.

Wilkerson, David, with John and Elizabeth Sherrill. *The Cross and the Switchblade*. New York: B. Geis Associates, 1963.

Wilkinson, Michael. *Canadian Pentecostalism: Transition and Transformation*. Montreal and Kingston: McGill-Queen's University Press, 2009.

Wilkinson, Michael, and Linda M. Ambrose. *After the Revival: Pentecostalism and the Making of a Canadian Church*. Montreal and Kingston: McGill-Queen's University Press, 2020.

Wilson, Lois. *Turning the World Upside Down: A Memoir*. Toronto: Doubleday Canada, 1989.

Index

Figures and tables indicated by page numbers in italics.